ECSTATIC OCCASIONS, EXPEDIENT FORMS

ECSTATIC OCCASIONS, EXPEDIENT FORMS

85 Leading Contemporary Poets
Select and Comment on Their Poems

EDITED BY DAVID LEHMAN

Ann Arbor

THE UNIVERSITY OF MICHIGAN PRESS

Second edition of *Ecstatic Occasions, Expedient Forms:*
65 Leading Contemporary Poets Select and Comment
on Their Poems, originally published in 1987 by Macmillan
Publishing Company. Copyright © 1996 by David Lehman.

Permissions and acknowledgments appear on pages 259–66.

All rights reserved
Published in the United States of America by
The University of Michigan Press
Manufactured in the United States of America
⊗ Printed on acid-free paper
1999   1998   1997   1996   4   3   2   1

A CIP catalog record for this book is available from the British Library.

Library of Congress Cataloging-in-Publication Data

Ecstatic occasions, expedient forms : 85 leading contemporary poets
    select and comment on their poems / edited by David Lehman. — 2nd
    ed.
        p.   cm.
    Includes bibliographical references.
        ISBN 0-472-09633-8 (hardcover : alk. paper). — ISBN 0-472-06633-1
    (pbk. : alk. paper)
        1. American poetry—20th century.   2. Poetry—Authorship.
    I. Lehman, David, 1948– .
    PS615.E374   1996
    811'.5408—dc20   96–31099
                                                                            CIP

for Glen Hartley

CONTENTS

PREFACE
to the Second Edition

Ecstatic Occasions, Expedient Forms was first published by Macmillan in hardcover in 1987 and in paperback a year later. Consisting of a poem and a comment on the poem from each of sixty-five contributors, the book aimed to define the range of formal possibilities available to poets today. The title was adapted from Marianne Moore's line about the origins of a poem: "Ecstasy affords the occasion and expediency determines the form." When the book slipped out of print, the University of Michigan Press agreed to publish a new edition, and I took the opportunity to enlarge the contents.

In addition to the original sixty-five contributors, twenty poets appear in this edition for the first time: Eavan Boland, Wyn Cooper, Jim Dolot, Rita Dove, Amy Gerstler, Donald Justice, Yusef Komunyakaa, Heather McHugh, W. S. Merwin, Susan Mitchell, Thylias Moss, Harryette Mullen, Charles North, Katha Pollitt, Charles Simic, Elizabeth Spires, Mark Strand, James Tate, Rosanna Warren, and Susan Wheeler. Three other poets—Tom Disch, Debora Greger, and William Logan—have revised their entries. There are a half-dozen new categories and other changes in the "Brief Glossary of Forms and Other Terms." The biographical notes are fuller; the original afterword has been omitted to help make room. We mourn the passing of five contributors: Howard Moss first, then John Cage in August 1992, Donald Britton in July 1994, Amy Clampitt in September 1994, and James Merrill in February 1995.

In this book you will find villanelles, pantoums, prose poems, sonnets, songs, narratives, commentaries, rhymed poems, free verse, a poem in the form of a musical fugue, a poem in the form of baseball lineups, a poem in the form of an index to a nonexistent book, a poem based on a principle of alliteration, and a sonnet containing fewer than fourteen words.

A number of the entries demonstrate that the process of creation and the process of revision may coincide. This may be what Paul Valéry meant when he said that poems were never finished, merely abandoned. Charles Simic, for example, allows the reader to compare the first version of his work, a prose poem, with the finished product. The reader can see how the materials of "Theseus and Ariadne" were refashioned into the much fuller, more complex and beautiful poem "The Anniversary." The result is an object lesson in the value of revision. The process is never ending: the version of "The Anniversary" published here has an additional stanza that the poem did not have when it appeared in *The New Yorker* in 1995.

I'd like to thank Maggie Nelson, who assisted in this undertaking, and to acknowledge all the poets and editors whose collaboration was essential. "What is 'form' for anyone else is 'content' for me," Valéry once observed, summarizing an experimental approach that some poets have taken to heart. At the opposite extreme are those for whom form properly considered is an extension of content. "Form precedes language," Susan Mitchell contends. No, form and content "come into being simultaneously," Elizabeth Spires counters. For Heather McHugh, poetic form "is where resemblance and distinction intertwine," while for William Matthews, "form is play." James Merrill quietly insisted that "form's what affirms." Who is right? They can't all be, can they? You make the call. But remember, the point was never to settle the issue once and for all, just to show how much life there is in the perennial debate—and to renew the evidence of poetry's singular vitality in our time.

July 1995

PREFACE
to the 1987 Edition

Trying to come up with a working definition of form is a little like trying to measure the circumference of a deity whose center, Pascal tells us, is everywhere. In both cases, one is tempted to look for safety in tautologies. "For when we ask, in our hopeless way, what is *form*, what is it that at all holds poems together, echo answers," Howard Nemerov has written. "It appears that poems are held together by people's opinions of what holds poems together." Nemerov would counsel us to "talk, if we talk at all, not about sonnets or villanelles and so forth, but about the working-out of whatever is in hand to be worked out." This makes eminent good sense, although—or because—it leaves us right back where we started.

At a time when traditional poetic structures propose themselves as options rather than exigencies; when the author of a sonnet sequence may cavalierly break the rules or invent new ones as he goes along; when it is a commonplace argument that poems fashion their own requirements for the poet to apprehend only after the fact, then the need for an enlightened practical criticism establishes itself with a vengeance. Wisdom dictates that the question of form be addressed with reference to specific texts. And, in the absence of all other authority, who better to talk about the formal dimensions of a poem than its author?

Out of such thoughts emerged this anthology of poems and commentary by the poets themselves: a forum on form that has itself become a form. Each contributor was asked to provide a poem accompanied by a statement on the decisions that went into its making. The results, in all their variety, follow. As the volume's editor, I sought to establish a compelling context rather than lay the framework for polemic and debate; I wanted merely to create an expedient occasion for various poets to ruminate variously about a common concern. Accordingly, in my initial communication with the poets, I limited myself to raising, as possible points of departure, such questions as these about the poem at hand and its composition: What constraints, if any, did you impose upon yourself? Which formal choices preceded the act of writing, and which grew out of it? In the case of a traditional or exotic form, a given stanzaic pattern or metrical arrangement, what chiefly attracted you to it? To what extent did a principle of form, a technical stratagem, or a distinctive method of composition generate your momentum—and inspiration? I urged contributors to "feel free to construe 'form' broadly (as any strategy for organizing a poem) or in a narrow sense." I also gave them license to disregard my queries if they seemed uncomfortably like leading questions. It just about went without saying that "the poem needn't exemplify a specific verse form."

I realized from the outset that the sum of the statements I received in reply might work as easily to muddy as to clarify our abstract and finally unsolvable quandary: "What is *form,* what is it that at all holds poems together?" The questions would, in any case, constitute a useful pretext or preamble. What poets, when pressed, have to say on a subject that seems at once so nebulous and yet so rife with customary associations would, it seemed to me, inevitably tell us a great deal about themselves, their assumptions, and their procedures. How, I wondered, would the poets elect to approach the subject? What form would their comments take? What tone? Mightn't their statements prove revealing in ways that went beyond the writers' spoken intentions?

Given so diverse a group of poets as that assembled here, it would be folly to look for anything resembling consensus. Yet some conclusions are inescapable. From the practicing poet's point of view, form—as more than one contributor insists—is concomitant to composition. This opinion of the matter was stated definitively by Marianne Moore in her poem "The Past Is the Present." "Ecstasy affords the occasion" for poetry, Moore wrote, "and expediency determines the form." Form, in other words, proceeds not from theory but from the pressures of a specific occasion. Talking about their poems, most poets are empiricists, and it cannot surprise us to find one poet after another eschewing lofty pronouncements in favor of expedient explanations. That is certainly the case in this book.

In effect, the reader will have the chance to eavesdrop on poets talking shop, working out "whatever is in hand to be worked out," freely or grudgingly giving themselves away. It adds an extra dimension to our understanding of the individual poets to find X and Y talking in a crisp, matter-of-fact way about the nuts and bolts of their verse-making technique, while A and B lean back and take a longer view, risking an occasional aphorism, gingerly invoking an influence or a precedent. It's significant, too, that one poet may choose to reconstruct the actual circumstances of her poem's composition (an idle meal at a Holiday Inn dining room) while another will dwell on the nature of his self-assigned task (to animate a photograph of an artists' bar in Milan). The outcome could be described as sixty-five ways of looking at a blackboard on which, after a suitable number of false starts and frequent erasures, a poem tentatively emerges. Nor is it an accident that the question of form should trigger off such a range of disclosures. Precisely because form is so elusive a concept, so multilayered a term, it seems perfectly emblematic of the poetic process itself: something that can be illustrated but never rigidly defined, something that can best be grasped with a chosen instance in mind.

A few words are perhaps in order on the methods of selection that this anthology reflects. No effort was made to be comprehensive. I followed no quota system, invoked no specific criterion other than the sense that the poets' work be of a quality and kind that would make it somehow exemplary in this context. Clearly, this was a judgment call. What it boils down to is instinct—and nerve. "You just go on your nerve," Frank O'Hara wrote. "If someone's chasing you down the street with a knife you just run, you don't turn around and shout, 'Give it up! I was a track star for Mineola Prep.'" The remark seems as apposite for the maker of anthologies as for the poet.

If, in perusing the list of contributors to this volume, you spot the omission of a favorite name, please don't assume that I necessarily snubbed him or her. On the college admissions theory that you accept more applicants than you have places for, I solicited material from many more poets than the sixty-five I hoped to end with. Even so, not everyone whose work I admired could be reached; and, of course, not everyone I asked chose to participate. Still, I can't help expressing my satisfaction with the finished product. The poems and statements, illuminating or usefully dissenting from one another, delight as they instruct. They argue well for the healthy state of contemporary poetry.

Ecstatic Occasions, Expedient Forms

A. R. Ammons *was born on a farm outside*

Whiteville, North Carolina, in the New Hope Community in 1926. After working at the North Carolina Shipbuilding Company in Wilmington for some months, he was inducted into the U.S. Naval Reserve, where he served for nineteen months, mostly in the South Pacific on a destroyer escort. With the help of the G.I. Bill, he earned a B.S. in General Science in 1949 from Wake Forest College. He attended the University of California, Berkeley, until 1952, then worked at his father-in-law's glassware company until 1964. Garbage (Norton, 1993), his most recent book, won the National Book Award in 1994, the second time Ammons has been thus honored. He was the guest editor of The Best American Poetry 1994. *He lives in Ithaca, New York, and teaches at Cornell University. "I've never had a writing schedule," Ammons says. "I believe that a motion commences from deeper down than day-knowledge and that the figure of the poem to emerge has already been dreamed and rehearsed somehow and that it announces itself when it is ready. I feel it as it is about to unwind into my consciousness. I feel it as an urge, an imminent possibility, go to the typewriter, and follow through." Ammons and his wife, Phyllis, have one son, John Randolph Ammons.*

INSIDE OUT

Among the many kinds of poetic form are those that realize themselves in stasis (achieved by motion) and those that identify their shape, their intelligibility through motion, as motion. Sonnets, villanelles are inventions like triangles (these may be discoveries) and their use is to cause "nature" to find its form only if it can do so in arbitrary human terms. There is the famous possibility that internal, organic form and imposed, external form may on splendid occasions complement each other as in a single necessity. But arbitrary forms please us even when they are interposed and impositional because they reassure us that we can repress nature, our own natures, and achieve sufficient expression with no more than a trifling threat, or we can take delight that we, mere human beings, have devised systems nature (or energy) is clearly, truly, abundantly released through. The danger is that arbitrary forms may be boringly clever compensations for a lack of native force, boxes to be filled with crushed material, boxes which may be taken to exhaust the unlimited existences inventive prosody can find to station the arbitrary in the work of art.

There are gestural and figural forms, too, internal assimilations that are narratives shaping transactions. I've chosen a short poem of mine to

show how the figure of winding can suggest the manifold accuracy by
which a brook or stream summarizes the meteorological action of whole
terrains, so that wherever there are hills and valleys one can confidently
look to find the winding of this dragon of assimilation.

Serpent Country

Rolled off a side of mountains or
hills, bottomed
out in flatland but getting

away, winding,
will be found a
bright snake—brook, stream, or river, or,

in sparest gatherings,
a wash of stones or a green
streak of chaparral across sand.

The figures, though, in this poem are controlled by other progressions, and these progressions are the real form of the poem. In one
motion, the figure enlarges from brook to stream to river, but then the
figure disappears till the only "stream" in the landscape is a trace of
green in the brush where an underground stream once briefly moved.
The form of the poem is the motion from the indelible river to the nearly
vanished green. It is a figure of disappearing. That is one kind of internal
form. It allows to nature full presence and action, it excludes nothing a
priori and imposes nothing. It discovers within. It uses human faculties
to imagine means, analogies to simplify so much material, to derive from
the broad sweep of action the accurate figure and the ineluctable, suitable form of motion.

John Ashbery *was born in Rochester, New York, in 1927. He is the author of fifteen books of poetry, including* And the Stars Were Shining *(Farrar, Straus and Giroux, 1994) and* Flow Chart *(Knopf, 1991). Self-Portrait in a Convex Mirror (1975) received the Pulitzer Prize, the National Book Critics Circle Award, and the National Book Award. A collection of his art criticism,* Reported Sightings, *was published by Knopf in 1989. He has delivered the Charles Eliot Norton Lectures at Harvard University*

and is currently the Charles P. Stevenson, Jr., Professor of Languages and Literature at Bard College. "I am aware of the pejorative associations of the word 'escapist,'" Ashbery has said, "but I insist that we need all the escapism we can get and even that isn't going to be enough." He was the guest editor of The Best American Poetry 1988.

Variation on a Noel

"when the snow lay round about,
deep and crisp and even . . ."

A year away from the pigpen, and look at him.
A thirsty unit by an upending stream,
Man doctors, God supplies the necessary medication
If elixir were to be found in the world's dolor, where is none.

A thirsty unit by an upending stream,
Ashamed of the moon, of everything that hides too little of her
    nakedness—
If elixir were to be found in the world's dolor, where is none,
Our emancipation should be great and steady.

Ashamed of the moon, of everything that hides too little of her
    nakedness,
The twilight prayers begin to emerge on a country crossroads.
Our emancipation should be great and steady
As crossword puzzles done in this room, this after-effect.

The twilight prayers begin to emerge on a country crossroads
Where no sea contends with the interest of the cherry trees.
As crossword puzzles done in this room, this after-effect,
I see the whole thing written down.

Where no sea contends with the interest of the cherry trees
Everything but love was abolished. It stayed on, a stepchild.
I see the whole thing written down
Business, a lack of drama. Whatever the partygoing public needs.

Everything but love was abolished. It stayed on, a stepchild.
The bent towers of the playroom advanced to something like
    openness,
Business, a lack of drama. Whatever the partygoing public needs
To be kind, and to forget, passing through the next doors.

The bent towers of the playroom advanced to something like
    openness.
But if you heard it, and if you didn't want it
To be kind, and to forget, passing through the next doors
(For we believe him not exiled from the skies). . . ?

But if you heard it, and if you didn't want it,
Why do I call to you after all this time?
For we believe him not exiled from the skies.
Because I wish to give only what the specialist can give,

Why do I call to you after all this time?
Your own friends, running for mayor, behaving outlandishly
Because I wish to give only what the specialist can give,
Spend what they care to.

Your own friends, running for mayor, behaving outlandishly,
(And I have known him cheaply)
Spend what they care to,
A form of ignorance, you might say. Let's leave that though.

And I have known him cheaply.
Agree to remove all that concern, another exodus—
A form of ignorance, you might say. Let's leave that though.
The mere whiteness was a blessing, taking us far.

Agree to remove all that concern, another exodus.
A year away from the pigpen, and look at him.
The mere whiteness was a blessing, taking us far.
Man doctors, God supplies the necessary medication.

I first came across the word *pantoum* as the title of one of the movements
of Ravel's "Trio," and then found the term in a manual of prosody. I
wrote a poem called "Pantoum" in the early '50s; it is in my book *Some
Trees*. "Variation on a Noel" is the only other time I have ever used the
form. The poem was written in December of 1979. I was attracted to the
form in both cases because of its stricture, even greater than in other
hobbling forms such as the sestina or canzone. These restraints seem to
have a paradoxically liberating effect, for me at least. The form has the
additional advantage of providing you with twice as much poem for your
effort, since every line has to be repeated twice.

Frank Bidart *was born in Bakersfield, California, in 1939. He was educated at the University of California, Riverside, and Harvard University. In 1990 he published* In the Western Night: Collected Poems, 1965–90 *(Farrar, Straus and Giroux, 1990). He is now completing a new collection entitled* Desire. *He received a three-year writer's award from the Lila Wallace–Reader's Digest Fund in 1991. He teaches at Wellesley College and lives in Cambridge, Massachusetts.*

THINKING THROUGH FORM

I am still a boy lying on his bed in a dark room every afternoon after school.

I am listening to radio-dramas one after the other, for hours, before dinner. Then after dinner—until my mother and grandmother try to force me to go to sleep. They don't understand why after school I insist on listening to "my programs" on the radio instead of staying outside and playing with my friends.

Later—Olivier's "To be or not to be." Garland's *A Star Is Born.* The ironic, massive outraged fury of Brando's "Friends, Romans, countrymen" on the soundtrack of MGM's *Julius Caesar.* Much later—arias sung by Maria Callas. The *shape* of these songs, soliloquies, arias heard thousands of times when I was discovering what I loved.

Toscanini's Beethoven Ninth. Kazan's *East of Eden*—read about for months, and at last seen, again and again.

How thin the actual poems I've written are next to the intensities, the symphonic panoramas of ecstasy and conflict and denouement in the works of art that as a boy I imagined someday I would make!

Soliloquies. Arias. Father-son dramatic *agon.* Symphonies—whatever we crave to experience over and over as we discover what art can be. *Love buries these ghost-forms within us.* Forms are the language of desire before desire has found its object.

"Form": I feel my brain always slightly short-circuits in front of this word. Like "freedom" or "Romanticism," it is full of contradictions, necessary, and trails behind it a long, bloody history of passionately held opportunities for mutual contempt and condescension. Is there some way to think about "form" in which we can escape habitual assumptions, predilections, the hell of "opinions"? Perhaps all we can do is ask the use or practice our ideas are meant to serve—and the conceptions they

contradict, or try to enlarge. What poets say never satisfies theorists. Most present-day theory seems to most poets a remote, rival universe.

The idea about form that has been most compelling and useful to me as a poet—the idea that, when I discovered it in graduate school, seemed to describe something like what I already had experienced—is Coleridge's notion of "organic form." It finally rests, I think, on a poetics of embodiment. The crucial texts are his lectures on Shakespeare and wonderful essay "On Poesy or Art."

For Coleridge, the artist "imitates," but must not "copy" the subject of the work of art. "The artist must imitate that which is within the thing, that which is active through form and figure. . . ." If Shakespeare had imitated merely the external "form or figure" of his characters, he would have produced dead copies, figures in a wax museum. The Nurse in *Romeo and Juliet,* for example, doesn't talk the way real nurses (or any human being) talked: "We know that no Nurse talked exactly in that way, tho' particular sentences might be to that purpose."

In the true work of art, "that which is *within* the thing" *takes on form* (just as "that which is active" in it took on form in the living world, in "nature")—and by a kind of self-manifesting, shows itself to us: "Each thing that lives has its moment of self-exposition, and so has each period of each thing, if we remove the disturbing forces of accident. To do this is the business of ideal art. . . ."

Such "self-exposition"—the *thing that lives* embodying its being by finding its shape in a work of art—is "organic form." Coleridge opposes it to "mechanical regularity," form that is imposed from without, predetermined:

> The form is mechanic when on any given material we impress a predetermined form, not necessarily arising out of the properties of the material, as when to a mass of wet clay we give whatever shape we wish it to retain when hardened. The organic form, on the other hand, is innate; it shapes as it develops itself from within, and the fullness of its development is one and the same with the perfection of its outward form. Such is the life, such the form.

By attacking "pre-determined form" Coleridge is *not* attacking traditional forms like meter or formal stanzaic patterns. (He can't imagine poetry without meter, arguing that "all nations have felt" that "the invention of metre and measured sounds" is "the vehicle and involucrum of poetry.") His point is that *only by the appropriate form* can the subject of the poem reveal itself—the poem's formal means must embody the form *that is already there,* the innate structure at least implicit in "the properties of the material." The difference between the work of art and "nature" must never be obscured:

> If there be likeness to nature without any check of difference, the result is disgusting. . . . Why are such simulations of nature, as waxwork figures of men and women, so disagreeable? . . . You set out with a supposed reality and are disappointed and disgusted with the deception, whilst in respect to a work of genuine imitation, you begin with an acknowledged total difference, and then every touch of nature gives you the pleasure of an approximation to truth.

But to have "*genuine* imitation" (the phrase catches that reconciliation of the seemingly irreconcilable Coleridge so often insists is necessary—and possible), the source or ground of form must always be beyond form: "The idea which puts the form together cannot itself be the form."

When form *proceeds* from subject, "developing itself from within," what speaks, what the work "witnesses" is the at-last-manifested *thing that lives* itself. The subject "witnesses itself," as if without the intervention of the author: "Remember that there is a difference between form as proceeding, and shape as superinduced;—the latter is either the death or the imprisonment of the thing;—the former is its self-witnessing and self-effected sphere of agency."

Coleridge's language often implies that self-witnessing "organic form" has an inner life of its own, independent of the will of the artist: "*it* shapes as it develops itself from within. . . ." Similarly, the work of art has its own laws, the organic laws of a living body:

> Imagine not I am about to oppose genius to rules. No! . . . The spirit of poetry, like all other living powers, must of necessity circumscribe itself by rules, were it only to unite power with beauty. It must embody in order to reveal itself; but a living body is of necessity an organized one,—and what is organization, but the connection of parts to a whole, so that each part is at once end and means!

"It must embody in order to reveal itself"—for Coleridge, this is the fundamental process, the great principle lying beneath the making of a poem, and all art. It is a generous and enabling principle, for it says that "the world," reality, what is real beyond words or the medium of an art, can get into art—can take on its appropriate form and reveal its life. There is no single formula or paradigm, in Coleridge, for *how* this happens, the artist's role in or control over it. In a typically pregnant,

semi-opaque, for me extremely eloquent passage, he meditates the mystery of the relations between the power of law and the power of something original, of creation:

> No work of true genius dare want its appropriate form; neither indeed is there any danger of this. As it must not, so neither can it, be lawless! For it is even this that constitutes it[s] genius—the power of acting creatively under laws of its own origination.

How does *"organic form"* bear on what I experience when I try to write a poem? The "subject" of most poems is not as defined, or nameable, as the character in a drama—so the fact that Coleridge's discussion of organic form is embedded in his lectures on Shakespeare's plays leaves a great deal unexplored, unsaid.

In what sense is the *form* of a lyric the "self-witnessing" of its subject?

I know that when I read a poem I want the sensation that it is. I'm only able to write a poem when, in what I write, I have at least the illusion that it is. I'll try to explore this in relation to my poem "To the Dead" (printed at the end of this essay).

The form of the poem—though idiosyncratic, and undoubtedly not at first consciously taken in by the reader—is perfectly regular. It is made up of an opening of six lines, two middle sections of twelve lines each, and a closing section that is the same length as the opening. At the end of the two middle sections there is an extra line, which becomes a kind of "refrain"—it is the same as the last line of the opening. Aside from these "refrain" lines, set off as separate stanzas, the poem is made up of alternating two-line and one-line stanzas. The structure, in other words, looks like this:

> opening section (6 lines in 4 stanzas—alternating 2-line and 1-line stanzas throughout the rest of the poem)
>
> first middle section (about *The Gorilla*—12 lines in 8 stanzas)
>
> "refrain" line (same as last line of opening section)
>
> second middle section (about the "you" addressed by the poem—12 lines in 8 stanzas)
>
> "refrain" line
>
> closing section (6 lines in 4 stanzas)

This is the *stanzaic* structure of the poem.

I didn't, of course, begin by deciding to fill out so idiosyncratic and seemingly arbitrary a structure. (The other formal stanzaic patterns I've used have been either traditional—a sonnet, a villanelle—or very simple, like unrhymed couplets.) How did it happen?

The first lines I wrote were the last three of the poem.

The love I've known is the love of
two people staring

not at each other, but in the same direction.

At first I wrote them as two lines. They looked terrible—*lousy*. They didn't look the way I heard them.

The love I've known is the love of two people staring
not at each other, but in the same direction.

Nothing of the dynamic within the idea is present in how this looks on the page.

So I tried setting it up in three lines, with a stanza break after the second—as it now stands. Now I had something balanced ("The *love* I've known is the *love* of"), followed by something linked to it—because in the same stanza—which is not "balanced" but points *outside* the stanza ("two people staring"). After the gap, the slight pause of the stanza break, the sentence is completed by a line which—by denying an expectation—reestablishes "balance" ("not at each other, but in the same direction"). The denial of an expectation becomes the means of understanding the nature of the thing (love) that caused the expectation.

To my eyes, set up in three lines this *action* is present.

This didn't, of course, necessarily make them good lines. I had the sense that I was quoting *somebody,* but I wasn't sure who—Augustine? It turns out I was quoting Auden, as quoted in Rudy Kikel's "Local Visions." Auden, it turns out, was quoting Saint-Exupéry. (Was *he* quoting Augustine?)

I felt the lines should end the poem, but they looked hardly more than a moralism, or homily. When the words came into my head, they were accompanied by a very strong affect—bleakness, misery. *Loss.* But in themselves, on the page, they were curiously blank. The poem, the still-unwritten lines that came before them, would have to fill them—a little like Garbo's face at the end of *Queen Christina,* across which (during an extremely long tracking shot) one reads the most *opposite* emotions. (Her director, Rouben Mamoulian, told her to think of nothing, or a banana.) I wanted the lines to be denser than simply misery,

Frank Bidart   9

bleakness. The fact that I was probably quoting the lines didn't seem irrelevant; I wanted them to seem (in their "eloquence") a kind of given of the culture, of our life—just *there,* like a boulder. A boulder across which we read very different emotions depending on the light and air, depending on what we are already feeling when we come on it.

So the *poem* had still to be written. The poem I imagined was about love; and at least four people I was close to who were dead.

It has seemed again and again in my experience that the moments of greatest connection—the moments of intimacy that were the ground of later connection—happened when one of us (for whatever reason) had had to look straight *down,* into the nearly intolerable things that couldn't be changed. These things are always, in some way, "secrets"—even if only secret from our daylight selves. *This* was what we were staring at "in the same direction"; *this* was what I knew had to bear down on the reader of the poem as the reader read the final lines.

For a long time I had had banging around in my head a line I didn't know what to do with:

There is a NIGHT within the NIGHT . . .

Like the final lines, which looked so emotionally "blank" alone, this entirely "unexplicit" line was associated in my mind with a great deal— in part, with that intimacy, that "staring" I have been describing, the yearning to return to it and the sense that both of us were (for moments at least) in fact still alive there.

The line, for me, embodies this through the kind of violation of language common in mysticism—it is the night *inside* the night, like but unlike night. The movement of this line seemed a kind of ecstatic appre- hension of this night: the movement *inside* which is an opening *out.* I didn't want to "rationalize" the line in the poem—I hoped that by repetition, in different contexts, it would accrue the density of the things I associated with it.

For this to happen, the movement I have described couldn't be isolated in one line. The whole texture of the poem—the movement of the poem throughout—had to embody at least variations of this move- ment *inside* that is an opening out. Or, conversely, a breaking out that is also somehow a completion.

After I wrote a version of the three lines immediately preceding the final three, I saw that a pattern was possible—alternating two-line and one-line stanzas. This seemed to catch the motion of something partly "balanced," enclosed yet also partly "unstable"—out of which some- thing breaks that, in freeing itself, to some degree balances and "completes" what came before. I began to think of each group of two-lines followed by one-line as a "unit" of this motion.

Then I wrote the opening of the poem, which has a great deal of "balancing" in the lines ("What I *hope* (when I *hope*)"), and repetition across lines ("see each other *again*,— / . . . and *again* reach the VEIN"). The repetition and balancing partly betray uncertainty, over-assertion: "It existed. *It existed.*" The first single line of the poem, to a degree, "breaks out" of the opening couplet (". . . and again reach the VEIN"), but the second single line does this much more:

There is a NIGHT within the NIGHT,—

The section that follows is an elaborated parallel to the experience with the "you" addressed by the poem, its "mirror image" that—the reader should finally see—is its opposite. The parallel is optimistic and comic. It came out of *The Gorilla,* a not-very-good (but lively) movie starring the Ritz Brothers—who play detectives assigned to catch, or unmask, a gorilla threatening the inhabitants of a mansion. The detectives discover that there is a "house within the house," hidden rooms out of which the gorilla suddenly pops. The walls are not walls, but corridors. The "inner" house—on which the health of the "outer" house depends, where the secrets that threaten to destroy the life of the "outer" house lie hidden—*can* be penetrated. The parallel is optimistic because, when the "inner" house gives up its secrets, the act frees, "disenthralls" those who live there. (This happens even if the detectives are the Ritz Brothers.)

The passage as a whole imitates this movement *in* that is also a discovery, a freeing. The discovery is ecstatically, decisively grasped—and then the last line of the opening section is repeated, for the night *inside* night is its mirror:

that is the HOUSE within the HOUSE . . .

There is a NIGHT within the NIGHT,—

I still hadn't written the passage about the relationship with "you." The poem thus far was very "cold" (except, perhaps, for the opening lines). Obviously this was the most intense, painful material in the poem. I didn't want the passage to be a "portrait"—I thought that its center was a process, a pattern that had been true for me again and again. But I also found that I couldn't write it if I didn't in fact think about *one* person, a specific relationship.

I wrote it again and again. I felt that, ideally, this section should be exactly the same length as the *Gorilla* section—the reader should feel the parallel, the more passionate "inner" house like and unlike the colder "outer" house. But I wanted not to count lines—when the passage about the friend felt right, present, elaborated, *"there,"* if I had understood all this material in the right way the two passages *should* be the same length.

Well, they turned out to be. If, when I finally did count lines, the passage about the "you" had turned out to be a different length, perhaps I would have decided it wasn't "right." I don't know; I didn't have to face the question.

The house in *The Gorilla* finally is a measure of what didn't happen in the section addressed to "you." Insight *didn't* free the dead friend—but the next lines nonetheless insistently summon up the night of staring "in the same direction," because it is the night in which both are still alive, the night inside night whose secret became the place they both *inhabit.*

> . . . for, there at times at night, still we
> inhabit the secret place together . . .
>
> Is this wisdom, or self-pity?—

In this mixed light we come upon the poem's final three lines.

The poem, then, has many subjects: the nature of the relationship with the dead "you," *The Gorilla,* the night inside night, etc. But the fundamental subject of the poem is the (for me, intensely emotional) act of "apprehending" and ordering these materials, these "subjects"—the act that is the poem itself. ("Apprehending" that *is* ordering.) This act is not anterior to the poem; the poem is not an imitation of an action that happened *prior* to it. But the action "imitated" *is* "real"—as the poem came into existence, it happened in my soul or psyche, not simply on paper. It is not simply an "art emotion" (Eliot's phrase). It happened *through* the form the poem had assumed on the page. Writing the poem was the only way I could perform this action—for me, a necessary one.

Because the fundamental subject of the poem is an action, one cannot point to an element in the poem and say, "This is its form." The form of the "action" is inseparable from the form of the whole. The reader will have to decide whether the form of *this* poem "witnesses" the action that, for its author, animates it.

But working on the poem, I felt that the repeated formal elements—alternating two-line and one-line stanzas, "balanced" length of sections, etc.—were crucial to an essential quality of this action: the sense that I was high above the material, looking down, "seeing it as a whole," *at the same time* that I was next to it, at the center of its intensity, its being. I had this sense only when I had the illusion that I was apprehending *what was there,* that the elements of the poem had found their form and were indeed before me. They didn't seem to be the playthings of my will or invention; I couldn't decide that "There is a LIGHT within the NIGHT" was a lively variant. I felt that I had to submit to what was there, that the order I made out of it meant anything only if I had seen its nature. (It *was* there, I felt, only when I had given myself up to it.)

Form is one of the great antipodes of almost all our thinking.

It is an aspect of one pole of the dichotomies that dominate Western thinking: Apollo vs. Dionysus, Plato vs. Aristotle, body vs. spirit, super-ego vs. id. (Who said that each human being is either a Platonist or an Aristotelian?) Schiller thought that man's two basic drives are "the sensuous impulse" and "the formal impulse"—both of which are subsumed into "the play impulse," which responds to the "living shape" (*Lebensform*) of the world.

As Coleridge constantly suggests, art cuts across or bewilders these dichotomies. Recently I came across the following passage in Cioran's *Drawn and Quartered* (translated by Richard Howard):

> The real writer writes about beings, things, events, he does not write about writing, he uses words but does not linger over them, making them the object of his ruminations. He will be anything and everything except an anatomist of the Word. Dissection of language is the fad of those who, having nothing to say, confine themselves to the saying.

At first I said, *Yes.* I asked myself, angrily and rhetorically, what Dante, Keats, Chekhov (except in moments of despair) would have said about the currently fashionable notion that the end and impulse of language is language.

But then I had to recoil. Cioran's dichotomy between "the real writer" and the "anatomist of the Word" isn't convincing. Precisely what he leaves out is *form.* Every writer feels, I think, that the structure he is working within allows him to say some things—and does *not* allow him to say other things. The relation between "words" and "things" is mediated always, to some degree, by form. Without the "form" of "To the Dead," to my mind the fundamental subject—the action of the whole—would not have existed. (Some action of thinking through some of the materials in the poem would exist, but not *this* action.) I certainly "lingered" over the language of the poem, and even felt that I had to "submit" to the nature of what the words "witnessed" (especially in a line like "There is a NIGHT within the NIGHT").

In our language, "form" jumps between categories associated with "idea" and categories associated with "matter." We speak of Platonic "forms" and formal *means*. In the body vs. spirit dichotomy, form is associated with "body," not "spirit"—to be *born* is to assume a *form*. To create a work of art is to kill those shimmering possibilities, that glowing penumbra of mystery that the not-yet-formed, not yet *real* work of art can have. (Picasso calls a painting a "hoard of destructions." This essay destroys the essay it might have been.) Chaos (the not-formed), for us, isn't life—but it's hard, once something is born, not to feel dissolution isn't all-too-imminent. The relation between "meaning" and *formal means* is a kind of bewildering dialogue—like form's mediation between words and things.

The point of this essay is not to bring order out of chaos by making a plea for "organic form." Catchphrases get separated from the discussion that gave them substance, and then seem so misleading they have to be obliterated. Basil Bunting says in an interview, "I have never supposed a poem to be organic at all. I don't think the thing grows, it's built and put together by a craftsman. . . ." I don't think Coleridge uses the word "grows"—he says that organic form "shapes as it develops itself from within." Certainly *craft* isn't the alternative to "organic form," as Coleridge understands the term. "To the Dead" was constructed, "built," not written starting at the beginning and ending at the end. Certainly Coleridge would agree that a poem is "built and put together by a craftsman."

But Bunting's impatience with the term betrays an impatience with at least its implications that is implicit in modernism. The term "organic" doesn't quite acknowledge how much violation of the formal surface may well be necessary for the *thing that lives* to find its authentic, startling form—to assert its irresistible, dismaying life. The *thing that lives* isn't necessarily anterior to its "form," and has often lived in this century by violation, juxtaposition, disjunction—not by a process that feels "organic."

Forms seek subjects. Milton wanted to write an epic before he knew what it would be about; he made a list of subjects. The opening of *The Prelude* is about Wordsworth's similar desire, his dismayed sense that he has no subject adequate to his will to write a long poem. Then he begins the long narrative of the growth of his own mind—for the human mind (he asserts in "The Recluse") *is* a subject of epic importance, if we have looked down into it and dared to see it correctly.

No dichotomy, no term like "organic" or "craft" seems right.

The image that haunts me is Brünnhilde in the circle of fire—the fire that keeps her alive, but that cuts her sleeping figure off from the rest of life. *Form* is the magic circle—the life-giving but otherlife-excluding Circle of Fire—within which the poem can exist in the world. Form is body.

To the Dead

What I hope (when I hope) is that we'll
see each other again,—

. . . and again reach the VEIN

in which we loved each other . . .
It existed. *It existed.*

There is a NIGHT within the NIGHT,—

. . . for, like the detectives (the Ritz Brothers)
in *The Gorilla,*

once we'd been battered by the gorilla

we searched the walls, the intricately carved
impenetrable panelling

for a button, lever, latch

that unlocks a secret door that
reveals at last the secret chambers,

CORRIDORS within WALLS,

(the disenthralling, necessary, dreamed structure
beneath the structure we see,)

that is the HOUSE within the HOUSE . . .

There is a NIGHT within the NIGHT,—

. . . there were (for example) months when I seemed only
to displease, frustrate,

disappoint you—; then, something triggered

a drunk lasting for days, and as you
slowly and shakily sobered up,

sick, throbbing with remorse and self-loathing,

insight like ashes: clung
to; useless; hated . . .

This was the viewing of the power of the waters

while the waters were asleep:—
secrets, histories of loves, betrayals, double-binds

not fit (you thought) for the light of day . . .

There is a NIGHT within the NIGHT,—

. . . for, there at times at night, still we
inhabit the secret place together . . .

Is this wisdom, or self-pity?—

The love I've known is the love of
two people staring

not at each other, but in the same direction.

Eavan Boland *was born in Dublin in 1945,
though she spent much of her
childhood in England, where her father was an ambassador. She has
published six volumes of poetry, among them* Outside History, The
War Horse, In Her Own Image, New Territory, The Journey, *and*
Object Lessons: The Life of the Woman and the Poet in Our Time
*(Norton, 1995). In her poem "The Muse Mother" (1982), Boland
wrote of learning "a new language, /to be a sybil /able to sing the
past /in pure syllables, //limning hymns sung /to belly wheat or a
woman, /able to speak at last /my mother tongue." She reviews regularly for the* Irish Times *and lives with her husband and two daughters
in a suburb of Dublin that "is south enough to be near Wicklow but is
still at an angle from the coast and bay of Dublin. About two miles
from the house, traveling west, is Dun Laoghaire harbor—the man-
made granite harbor of the poem. Here the ships of empire anchored.
And here the Irish emigrants left for England. And this is the subject of
the poem '[The Harbor].' She teaches at Stanford University.*

The Harbor

This harbor was made by art and force
and called Kingstown and afterward Dun Laoghaire
and holds the sea behind its barrier
less than five miles from my house.

City of shadows and of the gradual
capitulations to the last invader,
this is the final one: signed in water
and witnessed in granite and ugly bronze and gunmetal.

Lord be with us say the makers of a nation.
Lord look down say the builders of a harbor.
They came and cut a shape out of ocean
and left stone to close around their labor.

Officers and their wives promenaded
on this spot once and saw with their own eyes
the opulent horizon and obedient skies
which nine-tenths of the law provided.

Frigates with thirty-six guns cruising
the outer edges of influence could idle
and enter here and catch the tide of
arrogance and empire and the Irish Sea rising

and rising through a century of storms
and cormorants and moonlight all along this coast
while an empire forgot an ocean and the armed
ships under it changed to salt and rust:

a seagull with blue and white and gray feathers
swoops down and rolls and finishes
its flight overhead and vanishes—
its colors stolen where the twilight gathers.

This poem is more rhymed and more metrical than most of my work. I chose the form for the speaker's cadence and outsiderly tone. This short, blocky four-by-four quatrain is familiar to me from when I was a young poet in Dublin. It stays in my mind as the stanza of telegrams, annunciations, and conclusions. And I suppose it is also, somewhere at the back of my mind, a cadet and junior version of the great Irish ballad stanza that begins with narrative and ends with summons.

Interestingly, that ballad stanza—many of them were revolutionary in purpose—aimed to draw in the hearer while firmly excluding the speaker from the action. It achieved a strange combination of street-corner rhetoric with a considerable degree of Greek choric detachment. I have always been interested in that aspect of the Irish ballad, and I probably moved toward it in "The Harbor," which is a poem about the decline of empire—as so many of those were also.

The way in which a poem is composed—I mean the actual, physical, and metaphysical act of putting it together—sometimes seems to me cultural more than anything else. The Irish bards, for instance, were journalistic in many of their functions. They made songs for christenings and weddings. They brought news from village to village. They recited invective against the enemies of their patron. But their methods of composition were strangely pure and uncompromising. They went into the darkened rooms and lay down and composed in their heads. How true that was in every case I have no idea, but even the legend has left a subtle influence on Irish poetry.

It influenced me when I was a young poet—I would do some work in my head before I wrote the poem—but my progress since has been very un-bardic. I think the line composed in the head is more symmetrical, has primary sound colors, and gives very little grays and half-tones and a fairly poor array of dissonance. In fact, when I returned to this poem on the page, having drawn a lot of it in my mind, I tried to include some of the dissonance. For instance, I changed the eighth line from "witness in granite and gun-metal" to what it is.

Donald Britton

was born in San Angelo, Texas, in 1951. He received his undergraduate degree at the University of Texas, Austin, and his Ph.D in literary studies at the American University in Washington, D.C., with a dissertation on John Ashbery. His poems appeared in the Paris Review *and* Christopher Street *and were collected in his book* Italy, *which was published by Little Caesar Press in 1981. In 1988 he moved from New York City to Los Angeles, where he was an executive in the firm of Brierley and Partners. "The Dark Side of Disneyland," his two-part essay about the death imagery on some of the rides, appeared in* Art Issues. *He died of AIDS on July 22, 1994.*

Winter Garden
for Robert Dash

A permanent occasion
Knotted into the clouds: pink, then blue,
Like a baby holding its breath, or colorless

As the gush and pop of conversations
Under water. You feel handed from clasp to clasp,
A concert carried off by the applause.

Other times, half of you is torn
At the perforated line and mailed away.
You want to say, "Today, the smithereens

Must fend for themselves,"
And know the ever-skating decimal's joy,
To count on thin ice

Growing thinner by degrees, taking its own
Sweet time and taking us with it,
To navigate magnetic zones in which

Intense ecstatic figures touch, like worlds,
But don't collide, it being their devotion
To depend on you to name for each

A proper sphere. "Today, I turn to silence;
Let the language do the talking."
X the Unknown and his laughable, loveable crew,

The tumbling balconies of one-of-us-is-a-robot-
And-it's-*not*-me waves
(Spanking a beach so empty

If you weren't around to trip me
Would I really fall?) and days
When the wind is a bridge across our power

To enumerate, to dig, to plant, to hold
And to communicate the twill-and-tweed-
Colored field's coldness

Toward our game of enticing it indoors,
As if we could erect a rival gate to the departure
Whose uniform destination can't surprise,

Is blind, speaks not,
When on those white and sudden afternoons
I take your eyes, and see the sun set twice.

If "Winter Garden" has any claim at all to formal rigor, it would have to lie in my attempt to "non-personalize" or psychologically denature the poem—to detach it from any single speaker or communication context, yet maintain the illusion of a coherent, at times even elegant, discourse.

The poem has no "speaker," no "voice," no "persona," no "point of view." Rather, it is formally organized around a series of artificial statements, false-bottomed and meaningless in relation to ordinary purposive uses of language. It was my hope to take maximum advantage of the capacity of language to convey meaning, even when nothing is being said, e.g., "If you weren't around to trip me / Would I really fall?" Insofar as the poem flirts with nonsense in this way, it is almost a parody of a poem, its chief trope being to express at some length its own emptiness.

In fact, only in a poem does it seem possible to discuss the joy an illuminated quartz decimal point might feel as it skates back and forth across the display panel of a pocket calculator. To make statements about the "experiences" of such subjects, which are presumed not even to *have* experiences to report, is perhaps to conceive of poetry as the medium which expresses *"le langage des fleurs et des choses muettes."* But, to me at any rate, it is also to project oneself toward that point where one's words cease to comment on *any* experience, but become an experience in and of themselves: empty of discursive content, perhaps, but full of all manner of things *language* wants to say, but people usually don't.

Lucie Brock-Broido was born in Pittsburgh in 1956. She

received her M.A. from the Johns Hopkins University and her M.F.A. from Columbia University. She is the author of two books, A Hunger *(1988) and* The Master Letters *(1995), both from Knopf. She has received a fellowship from the Fine Arts Work Center in Provincetown, the Hoyns Fellowship from the University of Virginia, and a fellowship in poetry from the National Endowment for the Arts. She held the Briggs-Copeland appointment in poetry at Harvard University from 1988 until 1993. Currently she teaches in the graduate writing division of Columbia University. She lives in New York City and in Cambridge, Massachusetts.*

Hitchcock Blue

That these we take for granted:
The blue turn of the water at Three.
The bones of the lover alone, still
Life in Prussian Blue. The blonde in the
Fur cap at the northern seaport in
Late November.

These given which we have come to regard:
Anima, Animus
I have gone into the fire and lived
There. I told you in a letter
You touch it only once
You watch it for awhile you enter the
Flame. The blue part of the scald
The part that mars the skin, remembering
It will not forgive, forever. That's a
Pretty thing.

We imagined life without that auburn
Heat of the South, ultra
Marine by day, direct. Aniline and
Dangerous by dusk, midnight
Blue by midnight as we lay together in that
Blue of blues we said the soul, a girl, could
Travel anywhere, could read the hieroglyphs
Could dream the cornflowers out of
Nothingness, could weather any temperature or fire
Bombing, could watch the death of any small
Thing we were metaphysical when we were young
Like that.

Imagine this
That it is summer in the Arctic

Regions now. That all the ice
Has come down washing the earth
Clean of its hands. Even if I was alive
Then and loose
In Dresden as a little girl
Even if I had lived
Through that winter and
Come to the West to watch you in
White as you did your alchemies, even
Then I would want you as some
Thing I could write down, some
Palpable, milori blue substance
A metal, a stone.

Alfred Hitchcock gave a Blue dinner party years ago. Everything—the
steak, the mashed potatoes, even the silverware—was tinted a deep blue.
There were blueberries for dessert. As the story goes, not one of his
guests questioned the unnatural blueness of the meal, except perhaps to
wonder why he had chosen this particular hue.

The title "Hitchcock Blue" preceded the poem by several months. I
knew I wanted to create one small, finite, fairly intimate world which
would concern itself with that particular color in my mind. My invented
blue was a dark exotic one, one which might be visible only in the night.
I set about to incorporate all the cliche connotations of blue—water,
weather, yearning, blue imagination and even blue funk, with my own
private associations with Blues.

I made a list: direct blue, Dresden blue, Prussian blue, sapphire,
bleu d'azur, cerulean, cobalt, aniline, midnight blue, ultramarine, corn-
flower, milori blue. Most of these found their way into the poem. Only
milori proved elusive, for I could not even confirm its existence in the
Oxford English Dictionary. I began to think it was, perhaps, a fabrica-
tion. Eventually, a painter friend of mine found the color and sent me a
streak of it on a white board. Milori was the perfect blue to end the poem
with—a deep, substantial color, a romantic one, a word which sounded
like milord. "Hitchcock Blue" is, after all, a love poem.

The idea of making a love poem eventually dictated the form. I write
long poems which tell stories in personae which are rarely my own. This
is one of my first poems in my own voice. Admittedly, that voice is
shrouded, but it is mine nonetheless. The form was to be in the genre of
the poem addressed to the Second-Person-Absent Beloved, the un-

named, imagined "You." There isn't actually a story in the poem; rather, there's an obsession with the idea of "coloring a world"—no questions asked—as Hitchcock had once imposed his blue fantasy on his ever-accepting guests. The feminine speaker of the poem attempts to create something out of nothing; the masculine you is in absentia (my formulaic conception of love poems: a yearning). The idea of naming the soul a "girl" in opposition to animus/mind/male became the desire in the poem.

For me, this poem is a brief one; it was originally over twice its present length. I imposed no stanzaic length restrictions on myself, except to follow my decision that each of the four stanzas would end in one two-word phrase (with the fourth beginning the same way) with no enjambment between the stanzas. The line breaks were crucial to the motion of the poem. Since it is not my custom to capitalize the initial word of each line, I decided to experiment with this convention. By doing so, I found I could usually arrange to affix much more weight—a power to the words—not only on the line endings, but on the beginning of each line. There is minimal punctuation as I tried to pare the need for it down to the bone.

John Cage

was born in Los Angeles in 1912. In 1930, after two years at Pomona College, he departed for Paris, where he studied contemporary piano works, painting, and poetry. After returning to the United States, he developed an interest in the music of Arnold Schoenberg and in 1933 became his student at the University of Southern California. While working with a percussion band in Seattle in 1938, he began his lifelong collaboration with the choreographer and dancer Merce Cunningham. After his move to New York City in 1942, Cage grew interested in Eastern philosophy. By 1950, he had discovered the use of the I-Ching as a compositional device, and the method inspired the "chance" theory of composition for which Cage has become famous. Among Cage's earliest works using this principle were "Music of Changes" (1951), Imaginary Landscape 4 (1951), and "Radio Music" (1956). Cage continued to inspire disciples while infuriating critics with such pieces as "4 minutes, 33 seconds" (1952), in which a performer stands silently on stage for four minutes and thirty-three seconds, the only sounds coming from the audience and the environment. Cage was also a mycologist and taught classes in mushroom identification at the New School for Social Research in New

York. His later musical works include Etudes Australes *(1974–75, based on astronomical charts),* Roaratorio *(1979, based on sounds mentioned in Joyce's* Finnegans Wake*), and the five* Europera *works composed from 1987 to 1991. His books include* Empty Words *(1979),* Theme and Variation *(1982),* X *(1983), and* I–IV, *a collection of the Charles Eliot Norton Lectures he delivered at Harvard in 1988–89. Cage lived with Cunningham from 1970 until Cage's death from a stroke on August 12, 1992.*

Writing through a text by Chris Mann

n blo Win
tHru a
brownIe
Sod
Th box n
bLue
a bIt
a spooN

hump arguIn
bunS n juice

fuDge
lIght
D

tWos a
cHeek
a one jump sIt

factS
double duTch
as shouLdnt
bIggst
dowN
large lIke
n Stuff

kit pox Doctors clerk
than on It tell
so meD

Chris Mann (Launching Place 3139 Australia) sent me an untitled text which begins as follows:

"whistlin is did be puckrin up th gob n blowin thru a ol a brownie sod th box n i seen a compo front up n stack on a blue a bit of a spoon th doodlers hump arguin by buying up all buns n juice crack a fudge a droopie go th roy n late th light not worth a pinch a shit the Big H geech n thats a fine how d y do 1234 doin twos a whos up who n blinkin cheek a one jump sit y ring n warby kinda facts that double dutch or wear th daks n though I says it as shouldnt th lips yd smack d be the biggest dill y meet a boo goose urger with a down on by an large like intro d plonk n stuff it up some rat face kit pox doctors clerk gone polc on plug t wage a thru n thru a you know th news n do a turn than on it tell the truth so med"

Using MESOMAKE, a program made at my request by Jim Rosenberg after consultation with Andrew Culver, I chose to have it triggered with the first three words of the text, and separately with Chris Mann's name and the name of the place where he lives. Given two different outputs from an IBM PC, I chose to keep the first: "whistlin is did." Then using the word processor MultiMate I added words from the original text which directly preceded or followed the words already extracted and which did not, as they didn't, break the Mink* rule for a pure mesostic, that is, not to permit the appearance of either letter between two of the spinal name or phrase.** These decisions to add words were not made in any systematic way. The fragment given above is about one twenty-eighth of Chris Mann's total text. My "Writing through a text by Chris Mann" will express "whistlin is did" thirty-six times. Incidentally thirty-six is the number of wakas necessary to make renga. MESOLIST, not yet written, will permit the making of a new "whistlin is did" (a short poem, that is, a haiku) at the drop of a hat or, more exactly, in conjunction with I (a program by Andrew Culver which simulates the *I Ching* coin oracle and relates the numbers one to sixty-four to any other numbers). Thus all words in Chris Mann's text which satisfy the requirements for a W (preceded by a D and followed by an H) will be listed and numbered, and when one is in need of the first

*The late Louis Mink, author of *A Finnegans Wake Gazetteer* and Professor of Philosophy at Wesleyan University, Middletown, Connecticut.
**A mesostic (row down the middle, not down the edge) is like, but is not, an acrostic, which the dictionary (Webster's) defines as "a composition, normally in verse, in which one or more sets of letters (as the initial, middle or final letters of the lines) when taken in order, form a word or words."

spinal word of a new "whistlin is did" mesostic, I (I the program, not I myself) will determine which one is to be used. The stage is then set for the nonsystematic addition of words mentioned above.

Maxine Chernoff *was born in Chicago in 1952. Her six books of*

poems include New Faces of 1952, *which won the 1985 Carl Sandburg Award for Poetry.* Leap Year Day: New and Selected Poems *appeared in 1991. In addition to poetry, she has written a novel,* Plain Grief, *and two collections of short stories, including* Bop, *which won the* Sun-Times/Friends of Literature Award *for 1993 and was a* New York Times *Notable Book of that year. She and Paul Hoover coedit* New American Writing. *She is an associate professor of creative writing at San Francisco State University and is working on her second novel, to be published by Simon and Schuster.*

Phantom Pain

After the leg is lost, the pain remains as an emblem; so the kidnapper cannot part with his ransom notes. The high diver, lost on the subway, flexes his muscles defensively. The crowd fades to waves in a pool eighty feet below. "There," pointing to the nose of a seated passenger, "is where I'll land." The mad bomber turns to his wife and says, "I'll give up my career for you." She pictures his delicate bombs defusing, like scenes in a home movie played backwards. Meanwhile, the kidnapper, grown careless with sentimentality, drops a ransom note on the subway seat. The train conductor, who last night dreamed of a murderer, hides the note like a stolen pistol under his cap. Later the bomber stops at a diner full of known bombers. Anxious, he drops a coffee cup, white fragments exploding at his feet.

In writing prose poems, I am indebted to the work of Henri Michaux and Julio Cortazar, among others who create alternative universes that are as surprising, banal, stupid, and true as our own. A prose poem shouldn't be an excuse for self-indulgent retelling of one's own experience or for dwelling on memory alone; nor should it be mere fancy. Even as prose poems rewrite, dismember or otherwise refer to a long tradition of fable, parable, and other "symbolic" forms, they must exist independently by creating self-contained worlds. A prose poem can aspire to enlarge experience—both the author's and the reader's—rather than merely to mirror it.

Prose poems may be a contemporary equivalent of metaphysical poetry, since in both cases metaphor can expand to become the central concept (conceit) of the writing. The yoking of disparate elements—such as "phantom pain" and a kidnapper's lost ransom notes—is characteristic of both metaphysical poetry and surrealist collage. Nor is that the only thing the two have in common.

Writing "Phantom Pain," I extrapolated from the clinical sense of that term to other applications. The lost high diver looking for a place to land, the mad bomber giving up his career, and the kidnapper "grown careless with sentimentality" are all acting out of nostalgia, as is a person experiencing phantom pain after the loss of a limb. At the same time, there is an ironic undercutting of the concept as it collides with the narrative: the kidnapper's lost note is found and reinterpreted by the train conductor; the mad bomber returns symbolically to his career at the end of the poem.

Finally, "Phantom Pain" is a poem in prose because at the time it was written I felt that attention to line breaks, syllables in a line, end rhyme and stanzas would limit or distract attention from the narrative development and metaphoric density. These are the key ingredients of prose poems as I write them.

Amy Clampitt *was born in New Providence,*

Iowa, in 1920. After graduating from Grinnell College, she moved to New York City in 1941. She worked as an editor and as a reference librarian, wrote novels that were not published, and turned to poems in the late 1960s. Recognition came late; she was in her sixties when The Kingfisher *appeared in 1983, but this was a spectacular debut, vaulting her to the center of critical attention. She had stints of teaching at William and Mary, Amherst, and Smith. Her other books of poetry include* What the Light Was Like *(1985),* Archaic Figure *(1987),* Westward *(1990), and* A Silence Opens *(1994), all published by Knopf.* Predecessors, Et Cetera *appeared in the University of Michigan Press's Poets on Poetry Series in 1991. A play,*

Mad with Joy, *concerning the life and times of Dorothy Wordsworth, was given a staged reading by the Poets' Theatre in Cambridge, Massachusetts, in March 1993.* "I feel a certain kinship with Elizabeth Bishop's *nomadism,*" Clampitt told an interviewer. *"Though I've been in New York for many years, I feel less and less as though I've really* lived *anywhere."* Amy Clampitt died of cancer in September 1994.

Portola Valley

A dense ravine, no inch
of which was level until
some architect niched in this
shimmer of partition, fishpond
and flowerbed, these fording-
stones' unwalled steep staircase
down to where (speak softly) you
take off your shoes, step onto
guest-house tatami matting,
learn to be Japanese.

There will be red wine,
artichokes and California
politics for dinner; a mocking-
bird may whisper, a frog rasp
and go kerplunk, the shifting
inlay of goldfish in the courtyard floor add to your vertigo;
and deer look in, the velvet
thrust of pansy faces and vast
violet-petal ears, inquiring,
stun you without a blow.

Here, a dinner party in California was the ecstatic occasion—a small one, which seemed to call for relatively short lines and a neat look on the page. The form taken by the first stanza pretty much found itself, and the visual end-rhymes (staircase/Japanese, fording/matting) were, as I recall, quite accidental. The concluding rhyme (vertigo/blow) was consciously arrived at, however: the surprise of seeing those deer looking in at us was the effect I knew I was working toward. And in fact, throughout this as in almost everything I've written, I was writing for the ear. It's as though a magnetic chiming device went into operation, and all the waiting possibilities of assonance simply presented themselves: *i*nch, wh*i*ch, unt*i*l, n*i*ched, th*i*s, sh*i*mmer, part*i*tion, f*i*shpond, and so on. Similarly with the consonants, especially the *v*s in the second stanza (*v*ertigo, *v*elvet, *v*ast, *v*iolet-petal). When the occasion is less simple—when I don't have so clear an idea of what I'm going to say—I'm more likely to feel the need of some constraint, and to settle on a more recognizable stanza form, with or without a rhyme scheme that anyone will notice. Except as a concluding device, I tend to avoid rhymes that draw attention to themselves.

Marc Cohen was born in Brooklyn in 1951. He is the author of On Maplewood Time

(Groundwater Press, 1988) and the forthcoming Mecox Road, *also from Groundwater. His work was chosen by John Ashbery, Mark Strand, and Louise Glück for the 1988, 1991, and 1993 volumes of* The Best American Poetry. *From 1987 to 1992 he served as codirector of the Intuflo Reading Series in New York City. He edits Intuflo Editions. He was the director of operations for Rumarson Technologies, Inc., a computer manufacturer in Kenilworth, New Jersey. He lives in New York City.*

Silhouette

All because I think of you
making love to another man
doesn't declare a false brocade
while I give myself up true.
The imaginary whim is an ontological
partner on sea and land
sure as my house's coat fades.
Then we think he has come
to separate root from follicle.
It's sad how he attacks,
the very moment turning numb
realizing the ceiling is cracked.
Now all the noise that silence locks
is also silent and catches flak.

To tell the truth he seems to know
the guest, the host and chamber.
I never ask him to stay or go,
you don't even know him.
Again I see that ghostly stare
with the gilded edge and clamor.
He has been in and out
perhaps when your hair was trimmed.
Does this mean we are less
than what we are, all about
the twitch that fills the driveled air?
What a sanctified mess
thanking the other one every day
and emptying the shadow with candlelight.

I decided to write this particular double sonnet after coming across Elizabeth Bishop's poem "The Prodigal" in a modern anthology. I admired Bishop's honesty and wanted to emulate her humble, unembarrassed tone. I was also captivated by her poem's innovative rhyme scheme and the sudden dropping of that scheme at the poem's end. In "Silhouette," I tried doing the same thing. Rather than adhering rigorously to a preordained rhyme scheme or stressed, unstressed sequence, I established my own conscious liberties within the form. In the act of meeting the requirements of an imposed formula, I began to see what my poem's "original meaning" might be; and as the content of my poem emerged, I paid less attention to the formal rules that had guided me this far. Forms exist, after all, not so much as ends in themselves but as the known means toward an unknown end. The laws of any form are made to be broken, and break they do in a natural course of movement within the structure.

Classical notions of form can be misleading. Perhaps a better word for my purposes is process—the process of plodding on to the next word as one would paint a wall or sound a horn. And perhaps process is what we talk about when we talk about history. Do we make history or does history make us? The question can be argued back and forth for eternity. The important thing is that the doctrines of fate and of free choice are both fair templates to pattern the mystery that surrounds ourselves and everything around us.

I like comparing the action of my poem to a visit to the barbershop: the shave and haircut will be to my specifications, so the silhouette's shadow has no jagged edges as it speaks in the offstage presence of light and you. The shadow as well as the silhouette must be dealt with, and the language of its landscape will be less important than the fact that its form, cut with the proper light, can be traced on a surface and to the heart.

Wyn Cooper *was born in Detroit in 1957. He was educated at the University of Utah (B.A., 1979) and Hollins College (M.A., 1981). At a second stint in Utah, he studied with Mark Strand ("Just don't bore me," was Strand's advice). Cooper's book of poems,* The Country of Here Below, *was published by Ahsahta Press in 1987 and is now in its third printing. The book includes "Fun," which became Sheryl Crow's hit song "All I Wanna Do," winner of the 1995 Grammy Award for Record of the Year. He has taught at Bennington College and is now on the faculty of Marlboro College in Marlboro, Vermont.*

Fun

"All I want is to have a little fun
Before I die," says the man next to me
Out of nowhere, apropos of nothing. He says
His name's William but I'm sure he's Bill
or Billy, Mac or Buddy; he's plain ugly to me,
And I wonder if he's ever had fun in his life.

We are drinking beer at noon on Tuesday,
In a bar that faces a giant car wash.
The good people of the world are washing their cars
On their lunch hours, hosing and scrubbing
As best they can in skirts and suits.
They drive their shiny Datsuns and Buicks
Back to the phone company, the record store,
The genetic engineering lab, but not a single one
Appears to be having fun like Billy and me.

I like a good beer buzz early in the day,
And Billy likes to peel the labels
From his bottles of Bud and shred them on the bar.

Then he lights every match in an oversized pack,
Letting each one burn down to his thick fingers
Before blowing and cursing them out.

A happy couple enters the bar, dangerously close
To one another, like this is a motel,
But they clean up their act when we give them
A Look. One quick beer and they're out,
Down the road and in the next state
For all I care, smiling like idiots.
We cover sports and politics and once,
When Billy burns his thumb and lets out a yelp,
The bartender looks up from his want-ads.

Otherwise the bar is ours, and the day and the night
And the car wash too, the matches and the Buds
And the clean and dirty cars, the sun and the moon
And every motel on this highway. It's ours, you hear?
And we've got plans, so relax and let us in—
All we want is to have a little fun.

It began as a poem, became a song, and now it's a poem again. Here's how it happened: I was living in Salt Lake City in the mid-1980s, going to graduate school, and having serious doubts about the way I was living my life. One night I was sitting up late with a friend who urged me to stay a little longer, drink a little more. I begged off, but he was persistent. Then he said the magic words: "All I want is to have a little fun before I die."

That was all I needed. I wrote down the line the next day and kept writing. "Fun" was a gift; I wrote it in about two hours. Though I had no luck placing it in a magazine during the next two years, I included it in my book, *The Country of Here Below,* which was published in 1987. And that, I figured, was that. Five hundred copies were printed, and six years later they were still available.

Meanwhile, in Pasadena, an unknown singer named Sheryl Crow was recording her first album, *Tuesday Night Music Club,* in producer Bill Bottrell's studio. She didn't like the words she had come up with to match a catchy melody, so Bill handed her my book and said, "Try reading 'Fun'—this guy writes like us." Bill and fellow band member Kevin Gilbert had found my book at Cliff's, a used bookstore in Pasadena. The poem matched the tune almost perfectly. They dropped a few lines from the poem, added a chorus that placed the action in Los Angeles, and called for my permission.

The album appeared in August 1993 but not much happened until "All I Wanna Do" was released as a single. Sheryl sang it on "The Tonight Show," on "The Late Show with David Letterman," and at Woodstock II, and soon it was at the top of the charts. On March 1, 1995, I sat in the audience at the Shrine Auditorium in Los Angeles and watched Sheryl win two Grammys for the song and another for Best New Artist. To date, the single has sold over a million copies, the album more than seven million.

The press loves this story, from the high culture of *"All Things Considered"* and the *New York Times* to the low culture of *People* and *USA Today*. I have done more than 60 interviews, and both the song and references to the song have appeared in the strangest places. Recently, on cable station VH-1, the cast of the TV show "Frasier" was watching rock videos and making jokes and comments about them. After seeing the "All I Wanna Do" video, the woman who plays Frasier's producer on the show said, "Hey! Did you guys know that this song is based on a poem by Charles Bukowski?"

And how is "Fun" turning back into a poem? When Sheryl performed on "MTV Unplugged" shortly after the Grammys, her version of "All I Wanna Do" was almost unrecognizable. While Bill Bottrell and her touring band played funky jazz riffs, Sheryl sat in an easy chair and recited—that's right, she spoke—the words to the song, minus the refrain. As the music faded out, the band began to chant a single word over and over—Fun . . . Fun . . . Fun . . . Fun . . . .

Alfred Corn *was born in Bainbridge, Georgia, in 1943. He earned his undergraduate degree at Emory University and his M.A. in French literature at Columbia University. His most recent collection is* Autobiographies, *which appeared in 1992. He is also the author of five other volumes of poetry, plus a collection of essays entitled* The Metamorphoses of Metaphor, *all published by Viking-Penguin. He has received a Guggenheim Fellowship. He has taught poetry writing at Yale University, the University of Cincinnati, University of California, Los Angeles, and the City University of New York. A frequent contributor to the* New York Times Book Review, *the* Washington Post Book World, *and the* Nation, *he writes art criticism for* ArtNews *magazine. Currently he lives in New*

*York City and teaches in the graduate writing division of Columbia
University.*

Infinity Effect at the Hôtel Soubise

A destination or an origin?
A mirror faces a mirror to divide
The chandelier, which drips in crystal
Tiers under the thaw of lights and lights,
Itself multiplying illustrations of itself,
But always smaller—false worlds of even
Balanced on the real one, which is odd;
At least to me, alone here for a space in summer,
At home with the ease of being foreign,
Visiting monuments no one visits,
With no purpose, guide, no *sens de la visite,*
Waiting to go back to the life I left. . . .

Many a self holds its breath in this room—

Brilliance in mirror with splendid ranks
Bending endlessly down greener halls
That recede underwater, approach a limit
Where light is less and mood more; though I may
Have lost my balance, a victim of decrease,
With a mind regularly double and nothing
Easy, even when at "home," for a moment
The telescope collapses, gets me where I live,
As everything pivots, the candles released
In radiance through veils of living water:
I do not know whether to call this
An origin or a destination.

In "The Philosophy of Composition" Poe comes close to saying that
content should be nothing more than an aspect of form. The risk of
taking his view is that you may end up writing "The Raven," forced to
find a poem in which the word "nevermore" is prominently featured
because *o* and *r* are the most sonorous phonemes in English. The poet is
put in the position of having to be a master detective, intent on discovering the "crime," the poem a flawless aesthetic dictates that he should

write. Assuming that for most poets the subject of a poem comes first, still we hope for a seamless fusion of content and form and certainly consider that form is an aspect of the content. Writing the poems in my first book (from which this poem is taken), I avoided set forms almost entirely; instead, I tried to discover formal correlatives for the subjects treated. That's one way to make things hard for yourself, and the result is that every poem is different in form from all others. In some instances, the effort seems to have justified itself—as I believe it did in "Infinity Effect at the Hôtel Soubise."

The Hôtel Soubise is an eighteenth-century private residence in Paris, now open to the public, though not much visited (at least not back in the early seventies). In one of the rooms a low-hanging chandelier is reflected in facing mirrors, producing a series of reflections *en abyme,* theoretically infinite in number. I remember the first time I encountered that effect: there was a mirrored gallery in my father's place of business, and I always used to be fascinated (and disturbed) by the spectacle of seeing any number of duplicated selves striding along on my right and left sides as I went to see a parent who himself made me feel self-conscious even without facing mirrors. In any case, there I was during a stay in Paris by myself, trying to fill the time by seeing things I had missed during the year my wife and I had lived there. We were taking separate vacations, and there was a depressing sense that the marriage was coming to an end. For whatever reason I was suddenly struck by that image of myself underneath a brilliantly lit chandelier, stretching out to "infinity." I saw the two series of images on either side as a sort of seesaw or balance-scale, poised on the real scene like a pivot. Elementary arithmetic informed me that there would be an even number of reflections corresponding to the unitary scene, which the poem calls "odd" in a pun. So, when I was composing the first draft, I decided to group it in two stanzas of equal line length, with a single line set off between them, as a sort of graphic reconstruction of the scene. (To be strictly accurate, the facing stanzas *should* have had an infinite number of lines, but form can only do so much.) The central, pivotal line had the only "singular plural" idiom I can think of, "many a . . . " That seemed to express the many-but-one sensation being described. Another formal correlative to the mirroring situation is found in line five, which begins and ends with "itself," and there is a hidden pun in "illustrations," which contains the word *lustre,* French for "chandelier." Then, the last line of the poem is something like a mirror reverse of the first. When we travel, we move from a point of origin to a destination; and when we return home, our first destination becomes our origin, another "mirror reverse." I was just about to return home and "go back to the life I left." I think I felt more at home being in a foreign country than in my own at that time. The words "destination" and "origin" have other meanings as well. Looking at the infinitely receding reflections, one can imagine them as a hallway from which one has emerged or into which one is going—I mean, in an unusual state of mind. That is what is described in the final nine lines of the poem. It seemed as though the balance-scale of the scene had tipped and the "telescope" of the interlocking, ever-smaller reflections had "collapsed." The sensation of being, for a moment, beyond limitation brought the release of tears or "veils of living water," which could be confused with the surface of the mirrors, as though they were permeable, allowing free entry or exit. (I had seen Cocteau's movie *Orphée*.) And the mind that felt itself usually double or divided for once was unitary and "at home." The poem probably owes something to Cavafy's "Candles," but not, I think, to his "Chandelier."

Douglas Crase

was born on July 5, 1944, in Battle Creek, Michigan, raised on a nearby farm, and educated at Princeton. He studied at the University of Michigan Law School but left to serve as staff writer to the Political Reform Commission of the Michigan Democratic Party. He moved in 1974 to New York City, where he has been a freelance industrial speechwriter. His book, The Revisionist, *was published in 1981 by Little, Brown and nominated for the National Book Critics Circle Award and the American Book Award in poetry. His essays have appeared in the* Nation *and* Poetry, *and he wrote the introduction for the Vintage/Library of America edition of Emerson's* Essays. *He has received fellowships from the Guggenheim and MacArthur Foundations.*

Once the Sole Province

of genius here at home,
Was it this, our idea of access to a larger world,
That invented the world itself (first, second,
Third) past accuracy we are bound to inhabit now
As targets, positioned in a trillionth
Of the smallest measuring—microresults
Made in the least, most unimaginable chronology?
No more time-outs. For we are either ready or

We must be ready or not, an expensive mix
Of life-based chemistry perpetually on the verge
Of going to heaven in a vapor, and almost making it.
Almost, except there's that one true destiny
Incontestably driving down on us,
The finally collapsible ones,
Who are lumped in a uniform density at last,
At last coherent to desire. It is a density
Greater than the sun's.

       But, Day,
There must be some other reference,
Which is why you so nervously dwell on us,
On earth which keeps turning, embarrassed, from the light:
Indiscriminate shine on Shiite, Methodist, Hun,
And pump of excitability. Dissatisfied
As all things are on earth,
Is there anything earthly that can't be made to rise,
Emit disciples—the collimated and the laser lean?
They march to you, old outside agitator,
While you who pump the world with promises
Are simply not to be believed. All those diversions,
The years and decades, the manifold span of life
—These were the dialectic of a fold
Formed out of almost nothingness, a fold of hours
In a space where the "hour" is eccentricity. So
Pity the day, beyond which we can see,
For if time is distance then distance must be life
And who is there on earth who will not go
In answer to its call? Call this
The aim of every reverence:
That outside ourselves there be a scale more vast,
Time free of whimsy, an endless unbended reach
In which to recollect our planet, our hours and ourselves.

Since a poem is delivered in form, I can't imagine trying to write one
without an expectation of its dimensions. Most of the time, the dimensions I'll have in mind are like those of the poem printed here, though
I'm not the first or only one to use them. In fact, because these same

dimensions can be repeated for making different poems, they must add up to a form, even if it so far has no name.

The initial dimension is revealed in line length, determined by meter. Of course, if you try to scan these lines as customary accentualsyllabic, you are in for trouble, though the trouble is mainly one of definition. Einstein arrived at relativity by starting with definitions. Distance, he said, is what we measure with a ruler. And time is what we measure with a clock. Likewise, one could say that meter is what we measure with a stroke. I even write by measuring lines with the stroke of the fingers (the *ictus,* to fall back on Horace's word for this action), and since my dominant count in the lines here is four, they must be tetrameter. They may not look like the tetrameter you're used to, but if meter is what we measure with a stroke then meter too can be relative. No line stands alone. Instead, its stresses are variable according to the diction that clothes it, the sense that occupies it, or the line that precedes it; and this variability will also affect the length of the foot, which expands or even contracts as it reaches up to or falls away from each stroke. Shades of William Carlos Williams, which is okay, because I'm content to know the measure of these lines as variable tetrameter. But I would also call it the "civil meter" of American English, the meter we hear in the propositions offered by businessmen, politicians, engineers, and all our other real or alleged professionals. If you write in this civil meter, it's true you have to give up the Newtonian certainties of the iamb. But you gain a stronger metaphor for conviction by deploying the recognizable, if variable patterns of the language of American power. And to say that this civil meter is a metaphor for conviction is to acknowledge that it, just like iambic measures, is a unit of artifice and one dimension of a form.

A second dimension is measured down the page. Despite its division into two parts, the poem is not stanzaic, but stichic—the strategy being, as with the choice of meter, to exploit one of the strongest of American metaphors for conviction. In her lecture on *The Making of Americans,* Gertrude Stein wrote that it was strictly American to conceive "a space of time filled always filled with moving," and, as examples, she told us to think of cowboys, or detective stories, or movies. I like to think also of a keynote speaker delivering his pitch, or an anchorman delivering his news. In either case, the persuasion of the voice is proportional to its uninterrupted (or call it "highly enjambed") flow. Let a stretch break or station break intervene, try to pick up where you left off, and your news may no longer be true—exactly what has happened to the speaker in this poem when he breaks for his apostrophe to Day. For credibility, he has to turn against his initial message in a second delivery that will also be stichic and highly enjambed. Stanzaic shapes may betray their "wind-

and-rewind" feature, as though the audience could see you paging your script or reading the prompter. By contrast, the stichic shape *un*winds, appearing so spontaneously to fill a space of time with a moving argument that the delivery comes to seem inevitable and, being inevitable, true.

Persuasion, however, is supposed to be the characteristic of rhetoric, and imitation the characteristic of poetry; so you could argue that the form I'm promoting has confused the distinction between the two. But after Whitman—after Lucretius, for that matter—the distinction doesn't seem very useful, and even poets who only "imitate" must be hoping their imitations will persuade somebody. No surprise, then, if you see the devices of rhetoric—alliteration, assonance, sheer repetition itself—standing in as this form's third dimension, replacing end rhyme as a mechanism for moving the argument along. End rhymes tend toward something like stations of the cross: instead of a space filled with moving, they define a space filled with stopping and bowing. But the rhetorical devices (think of them pushing onward in the Gettysburg Address) are taken seriously in American civil discourse, even when shamelessly employed, because their placement internally or at the head of the line is consonant with, and yet another metaphor for, our sense of movement continuously filling its space of time. William James (who probably inspired his student Stein to the observation I've quoted) taught that truth was something *made,* and made in experience. In poetry, too, truth or the conviction of truth is something made in the experience of form. When we add up the civil meter, the stichic space, and the rhetorical momentum that identify this poem and others like it, I think we have a recognizable and repeatable form for making that kind of truth. With a form for truth, we are halfway home—and beauty is just around the corner.

Robert Creeley was born in New England in 1926. Though a "New Englander by birth and disposition," he has spent most of his life in other parts of the world, including Guatemala, British Columbia, France, and Spain. In the 1950s he taught at Black Mountain College, where he met Charles Olson, Robert Duncan, and Edward Dorn. He also edited the Black Mountain Review, *a crucial gathering place for alternative senses*

of writing at that time. Subsequently he taught at the University of New Mexico, and then at the State University of New York, Buffalo, where he still teaches as the Samuel Capen Professor of Poetry and the Humanities. Although usually identified as a poet (his collections include For Love, Pieces, Windows, *and* Selected Poems), *he has written a significant body of prose, including a novel,* The Island, *a collection of stories,* The Gold Diggers, *and a collection of interviews,* Tales Out of School, *in the Poets on Poetry Series. His critical writings are published in* The Collected Essays of Robert Creeley *(University of California Press, 1989), and his correspondence with Charles Olson is now available in nine volumes continuing* (The Complete Correspondence).

The Whip

I spent a night turning in bed,
my love was a feather, a flat

sleeping thing. She was
very white

and quiet, and above us on
the roof, there was another woman I

also loved, had
addressed myself to in

a fit she
returned. That

encompasses it. But now I was
lonely, I yelled,

but what is that? Ugh,
she said, beside me, she put

her hand on
my back, for which act

I think to say this
wrongly.

Form has such a diversity of associations and it seems obvious enough that it would have—like *like.* Like a girl of my generation used to get a formal for the big dance, or else it could be someone's formalizing the situation, which was a little more serious. Form a circle, etc.

It was something one intended, clearly, that came of defined terms. But in what respect, of course, made a great difference. As advice for editing a magazine, Pound wrote, "Verse consists of a constant and a variant . . ." His point was that any element might be made the stable, recurrent event, and that any other might be let to go "hog wild," as he put it, and such a form could prove "a center around which, not a box within which, every item . . . "

Pound was of great use to me as a young writer, as were also Williams and Stevens. I recall the latter's saying there were those who thought of form as a variant of plastic shape. Pound's point was that poetry is a form cut in time as sculpture is a form cut in space. Williams's introduction to *The Wedge* (1944) I took as absolute credo.

"The Whip" was written in the middle fifties, and now reading it I can vividly remember the bleak confusion from which it moves emotionally. There is a parallel, a story called "The Musicians," and if one wants to know more of the implied narrative of the poem, it's in this sad story. The title is to the point, because it is music, specifically jazz, that informs the poem's manner in large part. Not that it's jazzy, or about jazz—rather, it's trying to use a rhythmic base much as jazz of this time would—or what was especially characteristic of Charlie Parker's playing, or Miles Davis's, Thelonious Monk's, or Milt Jackson's. That is, the beat is used to delay, detail, prompt, define the content of the statement or, more aptly, the emotional field of the statement. It's trying to do this while moving in time to a set periodicity—durational units, call them. It will say as much as it can, or as little, in the "time" given. So each line is figured as taking the same time, like they say, and each line ending works as a distinct pause. I used to listen to Parker's endless variations on "I Got Rhythm" and all the various times in which he'd play it, all the tempi, up, down, you name it. What fascinated me was that he'd write silences as actively as sounds, which of course they were. Just so in poetry.

So it isn't writing like jazz, trying to be some curious social edge of that imagined permission. It's a time one's keeping, which could be the variations of hopscotch, or clapping, or just traffic's blurred racket. It was what you could do with what you got, or words to that effect.

Being shy as a young man, I was very formal, and still am. I make my moves fast but very self-consciously. I would say that from "Ugh . . ." on the poem moves as cannily and as solidly as whatever. "Listen to the sound that it makes," said Pound. Fair enough.

Tom Disch *was born in Des Moines, Iowa, in 1940.*
He grew up in various parts of Minnesota and moved to New York City in 1957. There he worked at odd jobs and attended New York University but dropped out without a degree in 1962, having sold his first fiction story to a San Francisco magazine. Since 1964 he has been a full-time freelance writer. He says he has "no Guggenheims, no awards or stipends, and only occasional part-time jobs teaching, but a longish bibliography." In the 1960s and 1970s he spent time in Mexico, Spain, England, Austria, Turkey; then, with Charles Naylor, England again, Rome and Florence, and then from 1975 to 1978, a long spell in London, where they wrote their collaborative novel, Neighboring Lives *(reprinted by Johns Hopkins University Press). Since 1978, he's led a more settled existence in New York City and in the Catskills area, where "Buying a Used Car" was written. His seventh and most recent collection of poems was* Dark Verses and Light *(Johns Hopkins University Press, 1991). His latest novel is* The Priest: A Gothic Romance *(Knopf, 1995).* The Castle of Indolence, *a collection of his essays and reviews on poetry, appeared from St. Martin's Press in the fall of 1995 and was nominated for the National Book Critics Circle prize in criticism. From 1987 to 1992 he was the theater critic for the* Nation, *and he is now a theater reviewer for the* New York Daily News. *He has yet to decide on his favorite color.*

Buying a Used Car

My idmost wish is not to live
Life is very often nice
But leads to grief   Let me be brief
    I want to die

But not this minute   Now I'll eat
Or watch TV or read a book
Until my brain has fogged and then
    I'll want to die

Or sleep which is as Hamlet notes
Akin to death   A test drive for
Those who aren't entirely sure
    They want to die

The salesman's suave   The price is low
It corners like a dream
You get to feel if you let go
          The thing would fly

But then you look beneath the hood
The engine is a piece of shit
Snap out of it you tell yourself
          And say good-bye

According to my log, I wrote "Buying a Used Car" on July 21, 1990. Soon after it was written I sent it, with some other poems, to Richard Burgin, the editor of *Boulevard*. He accepted it, then sat on it a long while. When it appeared in the fall 1994 issue of *Boulevard,* I had no recollection of having written the poem. Given the sentiment it declares, that was an unnerving sensation.

My diary also is a blank from mid-June through early September of 1990, from which I infer that I did not take my Kay-Pro computer and its bulky daisy-wheel printer to my summer rental in the Poconos. That might also explain why I had no other copy of the poem: it wasn't on a disk.

I think there must also have been an element of simple repression. The poem begins with a boast that it's straight from the id: it segues into a dream, and ends by recommending amnesia or denial. Little wonder that I stuffed the manuscript in a bottle, cast it out to sea, and forgot it existed.

Reading it now, as though it were someone else's, I am able to admire it as though it were someone else's. I feel a little like a bicyclist attending a seminar on bicycling: Oh, so, *that's* what it is that I do!

One mounts the machine without hesitation, with one decisive motion. *Idmost,* in this case, or, rather the phrase, "my idmost wish." A one-letter substitution in a common phrase, the sort of recombinant ding-dong that dyslexics and other poets keep emitting, usually without noticing. But in this case I did notice and at once, and quite simply, answered the question, "What is it?" *Not to live.*

That is simple Freudian dogma and a staple of romantic poetry, where Freud got it from. Indeed, before Keats's luscious "to cease upon the midnight with no pain," there is Hamlet's soliloquy, which is surely the archetype this poem is gazing at. What could be more forthright, more simple in an atomic sense, than "To be or not to be, that is the question"? It's a hydrogen atom, a fusion of the simplest positive and the simplest negative.

That anyhow is what I seem to have been after ("Let me be brief"), and in the dimeter fourth line (which follows a line that is, itself, a dimeter couplet) the poem declares its idmost wish with a maximum of concision. But where to go from there?

At such moments the bicycle's own momentum can take over. I had a quatrain that I could both admire and want to deny I'd written. Another quatrain then, as elementary as possible, that denies the first but has to echo, refrainlike, the last line of the first, with a suitably qualifying difference. Not the present but the future tense.

The third stanza opens not with *but* but "or" and offers the same lifesaving compromise that Shakespeare and Keats propose. To sleep: perchance to dream. So, a dream seems to be called for here, and even an explicitly Freudian (as per "idmost") dream.

In the dream-world of America the equation of ego and automobile is only a few degrees less elemental than hydrogen. What movie is without it? What is a boy's first toy? Better than that (for me) my father was a salesman; not a car salesman, but close enough to be untrustworthy. My father's dead. His ghost appears as a used-car salesman, selling me his product, the dream of easeful death. But the customer now isn't entirely sure, and the refrain distances him a little more from the wish. Now it's not *I* but "They."

The fourth stanza is the test drive itself, and already in the second line the machinery does something funny. In a poem that has been insistently regular and foursquare ("it corners") there is a three-foot line. A mechanic would notice. This is followed by two lines, all monosyllables, but again with a slight misfiring: the rhyme of "let" to "get" happens off the iambic beat. And when the refrain comes, the verb is conditional, and *die* has been altered (blessedly) to its dream-cognate of "fly."

Do I wake or dream? In the fifth stanza, I wake and look beneath the hood. Fortunately, I am an American and don't look under the bonnet, for the Grim Reaper doesn't wear a bonnet. And there is the skull (I knew him, Horatio), all worms and corruption. A revolting spectacle, and I can leave the poem with a parting equivocation: "And say good-bye."

Is it a good-bye to the salesman and his pitch for his BMW Liebestod? Or is it the larger good-bye the poem first contemplated? Only the shadow knows, and he isn't saying.

Jim Dolot was born in Detroit in 1965. He graduated in 1986 from Tufts University, where he majored in sociology. After working in public relations for two years in New York City, he went to the University of Iowa Writers' Workshop. He has lived in Texas and Florida and is currently teaching in Providence, Rhode Island. Two of his books, Beach Watch and LS, have been published by Remote Control Press.

Dictionary Jazz

Jack Derrida
Identifies himself
To the police
Of Jewish Dreams
As John Doe.

A jackdaw
Hits the jackpot.
(O my jelly donut
How sweet it is
Just to die!)

Jeanne d'Arc
A jailbird—
A jackdaw too—
Her jeremiads
Became his
Jeux d'esprit.

Juvenal dead,
Judah and dialogue
Just deleted,
J.D.
Junkered down

With dirty jokes.
No disc jockey
Deferring justice,
Not deranged—
De Stijl.

Indigestible
In dinner jacket
Jotting down
"There are no
Just desserts,"
Dirge jive
Disjointed,
He does the job:

Jihad!
Jet's dream.
Divine justice
Divulges
Jovial dividends.

Don Juan,
Dork jutting,
Double josser,
Juvenile delinquent,
Dryads juiced,
Dulcimer jigging
During jouissance,
Deep joy dirging
Deity's jujubes,
He dicks jane.

Double Alliteration

Alliteration foregrounded to the point of doggerel (W. S. Gilbert's "To sit in solemn silence in a dull dark dock") is of course a standard device in parody, and I'm not sure this exercise is much anew about anything. Still, phrasal or double alliteration, as here, seems to me to bring out something about contemporary language not otherwise easily available to poetry.

Let me explain double alliteration to the D.A. before I'm pronounced d.o.a. by the dadaists. American English, whatever it is, now may have more two-word stockphrases than in the past. They ring together and they choir and they collide. They form an interhissing and plaintive pseudoset, not exactly classless, not exactly decadent, running the gamut from clichés, to official names, to brand names, and by extension on to phrases that don't show up in ornery language and that the poet has made up. *Rice Krispies, Republican Kennedys, roll calls.* So, mixing *b* and *w* phrases like *Washington Bridge* and *white bread* and *bear witness* and *bedwetting* and *whiffle ball* with *wisdom beeth* and *wild betrothals* like *wisdom booth* and *wistful brokers* and *woodbine* to make what might be called "falsereal echoes" replicates the experience of hearing the compounded language now as it is branding and naming and wedding its way (the world is a . . .) daylong. Actual phrases mix it up— what does *talk show* have to do with *T. S. Eliot*? Nothing and everything. Take any two letters, say *p* and *l.* Think of all the phrases you already know (Progressive Labor, pilot light, pickled lox, low blood pressure, lilypads, etc.); then make up your own nonstandard permutations (pool lusts, painted locks, polite ligatures, lioness puzzles) and combine these two classes (given and invented) still again with monosyllables or single words (lap, lapidary, leap, pale) to get the rhythms of combination of the public language as it alters the older etymological background. Choose a meter and some story; let this "artificial" lexicon help you tell it. That's it.

The public two-word names, like and unlike personal names, mask the solo words: *Notre Dame* and *nuclear disarmament* and *New Deal* are for better or worse almost as much the name-language we have now— invidious new doubloons—as their component words taken individually. In one sense to emphasize this surface wrongs and trivializes diction, making it classless, murdering etymology and therefore "history." It kills off the historical and class past of individual words in favor of a limbo rush of current simultaneities that are brand shallow, and that will appeal to the audience all too quickly now, but be incomprehensible in twenty years, let alone further on. It surrenders to the brand-name character of all current words. That's both its flaw and its interest. This criticism in place, as an exercise it's useful to have students try it out—to make up their own list and then find what they think is the best motive or narrative for that list—to listen for and reconstruct one of these sets, and work out of it, as on an armature, some plot or action. Among other things it can show that desublimation may have limits just as sublimation does.

In the past I strung these words onto a narrative line of nine syllables—to get away from more available rhythms. That was as far as I'd gotten theorizing my use of double alliteration as a way of orchestrating different classes and levels of Americanese to protect it from universalese. Again: the American idiom now may have such name-phrases choiring to a degree and in numbers not heard say in Stevens or Joyce, let alone earlier. The poem here is formally a lot different, the first one with very short lines, each one almost completely shaped by the alliteration. It scraps the nine-syllable-line narrative for a much quicker scherzo rhythm. The lines treat the whole method as a joke. They're part of a series of sketches of famous literary critics that I've done, catching them, in a very small-minded spirit of *ressentiment,* in various kinds of flagrante delicto. There is one, for example, in ottava rima about Mikhail Bakhtin's use during WWII rationing of his manuscript on Goethe for cigarette paper. The story may be apocryphal; Bakhtin is one of my favorite critics. But the hoax is wiser than the hex, as Bakhtin himself knew. In any case, the object of such a poem about a great literary critic is to be both for and against the critic's hexing interpretation of what language "is" by participating in it and farcing it at once, to transfer the critical mode, a little vindictively, into verse, or better still doggerel, and this goes back too, at least as far as to Pope's "Essay on Criticism" and *Peri Bathous.* Since criticism colonizes poetry, poetry can colonize criticism back, in a supposed age of criticism, without any qualms, jeeringly and amorally, about being as unfair to the reality of critical thought as critical thought always is toward poetry. Of course there's practical danger: whether Aristophanes helped murder Socrates is an old enough question, but there's no real politics in any of this: real politics is a long way off.

I'm not a great believer in "formal" poetics as this phrase is now narrowly used; on the contrary, I think real poetry, as opposed to verse, is very rare, and never really formally familiar or orthodox. It pushes forward against all sorts of given language orders inside and outside poetry in a way that reenacts the whole problem of "rationalization" of which it is a part. Poetry is not, for better or worse, and despite the naive appeal of the idea, a rescue of old myth, or of older formalisms, or of religion, for example, but is the most active way of moving language forward in its crises of rationalization as a self-critical study. Homer's similes are very different in their imaginative freedom and reason from the oracles of the priests he shows. This piece above is of course not a poem, but a snippet of versification: poetry is real and is a long way off.

Rita Dove *was born in 1952 and grew up in Akron, Ohio. She served as the U.S. Poet Laureate and Consultant in Poetry at the Library of Congress from 1993 until 1995. She received the 1987 Pulitzer Prize for her book of poems* Thomas and Beulah. *Recent publications include the novel* Through the Ivory Gate *(Pantheon, 1992),* Selected Poems *(Pantheon/Vintage, 1993), the verse drama* The Darker Face of the Earth *(Story Line*

Press, *1994*), and a new poetry collection, Mother Love *(Norton, 1995)*. *The Library of Congress will bring out her laureate lectures under the title* The Poet's World. *Dove is the Commonwealth Professor of English at the University of Virginia. She lives near Charlottesville with her husband, the German writer Fred Viebahn, and their daughter Aviva. "I think when we are touched by something it's as if we're being brushed by an angel's wing, and there's a moment when everything is very clear," she has told an interviewer. "The best poetry, the poetry that sustains me, is when I feel that, for a minute, the clouds have parted and I've seen ecstasy or something."*

Rive d'Urale

Cedar Waxwing

I am not a poem, not
a song, unsuspecting.
I am not a river, exactly.
I am not a stunned head on the wall. . . .

Pleasure arrives on wings of glass
and I pay with my red bead.

The Study

in the luminous wood the gay sparrow
in the middle of the afternoon a white room

too much paradise

I do not want to go out
I do not wish to stay in
shining grove
green sparrow

the face a dream before it reaches the mirror

One in the Palm

The bird?
The bird was

brown, not golden,
smoothed feathers in no wind.
Stilled, not still.
Stilled at the end of the seeing.

A brown ordinariness.
A cup of coffee.

Dying occurs
elsewhere, more quickly
than we in a lifetime
can imagine.

No angels.
A cup of coffee
and a bead of red:
perfect coherence.

The March of Progress

The wall went up sleekly,
              no hillside.
The wall went up like a bullet,
              magnificent.
The wall was recognized officially
for its achievement, the wall
slithered towards heaven on a glycerin pulley,
              efficient silicone.
The wall would be so kind as to let in
              Light.

Fingertip Thoughts

Sehr geehrte Zuschauer, do not believe
what you see before you: the very eyeball can deceive.
Somewhere in the picture
there is a bird, but not where
you'd have it. Also
a banner, presupposing a breeze.

Red-tipped birds from wet branches
singing, skimming the available light
into a cup. Catch up for an instant
the dark shawl . . .

What is the spirit?
The age's slow exhalation.
What bird is that singing
beyond my window,
small skull grinning through the leaves?

Assassinated Storylines

It begins with a bird who has something
to offer—a plump one, maligned,
whose plumage has grown sooty
along the beggar's path to the city.

Talon-clutch, blue bone ring:
a scrap of color—go on,
take it, pluck it away! There.
Patience: The song is rising.

Rive d'Urale

that which is cut out
that which is ravaged
that which has opened itself before the rippling blade

that which loiters
that which roves town to town
    abundant
    loosening

that which burrows
that which unlocks stone
    waters rising
    birds circling

too many cracks to think about along this spine
    each step
    a bead

In early 1989, the incumbent 1988–89 group of scholars at the National Humanities Center in North Carolina commissioned a work of art as their parting gift to the Center. Polish artist and independent scholar Ewa Kuryluk and I were asked to consider collaborating on an installation. After several weeks' deliberation, we decided to accept the challenge and chose as our motif the Center itself. Situated in a woodsy area "far from the madding crowd," this spacious, window-lined building was like a modern-day monastery with its two tiers of identical whitewashed offices, one for each visiting scholar. All those windows, all those teeming thoughts!

The final installation consisted of two Plexiglas boxes, each containing a fabric scroll. In the smaller horizontal case lies the text of "Rive d'Urale"; the scroll is partially unrolled, so that only twenty-four inches (approximately two "pages") are visible at any given time. Mounted directly above this case, a larger Plexiglas box contains a double-layered vertical scroll featuring cutout portraits of both artists as well as several objects that recur in the poem.

Ewa gave me a twenty-five-foot length of muslin for my poem. Writing on muslin posed several significant aesthetic difficulties. Since the blue and red pens dispensed indelible ink, there could be no corrections. Knowing that only a small (randomly selected) portion of the text could be read at any given time, I had to reconsider the concept of the page and, consequently, the concept of progression. Rather than compose a cohesive narrative, I decided to offer many glimpses into "windows"—a panoply of furtive probings into the human mind.

Naturally, I did not think of all this before beginning to write. I could not bear to compose directly on the cloth, so I spent many hours "sketching" my thoughts on computer sheets cut to specification; still, what happened during the course of this preliminary "composition" was unsettling: freed from the need to advance a narrative—or even to suggest an emotional trajectory—the images seemed to fly up from the text and dangle somewhere above the page, like angels who shed only a smidgen of their glory on those benighted souls below. But the *substance* of each image also refused to stay still: a bird in the palm flies off to become a skull grinning from a wet branch; a green sparrow transmogrifies into the brown ordinariness of a cedar waxwing, which then dons the sooty plumage of the pigeon. Or take the red bead, described in the third "window" as "perfect coherence"—how many things that red bead can be: a form of currency, a drop of blood, the tip of a wing, an ornament, a ball on an abacus, a step in time.

I could not shake the impression that the real poem was floating above the words. Once I accepted this phenomenon—this metatext—however, I was released from the compulsion to cohere, to persuade—those Aristotelian principles weighing down the wings of Shelley's skylark—and felt content merely to scratch my markings in the sand.

I began transferring the windows onto the muslin. Writing on cloth was a much more laborious process, and the text began to change as it "slowed down." The wall of language let in light, but no more than glimmerings, with an occasional flash. I began paring away unnecessary syntax: each image became totem or fata morgana, by turns. When I arrived at the final panel, there was nothing left to transfer. Ewa suggested a fantastical title for the entire installation: *A River of Mountains,* the mystical Urals rendered intimate by the melodious currents of the French language. In this last window, then, terra firma falls away; and what are we left with but scraps of language bound up in a scroll, which we clutch to our chests as we go about the Adamic task of naming the losses—"that which is cut out," "that which is ravaged"—though there are too many cracks in the firmament, and we have to watch our step.

"Rive d'Urale" was not intended to be viewed as a whole—that is, the poem is fashioned from fragments, indeed has made fragmentation its modus operandi. And yet when I read the poem on conventional pages, some sense of that fractured universe is still evident—a snatch of music wafting from the ineffable, thoughts just beyond one's fingertips.

Maria Flook *was born in Hamilton, Ontario, in 1952. Her first collection of poems,* Reckless Wedding *(Houghton Mifflin, 1982) received the Great Lakes Colleges New Writers Award in 1983.* Reckless Wedding *has recently been reprinted in the Classic Contemporary Series (Carnegie Mellon University Press). She is also the author of* Sea Room *(Wesleyan University Press, 1990). Her four books of fiction include* Family Night *(Pantheon), a* New York Times *Notable Book of 1994, which was awarded a PEN/Ernest Hemingway Foundation Special Citation, and* Open Water *(1995). A recipient of a Pushcart Prize and a National Endowment for the Arts fellowship, she teaches in the core faculty of the Writing Seminars at Bennington College. She lives in Truro, Massachusetts.*

Discreet

Today I wrote the ending of all poems.
It came like a strict rain
in an impersonal tone, and with the awkward
marks and small corrections of stars at night.
I unlinked the pendant from its chain
like an intimate word once fastened to a phrase.
There were inexcusable vowels, a slurring
beautiful lie.
Now rhymes fall to their knees
upon sharp glass, and a name rides bareback
out of sight.
I might tell a word too long to tell,
inform without information,
but I won't let a dream repeat itself
in a story.
I autographed my wish and gave it
to another, but it was whiter than paper.
I can no longer spell
the truth, or read myself to sleep
beneath dim lamps.
All unfinished days,
the formless, incompleted loves
have fallen to one corner of a page,
a loveliness or error
where the ink has deepened.
The unedited rains, the misprinted stars.

The first line of this poem appeared without any irony; it wasn't self-conscious. Its gloom was such a bold sort of gloom, I trusted it. I felt the line to be true and not simply metaphoric. This left me with a great deal of explaining to do.

I never begin a poem by worrying about how it should look on the page. In "Discreet," as in all my work, I was most concerned with the poem's meaning and with the language I might choose to express that meaning. For me, content makes the form of the poem. Content arranges the lines (at least in the first many drafts), and finally, content is the structure from which a poem rises or falls. I admire the pleasing architecture of the sonnet, if well-made, but I never choose to use those blueprints. I'm well aware of how easy it is to write a bad sonnet, and perhaps I am just avoiding that. I also distrust the use of an elegant language, which is like the brocade on a military uniform. This is why I shy away. I think a poem should have a natural speaking voice and the language should not be heightened except by its true meanings.

I made at least one hundred or more drafts of this piece; the first several of these worked through the "idea" of the poem. I had to learn my intention, question my thinking. I had to elicit and to restrain my intuition, which in my case is quite pushy. This first process holds the most pleasure and mystery because in these early drafts I have not met the full face of what I am addressing. It's like extending an invitation to a stranger, and yet I am already making demands on this stranger. The work goes nervously; there are many impolite intrusions upon memory, upon the past, upon whatever moment might be solicited in the process of writing the poem. As this is happening, I am also finding the language, the right sounds. I think it is with diction that curious choices are made, and both form and content are altered by the poet's selection of words. Language should sharpen and clarify a feeling, but if the words are wrong the poem might be lost behind a swirl of synthetic veils. This problem occurs most often with imagery when an authentic statement is confused by a lot of emotional scenery. I believe a good image requires a certain reticence, a privacy, but I want my images to be frank and to display the same security as in any of the more direct or flat statements the poem might also make.

In "Discreet," I seem to be talking about poetry itself, how I failed in it or how it was lost from me. There are references to a love or to a life diminished by repetitive error. I used images of rain and stars because these things, being so impersonal by their universality, helped to balance the more private details suggested in the piece. The personification of vowels and rhymes was a mocking of my art, but there is a good amount of buried rhyme and off-rhyme here. I did not seek a purposeful music when writing this poem; the musicality of these lines seemed to happen as in a dream. The repetition of words such as in the lines "I might tell a word too long to tell, / inform without information" seemed to assume the weight of a refrain. There is something dreamlike about this poem. I prefer the word *dreamlike* to the word *surreal,* because as in any dream, I believed the images to be pure, unquestionable, despite their peculiarity. I felt this poem to be very quiet at the edges while the movement of the narrative is at times aggressive. It is made less so by the speaker's voice, which is present tense, yet the voice seems to be retelling the situation and the events become distilled in recollection.

It is difficult to write free verse. I worry if a line stretches on, I worry if an entire poem cloaks the page instead of being snipped here and there into stanzas. It's foolish to think a line should break so that the reader might rest or so an end word can shiver and throb in order to call more attention to itself. I've learned not to consider these things. I try to break the lines of a poem in the same way they might lift or fall in ordinary speech. Depending on the speaker's voice, the lines might hover or lengthen, but it is only in response to an underlying meaning and to the more secret measurements of feeling that a line gains its resonance. When making a poem, I must first find its core, find an intuitive accuracy there, and the form any poem takes should deepen in its outlines.

Alice Fulton *was born in Troy, New York, in 1952. She studied with A. R. Ammons at Cornell University and was a fellow of the Provincetown Fine Arts Work Center and the Michigan Society of Fellows. Her books of poems include* Sensual Math *(Norton, 1995),* Powers of Congress *(Godine, 1990),* Palladium *(University of Illinois Press, 1986), and* Dance Script with Electric Ballerina *(University of Pennsylvania Press, 1983). Currently a fellow of the John D. and Catherine T. MacArthur Foundation, she has also received grants from the Ingram Merrill and Guggenheim Foundations. She is a professor of English at the University of Michigan, Ann Arbor.*

Everyone Knows the World Is Ending

Everyone knows the world is ending.
Everyone always thought so, yet
here's the world. Where fundamentalists flick slideshows
in darkened gyms, flash endtime mess-
ages of bliss, tribulation
through the trembling bleachers: Christ will come
by satellite TV, bearing millenial weather
before plagues of false prophets and real locusts
botch the cosmic climate—which ecologists predict
is already withering from the greenhouse effect as fossil fuels seal in
the sun's heat and acid rains
give lakes the cyanotic blues.

When talk turns this way, my mother speaks in memories,
each thought a focused mote in the apocalypse's
irridescent fizz. She is trying to restore a world
to glory, but the facts shift with each telling
of her probable gospel. Some stories have been
trinkets in my mind since childhood, yet what clings is not
how she couldn't go near the sink
for months without tears when her mother died,
or how she feared she wouldn't get her own
beribboned kindergarten chair, but the grief
in the skull like radium
in lead, and the visible dumb love, like water
in crystal, at one with what holds it. The triumph

of worlds beyond words. Memory entices because ending is
its antonym. We're here to learn
the earth by heart and everything is crying
mind me, mind me! Yet the brain selects and shimmers
to a hand on skin while numbing the constant
stroke of clothes. Thoughts frame and flash
before the dark snaps back: The dress with lace tiers
she adored and the girl with one just like it,
the night she woke to see my father
walk down the drive and the second she remembered
he had died. So long as we keep chanting the words
those worlds will live, but just
so long, so long, so long. Each instant waves
through our nature and is nothing.
But in the love, the grief, under and above
the mother tongue, a permanence
hums: the steady mysterious
the coherent starlight.

Until recently, I believed that Pound (along with Blake and Whitman, among others) had managed to establish beyond all argument the value of *vers libre* as a poetic medium. I thought that questions concerning the validity of free verse could be filed along with such antique quarrels as "Is photography Art?" and "Is abstract art Art?" In the past few years, however, I've heard many people—professors, poets, readers—speak of free verse as a failed experiment. To these disgruntled souls, free verse apparently describes an amorphous prosaic spouting, distinguished chiefly by its neglect of meter or rhyme, pattern or plan. Perhaps the word *free* contributes to the misconception. It's easy to interpret *free* as "free from all constraints of form," which leads to "free-for-all." However, any poet struggling with the obdurate qualities of language can testify that the above connotations of "free" do not apply to verse.

Since it's impossible to write unaccented English, free verse has meter. Of course, rather than striving for regularity, the measure of free verse may change from line to line, just as the tempo of twentieth-century music may change from bar to bar. As for allegations about formlessness, it seems to me that only an irregular structure with no beginning or end could be described as formless. (If the structure were regular, we could deduce the whole from a part. If irregular and therefore unpredictable, we'd need to see the whole in order to grasp its shape.) By this definition, there are fairly few examples of formless phenomena: certain concepts of God or of the expanding universe come to mind. However, unlike the accidental forms of nature, free verse is characterized by the poet's conscious shaping of content and language: the poet's choices at each step of the creative process give rise to form. Rather than relying on regular meter or rhyme as a means of ordering, the structures of free verse may be based upon registers of diction, irregular meter, sound as analogue for content, syllabics, accentuals, the interplay of chance with chosen elements, theories of lineation, recurring words, or whatever design delights the imagination and intellect. I suspect that the relation between content and form can be important or arbitrary in both metered and free verse. In regard to conventional forms, it's often assumed that decisions concerning content follow decisions concerning form (the add-subject-and-stir approach). However, poets consciously choose different subjects for sonnets than for ballads, thus exemplifying the interdependency of content and form. The reverse assumption is made about free verse: that the subject supercedes or, at best, dictates the form. But this is not necessarily the case. The poet can decide to utilize a structural device, such as the ones suggested previously, and then proceed to devise the content.

When we read a sestina, the form is clearly discernible. This is partly because we've read so many sestinas (familiarity breeds recognition) and partly because it's easy to perceive a highly repetitive pattern. More complex designs, however, often appear to be random until scrutinized closely. Much of what we call free verse tries to create a structure suitable only to itself—a pattern that has never appeared before, perhaps. As in serious modern music or jazz, the repetitions, if they do exist, may be so widely spaced that it takes several readings to discern them. Or the poem's unifying elements may be new to the reader, who must become a creative and active participant in order to appreciate the overall scheme. This is not meant to be a dismissal of the time-honored poetic forms. I admire and enjoy poets who breathe new life into seemingly dead conventions or structures. And I'm intrigued by poetry that borrows its shape from the models around us: poems in the form of TV listings, letters, recipes, and so forth. But I also value the analysis required and the discovery inherent in reading work that invents a form peculiar to itself. I like the idea of varying the meter from line to line so that nuances of tone can find their rhythmic correlative (or antithesis).

Given all this, I favor a definition of form as the components that make a poem harmonize and coalesce. In "Everyone Knows the World is Ending" I was interested in breaking down this expectation of formal harmony in favor of formal dissonance. I wanted a poetics that could include disruptive elements while maintaining a structural unity: a music akin, perhaps, to the surprising tonal focus of new jazz as opposed to the more predictable harmonies and modulations of the nineteenth century. I tried to lead the reader through an unpredictable yet unifiable whole, largely by the introduction and interweaving of several registers of tone and diction.

The first stanza contains a long, chaotic sentence in which the form imitates the apocalyptic content. The tone is ironic, with playful twists on biblical language and scientific diction. However, rather than continuing in irony, the second stanza moves into the realm of emotional truth or sincerity. This stanza of personal apocalypse broadens into the generic *we* and philosophical aphorisms near the poem's conclusion. These three large gestures are meant to convey the reader from cynicism to transcendence (a bumpy ride, I admit). The last line, a phrase with both scientific and poetic resonances, is intended as a unifying gesture. (In astronomy, when starlight reaches the top of the earth's atmosphere it is said to be coherent; its waves are in harmony. Then discordant cells in the atmosphere delay some parts of the wave front, destroying the order and corrupting our perception of it.) The term "coherent starlight" combines, I hope, the technical diction of stanza one with the more poetic registers of stanzas two and three. The phrase "under and above the mother tongue" is meant to serve a similar function. There's the punning reference to the mother of stanza two, recalling the irony of the poem's beginning, along with the serious reference to the language itself.

It seems fitting that this particular poem was chosen for inclusion, since, for me, the poem's meaning centers on ideas of form as defined by Kant: "the organization of experience from the manifold of sensation." Before writing it I was thinking of the way our memories impose selection on experience (we can't have total recall) and thus give form to our lives. I was struck by the fact that apparently amorphous phenomena have an organization. Even starlight, that most diaphanous stuff, has its formal qualities, though they prove too cagey, too wayward for calibration from the earth.

Jonathan Galassi was born in Seattle in

1949 and grew up in Massachusetts. After graduating from Harvard University in 1971, he spent two years at Cambridge University. Since then, he has worked in publishing, and for the last eight years he has served as editor-in-chief of Farrar, Straus and Giroux in New York City. He has published one collection of poems, Morning Run *(Paris Review Editions, 1988) and two volumes of translations of the work of the Italian poet Eugenio Montale. He lives in New York with his wife and their two daughters and is working on a translation of Montale's major poetry.*

Our Wives

One rainy night that year we saw our wives
talking together in a barroom mirror.
And as our glasses drained I saw our lives

being lived, and thought how time deceives:
for we had thought of living as the Future,
yet here these lovely women were, our wives,

and we were happy. And yet who believes
that what he's doing now *is* his adventure,
that the beer we're drinking is our lives?

Or think of all the pain that memory leaves,
things we got through we're glad we don't see clearer.
Think of our existence without wives,

our years in England—none of it survives.
It's over, fallen leaves, forgotten weather.
There was a time we thought we'd make our lives

into History. But history thrives
without us: what it leaves us is the future,
a barroom mirror lit up with our wives—
our wives who suddenly became our lives.

In my mind's eye, I can see the bar where "Our Wives" was first conceived, even if I doubt I could find it on the street. It was a new place on the Upper West Side of Manhattan that traded on someone's idea of nostalgia: frosted glass, green plush upholstery, very yellow lights and lots of mirrors. We were meeting our oldest friends for one of our periodic bouts of talk about life and love and work, and because it was raining we ducked in here, the first available place. We seem to do a great deal in tandem with this couple: we all got married the same summer and moved to the big city in fairly rapid succession. Now we've all become parents. "Our Wives" was written in homage to this friendship, and it takes its intimate, gently ironic tone from the mood and feeling of our (now institutional) evenings together.

The poem began out of the suggestiveness of the rhyme *wives/lives,* and it tries to explore the real-life relationship between these terms. I felt there was a potential poem in the conjunction, and sensed that the way to realize it lay in emphasizing the jarring closeness of the words, their strong and provocative resonance. The leap from this recognition to the notion of a repeating form like the villanelle isn't very far. But all I really needed was to repeat the rhyming words themselves, not whole lines as a true villanelle requires. Hence the bastardized form of "Our Wives," which allows for narrative movement in a way that a more fully repetitive structure might not, yet keeps turning back, revising itself, insisting in its intimate, knowing way on this arch rhyme, which seems to be just this side of a tautology. (Whether it is or not is one of the things the poem is about.)

The reader who is interested in analyzing how a poem achieves its effects will see that there are other kinds of repetitions and revisions at work in the poem (e.g., the related terms *history* and *future,* which appear both upper and lower case. Do they bear the same ratio to one another as *wives* to *lives?* If so, conscious intention isn't responsible.) And the regular rhythms contribute, too, to the equilibrium that the poem attempts to establish—or reestablish—as it progresses.

But there was nothing programmatic about my choice of a strict form for "Our Wives." The form chose itself: because the poem was an attempt to explore the "meaning" of a rhyme, I naturally gravitated to a form which could make extensive use of that rhyme. Much as we insist—and with reason—on seeing the contemporary world as jagged, uncentered and wrenched apart, there are rhythms and rhymes in contemporary experience that can find poetic counterparts within the vast repertory of our tradition, as more and more poets from across the entire spectrum of styles currently practiced in America have begun to discover. Is this a sign of weakness? Is the general vogue for form simply a desperate grasping for rejuvenation, for new blood? How much of a real rededication to formal principles does it represent?

Certainly there have been admirable contemporary revisions of conventional forms. A poem like "The Songs We Know Best" in John Ashbery's new book, *A Wave,* is an outstanding example of how a regular structure (in this case a song lyric) can be made resonantly new. (Ashbery has been doing this kind of thing from the beginning.) Bill Knott's "Lesson" in his book *Becos* is another example of creative appropriation of repetitive devices (there is often a degree of irony involved in poems of this type). These poems stand beside purer, less self-conscious examples of traditional form in poets like Elizabeth Bishop, James Merrill and Gjertrud Schnackenberg as proof that formal poems can be utterly contemporary in feeling and tone, that far from calling attention to itself, the rigorously delimited poem can appear so natural that one is aware of its structure only insofar as aesthetic pleasure dictates.

Unfortunately, there are far more counterexamples of so-called formal poems that seem to have been stuffed into clothes that don't fit them, poems that are splitting at the seams because their content and language are at war with their artificial, externally imposed restrictions. Equally bad are poems that glide along so effortlessly and mildly that they seem unaware of their surroundings, weightless. Robert Hass, one of our most discerning commentators on contemporary poetry, has referred to this kind of work as embodying "a private fiction of civility with no particular relation to the actual social life we live."

I believe there's no need for us to renounce the cadences and harmonies and resolutions that have enriched English poetry for hundreds of years, as long as we can make them express a meaning that is ours, that isn't borrowed along with these poetic tools. If meanings are imprinted on the tropes and rhythms we have inherited, the poets I've cited have shown us in their very different ways how those meanings can be usurped, subverted, inverted, transmuted, surpassed. Poetry, like any cultural activity, works by accretion, even when it seems most radical; even when it is reacting most against the past (and perhaps most eloquently then), it is speaking of the past's power. Yet that power can and does work for as well as against us. It's a burden, but also a patrimony, and we'd be mistaken not to exploit it in whatever way we can.

Amy Gerstler *was born in San Diego in 1956.*

She works as a freelance journalist, art critic, and teacher, and lives in Los Angeles. In 1991, her book Bitter Angel *(North Point Press, 1990) received the National Book Critics Circle Award in poetry. The book includes "Della's Modesty," a prose poem in which passages from three Perry Mason novels are interspersed with quotations from the likes of Havelock Ellis, Flaubert, and Montaigne in an effort to locate the relation between modesty as a virtue and sexuality as a transcendent idea. Gerstler's other books include* Nerve Storm *(Viking Penguin, 1993) and* The True Bride *(Lapis Press, 1986). Her work has appeared in three volumes of* The Best American Poetry *as well as in Paul Hoover's* Postmodern American Poetry *and Nicholas Christopher's* Walk on the Wild Side: Urban American Poetry since 1975. *She has worked at Beyond Baroque, the literary arts center in Venice, California, and has collaborated with artists. In 1996 she will teach at the University of California, Irvine.*

Commentary

"*Every blessed*
or blasted object's got
a mind of its own now,
a peevish will of iron.
The tin spoon's blank face
glints openly, meanly.
Clothing and skin develop
an adversarial relationship.
Each new item's designed
not to satiate, but to create
worse need, baser fears.
The beverage dribbling
down your chin like quicksilver
intensifies thirst. Newfangled
bandages increase bleeding . . ."

The ancient clay tablet
breaks off here, but we know
how this grievance ends
from corroborating texts.
Sleep blows over
the long-winded
complainer like a wet haze,
causing him to forget
the body and its little
problems, his minor
quibbles with the spirit
of his age. The clamor
in the field of rushes
across the stream
grows louder and wakes him.
He attends a party
at the summer palace,
but will not permit any
of the guests to approach
him. Later that night,
sequestered in his drafty
attic, he writes his famous
suite of "Four Serious Songs"
the first of which begins:
"How dare you have fun
in my absence!" and jots
down notes for what was
later to become his lively,
timeless cycle entitled
"Sixty Miseries," with
its many witty references
to boundary stones,
the fishing net, a grab-
bag lined with thorns,
and the mysterious victim
dug up by dogs, which
we will consider
in some detail
in the following chapter.

"Commentary" springs from my interest in old, fragmentary texts. How mysterious they are. They begin and end so abruptly, arbitrarily—what would the now-obliterated parts have said to us? The Rosetta Stone, the Dead Sea Scrolls—these tenacious ancient writings, making their way in bits and pieces through the centuries to our time and beyond,—move me.

The tone of "Commentary" is an affectionate takeoff on scholarly interpretive notes on ancient texts, where fact-finding, avidness, and pure conjecture merge. All biographers and historians, if they want their writing to have color, must project and imagine. They soberly collect information, and yet at some point they are driven to speculate about historical circumstances, and educated speculations may be stated in a passionate, authoritative way, as though they were truths, not musings.

I like the way the pissed-off voice of some character from the distant past (in the italicized lines that open the poem) may be interrupted midgripe by the eager, soothing voice of an admiring biographer. I often favor the diction and vehemence of complaint. A good rant can have such energy.

Dana Gioia

was born in Los Angeles in 1950. A Stanford graduate, he received an M.A. in comparative literature at Harvard before returning to Stanford to study business administration. After receiving his M.B.A., he moved to New York and began working for General Foods, where he put his business acumen in the service of marketing Kool-Aid and Jell-O and eventually rose to the rank of vice president. His two collections of poems, Daily Horoscope *and* The Gods of Winter, *were published in 1986 and 1991 by Graywolf Press.* Can Poetry Matter?, *a volume of his essays, was short-listed for the National Book Critics Circle Award in criticism for 1992. He has published a translation of Eugenio Montale's* Mottetti *and edited a posthumous volume of the stories of Weldon Kees. In 1992 he left General Foods to become a full-time writer. He lives in Santa Rosa, California, with his wife and two sons.*

Lives of the Great Composers

Herr Bruckner often wandered into church
to join the mourners at a funeral.
The relatives of Berlioz were horrified.
"Such harmony," quoth Shakespeare, "is in

immortal souls . . . We cannot hear it." But
the radio is playing, and outside
rain splashes to the pavement. Now and then
the broadcast fails. On nights like these Schumann
would watch the lightning streak his windowpanes.

Outside the rain is falling on the pavement.
A scrap of paper tumbles down the street.
On rainy evenings Schumann jotted down
his melodies on windowpanes. "Such harmony!
We cannot hear it." The radio goes off and on.
At the rehearsal Gustav Holst exclaimed,
"I'm sick of music, especially my own!"
The relatives of Berlioz were horrified.
Haydn's wife used music to line pastry pans.

On rainy nights the ghost of Mendelssohn
brought melodies for Schumann to compose.
"Such harmony is in immortal souls . . .
We cannot hear it." One could suppose
Herr Bruckner would have smiled. At Tergensee
the peasants stood to hear young Paganini play,
but here there's lightning, and the thunder rolls.
The radio goes off and on. The rain
falls to the pavement like applause.

A scrap of paper tumbles down the street.
On rainy evenings Schumann would look out
and scribble on the windows of his cell.
"Such harmony." Cars splash out in the rain.
The relatives of Berlioz were horrified
to see the horses break from the cortège
and gallop with his casket to the grave.
Liszt wept to hear young Paganini play.
Haydn's wife used music to line pastry pans.

A Tune in the Back of My Head

I had the form of "Lives of the Great Composers" in mind for several
years before I ever wrote a word of it. Like many writers I entered

adolescence burning with vague artistic ambitions which in my case directed themselves primarily toward music, the only art of which I had much practical knowledge. After several years of uncharacteristically serious application, I gradually found my interest shifting toward poetry, but this early training had exercised a lasting influence on my sense of how a poem should be shaped to move through time.

The musical effect I missed most in poetry was counterpoint, so it is not surprising that for years I fantasized about writing a fugue, the most fascinating of all contrapuntal forms, in verse. I say fantasize because for years it remained only that—a seductive daydream. I could imagine a poem where variations on a single theme would tumble down the page in elaborate counterpoint, but I had no practical notion of how to write it. The one example I knew of, Paul Celan's magnificent "Todesfuge," was too unique and lofty a model to provide any specific help, though its existence proved that the form could be approximated in verse.

Twice I thought I had the beginnings of my fugue, but neither poem developed as I had imagined. I ran into two problems. First was how to create a set of interrelated themes interesting in isolation that were also distinctive enough to stand out in counterpoint and be instantly recognizable in their many variations. Imagistic poetic language tended to lose its sharpness and blur together under these circumstances. Second was how to let the sense of the poem develop naturally out of the sound. Music alone, even contrapuntal music, was not sufficient to sustain the reader's interest through a poem of any length. I abandoned both poems, but the idea continued to haunt me like a half-remembered tune in the back of my head.

Several years later when "Lives of the Great Composers" was written in what for me was a short period of time (two weeks of evenings after work), I realized I had been making abstract formal decisions in the back of my mind for some time. My instructor had been Weldon Kees, a neglected poet who, I suspect, will ultimately be seen as much more influential on my generation than his more highly regarded contemporaries Lowell, Berryman, Schwartz, and Jarrell. Reading Kees I had learned how contrapuntal themes could easily be conveyed through two devices: contrasting diction, especially proper versus common nouns; and contrasting types of statements, especially the juxtaposition of prosaic facts and poetic images. (Pound offered the less useful means of counterpointing different languages, a notion I briefly played with in an early draft.)

The arbitrary nature of the poem's material dictated that it be written in regular stanzas, which I eventually patterned roughly after those of Kees's "Round" whose extravagant nonce form I felt might be repeatable. This initial decision set some helpful limits on how the unruly subjects were developed. Likewise, the unpredictable recurrence of characters and images only seemed satisfying to me when set to a strongly metrical tune where the regularity of the rhythms bestowed an air of inevitability to the otherwise jarring transitions. Rhyme I decided to use randomly both to surprise the reader by striking unexpected harmonies from time to time and to avoid the potential monotony of rhyming the same words over and over in the closed system of the poem. A regularly rhymed "Lives of the Great Composers" would have been a redundancy, like a rhymed sestina, since the poem was already an experiment in the structured repetition of sounds.

Finally the continual repetition of a small group of facts and images dictated that the poem have some progressive narrative or thematic structure. In this way statements could be repeated for a cumulative musical effect without exhausting their significance, since the words would take on a slightly different meaning each time. Without this "plotting" the poem would have become more arbitrary and less interesting with each stanza. I had no idea what this plot would be when I began the poem. I trusted the music to lead me to it. Luckily, this happened, but only in the course of extensive revisions, because ultimately a musically satisfactory plot was difficult to achieve. It led me to reduce significantly the number of characters and incidents (out went Mahler laughing at the end of *La Bohème,* Beethoven raving on his deathbed, and poor Saint-Saëns being mistakenly arrested for espionage) and then to play with the remaining elements until each fell into its proper perspective. Finally the poem was finished, and though there are undoubtedly some readers, suspicious of artifice, who wish it a fate not unsimilar to Haydn's scores, it remains one of my personal favorites.

Debora Greger was born in Walsenburg, Colorado, in 1949. Her first three books of poetry were published by Princeton University Press: Movable Islands *(1980),* And *(1986), and* The 1002nd Night *(1990). A fourth collection,* Off-Season at the Edge of the World, *appeared in 1994 from the University of Illinois Press. Her poems have been chosen for four volumes of* The Best American Poetry. *She is also an artist whose collages have appeared in several magazines. She lives in Cambridge, England, and Gainesville, Florida. She teaches in the creative writing program at the University of Florida.*

Memories of the Atomic Age: Richland, Washington

O weigh
down these memories
with a stone

—Olive Senior

Root Cellar

The night before, the garden had been caught
by frost. Now it lay blackened, slumped, a can
of rain's isotopes turned ice, a man's
work glove gone stiff, not even the fire hot.

The wet leaves slow to catch, he dug a well
in the not yet frozen dirt, more just a hole
with a door to keep out what would otherwise befall
the poor root vegetables. Now even hell

could freeze, my father said. A spark like a rocket
fell back to earth. Potatoes would grow eyes
to see in the dark, turnips turn coats like spies,
parsnips send out feelers in that dank pocket.

A shooting star—no, Sputnik raced the moon.
Time to wrestle with long division soon.

Blank Paper

He brought home paper from work, marked
    CONFIDENTIAL,
a briefcase full, now stamped DECLASSIFIED,
for us to draw on, mysteriously dull
but blank as snow on the other side.

Hoping we'd be quiet after work?
We played with the badge with his picture on it,
grew bored, and fought to be the dimestore clerk
you paid with paper coins. Would green win out?

Did he dread the Saturdays it snowed?
Where was the hush of a world brought to a halt

Debora Greger 69

at tomorrow's gate? What would he say he was owed?
He bundled up and spread the walk with salt.

My mother forced a paperwhite to bloom,
pure as the snow's irradiated room.

Forty Hours' Devotion

The altar blazed with flowers banked with lights
whose faith still flickered. Jesus wore a necklace
the gold of the monstrance holding the host in place
for forty hours. Like graveyard shift, those nights

in the desert guarding the reactor against sleep?
Your daughter prayed against communists at school,
and now you both stood a moment in the vestibule.
Out in the desert ranged the feral sheep

whose shepherd had been bought by the government.
Bought, the rancher and the orchardist. O bless
the stubborn, contaminated fruit. And bless
the gases kept secret, released by accident,

the heavy water censing the river it warms.
O bless and keep Your flock from any harm.

Burial Mound

And that, my father said, was a burial mound.
And there we dug, and sifted the dusty dirt
all afternoon, a few trade beads a start:
such was our Sunday trespass on holy ground.

A deep blue bead from Venice, out in the desert—
where you can't go now unless it's just to golf.
Gone the Black Robes. Gone the dust-hued wolf.
What's to keep the reactor's guard alert?

The red of cheat grass a mirage that stained
the heat that wavered down the road that shone
like water made of dust so sweetly bitter—

flying home, you see the mounds from the plane.
Reactor cores, nuclear submarines,
buried out there for want of anything better.

The Nuclear Sonnet

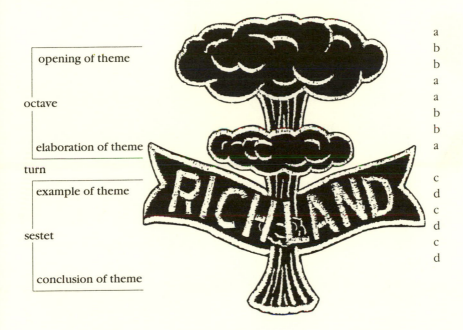

opening of theme   a
    b
octave   b
    a
    a
elaboration of theme   b
turn   b
example of theme   a

    c
sestet   d
    c
    d
conclusion of theme   c
    d

Marilyn Hacker *was born in the Bronx on Thanksgiving Day, 1942, to*

Jewish parents who were second-generation American citizens. She now divides her time between the Upper West Side of Manhattan and the Third Arrondissement in Paris. She is the author of eight books, most recently Winter Numbers *and* Selected Poems 1965–1990 *(both from Norton, 1994). Her collection* Presentation Piece *(1975) received the National Book Award and was also a Lamont Prize for Poetry selection of the Academy of American Poets;* Going Back to the River *(1991) received a Lambda Literary Award. In 1995 she was awarded the Lenore Marshall Prize for Poetry.*

Letter from the Alpes-Maritimes
I. M. James A. Wright

Carissima Joannissima, *ave,*
from a deceptively apolitical
solitude. (Must I be auto-critical,
having exchanged upper-Manhattan Soave
for Côtes de Provence?)

In this cottage with light on four sides I shared
for a conjugal fortnight three years ago,
I play the housewife-hermit, putter. I know
the pots, the plates, the water-heater. My third
midsummer in Vence

whose suburban villas fructify the hills
out the kitchen window, my perimeter
marked by an ivy-cloaked oak. Out the French door,
yellow exclamations of broom in scrub-wild
haphazard descent

down ancient rock-terraces to the ravine
where a cold brook sings, loud as the nightingale's
liquid vespers. When you go down the woods trail
to the water, it's a surprise to find
such small source for song.

I watch the sky instead of television.
Weather comes south over the mountains: that's news.
Today the Col de Vence was crystalline. Blues
stratospheric and Mediterranean
in the direction

of Nice. From Tourrettes, I could see Corsica.
Sometimes I take myself out to dinner. I write
between courses, in a garden, where twilight
softens the traffic beyond the begonias,
and my pichet, vin

ordinaire, but better than ordinary,
loosens my pen instead of tongue; not my guard.
I like eating alone; custom makes it hard

to be perceived content though solitary.
A woman alone

must know how to be cautious when she gets drunk.
I can't go rambling in night fields of horses,
apostrophizing my wine to their apples,
heaving an empty with a resounding thunk
in someone's garden.

Nor are, yet, establishments for grape and grain
the frequent settings for our lucky meetings.
I think of you, near other mountains, eating
breakfast, or warming the car up in the rain
to do your errands.

Both of us are happy in marketplaces.
In your letter, bargains at J. C. Penney's.
I'm in the town square early. Crowded Friday's
cheese-sellers and used-clothes vendors know my face's
regular seasons.

Djuna Barnes and the Equal Rights Amendment
died in the same month. Though there's a party Sunday,
why should I celebrate the Fourth of July?
Independence? No celebration without
Representation.

The exotic novel Barnes could have written
continues here: the old Countess and her child,
further than ever from being reconciled,
warily, formally, circle the old bone:
an inheritance.

Between mother and daughter I'd be a bone,
too. I cultivate pleasant neutrality,
reassuring each of them she can trust my
discretion, though I think they both know my own
clear preferences.

I gave the mother a blood-red gloxinia.
Hothouse perennial herself at ninety,
terrible on the roads, (Countess Báthory

is rumored to be a direct ancestor,)
a war monument's

long bones, selective eyes, a burnished ruin
in white jeans, along the lines of Katherine
Hepburn around the cheekbones and vulpine chin;
her style half-diplomacy, half-flirtation:
she gets what she wants;

which is what her daughter has never gotten:
bad marriage, penury, a retarded son,
father's sublime indifference and mother's scorn.
She's sixty-two now, and accused of plotting
"under influence

of a bad woman." That they are two old dears
goes without saying, and that daughter loves her
friend, but, avec amour, her wicked mother.
Add that one of them was a French officer,
one an ambulance

driver in the War, and that the property
where I live is the object of contention,
and that the penniless daughter is as handsome
as the mother who'd will her patrimony
to the state of France.

I'm thirty-nine and thin again, hair thinning
too, hélas, as when, in London, twenty-nine,
I paid a trichologist, wore long skirts, pined
in a Park Road bed-sit, and read, through waning
light, anti-romance

by Ivy Compton-Burnett, hoping to lose
(my American soul?) San Francisco-style
expectations, though the Sixties were a while
over. I didn't know I could change and choose
another ambiance.

Better celibate than a back-street girlfriend.
(I called myself that, ironic in self-scorn,
waiting for evasive letters across town.)

I know I'll never have to do that again.
At least two women

at least a while loved me reciprocally.
That I knew I could love them, I owe to you.
I see tomorrow's weather from the window.
I've found my spot—the kitchen, naturally.
I've put basil plants

in an orange juice jar to root. Though I said
I went wistfully under the flowering May
boughs in Central Park, single, while pairs of my
friends blissed out in rut, I don't think that I need
antidepressants!

I don't think I'm even frequently depressed
without the old objective correlative.
Perhaps I am as skinless and sensitive
—"sensitive"'s necessary—as you suggest.
Long-sleeved elephant's

hide coveralls I metaphorically wore
that month of committees, trysting visitors,
arrivals, entertainments and departures.
I can write poetry now, if I don't bore
the constituents

who never read it, though they all want to Write
Something. In all fairness, I'm not being fair.
Hendecasyllabics, Joannissima,
could ramble on for forty-three days and nights
until I leave France.

I'll stop, hoping to see you in October
face to face, with help from universities.
(Here, a word-play on "tenure" and "liberty.")
"Long bones," recalls you, too, once almost my lover,
happily my friend.

Form can be a medium of homage and challenge between poets. I think
American free-verse orthodoxy has minimized, for many, the pleasures

of good-natured bardic competition, where you, I, she or he will attempt to master and further the intricacies of a difficult form/meter/stanza proposed, in example, by her, him, me or you. Evelyn Ashford will never race Jesse Owens, nor will I trade epigrams with James Wright; but she can pace herself against his time, and I can match his metrics.

The first section of Wright's poem, "The Offense," named and exemplified the challenge: ". . . the difficult, the dazzling / Hendecasyllabic. / How in hell that we live in can we write it?" I was reading Wright in Vence in 1982. The Alpes-Maritimes have been one of my landscapes, in life and art, since 1971; they were the setting, too, I found, of one of Wright's last poems ("Winter Sunrise Above Vence"). I sensed proximity as well as challenge. I had an epistolary poem in mind. I picked up the glove cast by Wright in his lines, left by Wright at his death, and started in hendecasyllabics. They were a rhythmic tonic for me, refreshing after the iambic pentameter in which I'd largely, that summer, been working. To up the stakes, I made a five-line stanza, four hendecasyllabic lines, rhyming or slant-rhyming *a b b a,* with a five-syllable tail line keeping the same rhyme (on *Vence*) throughout the poem—for, it turned out, twenty-seven stanzas!

Though the "Letter" is not to James Wright, he is reading over my shoulder. The references to horses, apples and drink engage his work in dialogue, and "long bones," very apt in my poem, was his instruction for/description of the hendecasyllabic line in English.

I think this loose-limbed stanza unified my poem in its deliberate epistolary ramble from present to past, landscape to anecdote, vignette to statement. No question that the relation of the speaker as "woman" to the image of "poet" presented by Wright and other men of his generation is under examination as well, but in a spirit of mutual amity and respect established, I would hope, by the challenging meter.

Rachel Hadas was born in New York City in 1948. With the exception of college and four years in Greece, she has lived mainly in New York City. She majored in classics ("a fact for which I've never ceased to be grateful") at Radcliffe College and later studied writing at the Johns Hopkins University and comparative literature at Princeton University. She says, however, that her years in Greece between college and graduate school were probably her most abiding poetic education. She has taught classes at Columbia University and Princeton University, and has taught English at the Newark campus of Rutgers University since 1981. Her ten books include poetry, essays, and translations; her most recent book is The Empty Bed (Wesleyan University Press, 1995). She has been awarded a Guggenheim Fellowship, an Ingram Merrill grant, and an award from the American Academy of Arts and Letters. She lives in New York City and Vermont with her husband George Edwards, a composer, and their son, Jonathan.

Codex Minor

The headless bird flew back
to the winter root, its tree.
Strong red clay and bones:
stuff my foreign songs
sprang from, not understood
till now, nor now, but hard
against the tongue, the brain—
this late-returning pain
comes surely home to roost.

The village spoke and said:
Your roots are steeped in red,
your bones are benches, mugs,
a shawl, a hut, a tank,
a densely carved-on tree.
Think back to splintered wood.
No name, no family.
The tale not fully grown,
stories not understood.

What does it mean, this late-
night life, ungathered, turning?
Tardy recognitions in the dark?
The blood-red bird flies back to me and says:
Your roots are soaked in red.
I have no song, bird. Make the words for me.
Here is the body; you possess the head.
Escape but find my elemental tree.
Water the roots, blind groper; mouth and spout
beyond all hope of pushing in or out.

The beach in Ormos, then. A single gull
suspended in the air; a porcelain
brilliance; a limpidity; no motion
except Andreas and his son
were working with their hands
in wood. On wood. A boat. A big caïque.
They kissed a little cross
and propped it on the prow
and—gently, slowly—set the thing in motion.
I looked up at the sky again with knowledge.
Could I come here again, I said, to live?
Could I come here again?

Memory tells me that the first couple of lines of "Codex Minor" came to me at night, when I was already half-asleep after having been reading Northrop Frye's *The Great Code,* to which the otherwise impossibly obscure title of the poem obviously refers. But looking in my copy of Frye's book, I find the entire first draft of the poem (then twenty-three lines) penciled in the back. From the beginning the poem was personal and enigmatic but also, I felt, archetypal and thus somehow universal. The structure, what there was of it, consisted of a riddling sort of exchange, question and answer; rhetorical questions abound in my poems. The diction and meter imposed themselves from the start, though the lines loosen and lengthen as the poem goes on. The last stanza, as is perhaps too obvious, has a very different root: it is a vivid memory, inserted into the poem as a kind of answer to persistent questions, but itself ending in another question. All this I notice now; it was not planned, though of course I knew the texture of the final stanza was different. Possibly the relative sparseness of rhyme in the last stanza is another indication of the difference in style. Rhyme gives me great pleasure and I have to make an effort to shun it—not that formal rhyme schemes always work for me, but rhyme's wit and pacing, chiming and assonance so often enrich the meaning of a poem with music.

The sense of roots is double in "Codex Minor"—roots as one's forbears, roots as in roots of a tree or (after reading Frye) *the* tree. A phrase from Hopkins which I love, "send my roots rain," can also be discerned. The bird was not merely a proverbial chicken coming home to roost; it was peremptory, swift, muse-like, flying between me and some lost origin, perhaps in a grimly imagined Eastern Europe, homeland of my father's to me mysterious family.

The poem describes a bit, narrates a bit, but seems now mostly an incantation. As usual with me, I was aware of few formal choices or strictures. Perhaps the urgency with which the poem first imposed itself on me made me especially intuitive in my approach; I virtually took dictation from the bird. It's also relevant, I think, that when working on later drafts of "Codex Minor" I was teaching creative writing, and remembered a long talk with a student about the fascinating process and problems of capturing in language the incessant but not always verbal flow of ideas and images—all this without losing syntax, rhythm, and at least a faint shadow of sense.

Mac Hammond *was born in Des Moines, Iowa, in 1926. He earned his B.A. at the University of South Carolina and the University of the South, and his M.A. and Ph.D. at Harvard University. He has taught at the University of Virginia, Western Reserve University, and has had a long academic career at the State University of New York at Buffalo. He cites the New Critics, Auden, Yeats, and Stevens as his early influences; he also names Svatava Pirkova-Jokobson, an ethnomusicologist and folklorist, as an influence who taught him to see central myths in American pop culture. He writes, "I received early insights into the nature of poetic language from the structuralist linguist Roman Jakobson, with whom I wrote my dissertation on Stevens. I think some of my best poetry embodies Russian Formalist and Prague Structuralist theories." He is the author of three books of poems,* The Horse Opera *(1966),* Cold Turkey *(1969), and* Mappamundi *(1989). He is now making poetry videos and is one of the founding members of the Nickel City Poetry/Video Association in Buffalo. He lives in Buffalo with his wife, Katka.*

Golden Age

What's an old man like you doing
In *The Garden of Love,* Venus, Adonis
Dallying, nymphs and swains in postures
Of amor, dripping rivulets and reeds.
Alessandro Scarlatti, you can't fool me
With your classical allusions—I know,

At the beginning of my own old age,
That your neighbor's daughter inspired
Your serenata, her plump breasts,
Because, when I first heard the lift
Of this music—trumpets, two sopranos,
Strings—it was like meeting (what in
the) another st-stunning young face.

Form in the art of poetry to me these days is parallelism in sense, a notion come from Roman Jakobson's bipolar theory of language. Jakobson's poetics points to parallelism in sound, grammar, and metaphor; I have merely taken the next step to larger blocks of meaning. And thereby content is form, form content.

In *Golden Age* the parallelisms were present at the conception before the writing: 1) the eroticism of *The Garden of Love,* an allegorical mirror for 2) my make-believe about Scarlatti's late erotic life and 3) a revelation, in a simile, of my own surprises of that sort.

The title, "Golden Age," points to all three of the parallel ideas.

William Hathaway was born in Madison, Wisconsin, in

1944—"all I ever did in Madison," he says. He grew up in Ithaca, New York, with separate years in Rome, Locarno, and Paris. He earned degrees at the University of Montana and the University of Iowa. His books of poetry have been published by Ithaca House, Louisiana State University Press, and the University of Central Florida Press. For twenty-five years he taught writing and literature classes in Louisiana and New York; now he works for hotels.

My Words

Not pall, but shadows
and they do not cast, but sprawl
or stain, or balm or silent flow.
Oh, Hell, who knows? My words

cast a pall in long-shadowed afternoon, in the basement lecture hall

where heavy-lidded students sprawl.
Thoughts fly up, words drift below.

Indecision: the theme about the theme
is wrong. Madness is what sparkles
in such speech—wild spermous squirm
which seeming reckless makes a sting.

My enemy, your heart knows you!
I have not killed you yet, but do
not think that I forget. If hatred's ember
gives up its wisp in me, remember

my words. Then pure, I may leap
to the grave, proclaim to all my name.
Irony: that cherished absurdity you keep
will give Structure finally to your shame

in my finally aimless act. Even stars
can bump and my words could mesh
even in this chalky air, these students unslump
to crazed conviction poisoning their ears.

T. S. Eliot explained to us that "no *vers* is *libre* for the man who wants to do a good job." Free verse was never supposed to be free lunch. It cannot justify, for instance, repeated use of sentence fragments, discursive cliches, or mixed metaphors that are supposed to be "images" of unfathomable profundity. Indeed, free verse is supposed to challenge us to match our rhythms with the wild pace (shake, rattle and roll) of our times and to invite us to take on vastly more complicated responsibilities with form. Free verse was also never intended to give hip pedants— themselves oblivious to twenty years of passing fashions—permission to mock Tennyson's meters or Shelley's hyperbole for the entertainment of schoolchildren. Nobody who really loves poetry wants to blast away its history; the authentic impulse is to slough off some of the last generation's excess and straighten up for a fresh perspective. Robert Frost was right when he said that free verse "was like playing tennis without a net." The pace of the game has changed radically, and if you're going to be a contender now you've really got to move them feet. Without metrical tension, the poet who wants to do a good job must compensate for the loss by extremely artful use of other poetic elements. As there is no free lunch, there is no free verse.

"My Words" is deliberately cryptic in a less sophisticated manner than work which is now considered "formal," but I would rather defensively maintain that my *form* is as careful and clever as any egghead's. I used lapping rhymes and rhythms to whack out a tonal logic that I hope will balance undeveloped paradoxes and allusions in the content. I aimed for a voice that would sound highly organized, precisely ornate, a trifle finicky—the madman's Gordian-knot logic. The obsessive rhymes and repetitions are obvious, but in order to maintain some eccentric elegance I kept my enjambments understated and my punctuation a trifle irregular. At the end, when the voice seems objectively to observe its own "crazed conviction," I relaxed the rhyme and made the syntax less nutty, I think. I mean, that is what I finally *meant* to do—because an idea central to the poem's interest to me is about extreme Disorder cased in Order. A notion for this poem might owe a seminal debt to "April Inventory" by W. D. Snodgrass.

A teacher is teaching things profound and poignant to sleeping students and that is practically a cliched setup. But the teacher has suffered some irrevocable wrong, which seems to have arisen from a general indifference to his values, an antiphilosophic carelessness that nonetheless is armed with a rationalizing vocabulary. Personal and public griefs are hopelessly intertwined; Hamlet is still nothing but a puzzle. Smug, arrogant, paranoid, the voice, I certainly do pray, unwinds a horrible yearning for Order, which has slipped out of reach. Form may or may not be order, or perhaps more accurately, harmony. My form in this poem, which is not very typical of my poetry, is supposed to be a handhold on the aimlessness.

When I write poems, I search for a certain voice, brainstorming with diction, tones, poses and rhythms for the moment when I can feel it coming naturally on a steady roll. I think maybe method actors do something like this. I induce a meditative state, clearing my mind of everything but an (as yet) undefined sense of theme, and let sound particularize out of that sense. Most of my stuff, including lyric poems, has a narrative conception, in that a specific character speaks out of a specific place or event. If a form fails to materialize, the poem fails—it just obviously doesn't become a poem. I am a nonintellectual who grew up around intellectuals and still has daily contact with them. I've known many smart and extremely knowledgeable people whose minds and hearts have spun out in chaos. The popular logical fallacy is that their "braininess" drove them mad or silly—that limitation is the key to Order. Not necessarily so.

Anthony Hecht *was born in New York City*

in 1923. His B.A. from Bard College was granted in absentia (1944) while he was still overseas with the army; he later earned his M.A. from Columbia University. He has taught at the University of Rochester, where he was John H. Deane Professor of Poetry and Rhetoric from 1968 through 1986, and at Georgetown University. In 1992 he gave the Andrew W. Mellon Lectures in the Fine Arts, which were published as On the Laws of the Poetic Art *(Princeton, 1995). After forty years of teaching, he retired in 1993. Most of his poetry has been assembled in* The Collected Earlier Poetry of Anthony Hecht *and* The Transparent Man, *both published by Knopf. His other works include a prose volume,* Obligatti: Essays in Criticism *(Atheneum); a critical study,* The Hidden Law: The Poetry of W. H. Auden *(Harvard University Press); a translation (with Helen Bacon) of Aeschylus's* Seven Against Thebes *(Oxford University Press), and a coeditorship (with John Hollander) of* Jiggery-Pokery: A Compendium of Double Dactyls *(Atheneum). He wrote the introduction to* The Sonnets *(New Cambridge Shakespeare series, edited by G. B. Evans).* The Presumptions of Death *(Gehenna Press), with illustrations by Leonard Baskin, appeared in 1995.*

Meditation
for William Alfred

I

The orchestra tunes up, each instrument
In lunatic monologue putting on its airs,
Oblivious, haughty, full of self-regard.
The flute fingers its priceless strand of pearls,
Nasal disdain is eructed by the horn,
The strings let drop thin overtones of malice,
Inchoate, like the dense *rhubarb* of voices
At a cocktail party, which the ear sorts out
By alert exclusions, keen selectivities.
A five-way conversation, at its start
Smooth and intelligible as a Brahms quintet,
Disintegrates after one's third martini
To dull orchestral nonsense, the garbled fragments

Of domestic friction in a foreign tongue,
Accompanied by a private sense of panic;
This surely must be how old age arrives,
Quite unannounced, when suddenly one fine day
Some trusted faculty has gone forever.

II

After the closing of cathedral doors,
After the last soft footfall fades away,
There still remain artesian, grottoed sounds
Below the threshold of the audible,
Those infinite, unspent reverberations
Of the prayers, coughs, whispers and *amens* of the day,
Afloat upon the marble surfaces.
They continue forever. Nothing is ever lost.
So the shouts of children, enriched, magnified,
Cross-fertilized by the contours of a tunnel,
Promote their little statures for a moment
Of resonance to authority and notice,
A fleeting, bold celebrity that rounds
In perfect circles to attentive shores,
Returning now in still enlarging arcs
To which there is no end. Whirled without end.

III

This perfect company is here engaged
In what is called a sacred conversation.
A seat has been provided for the lady
With her undiapered child in a bright loggia
Floored with *antico verde* and alabaster
Which are cool and pleasing to the feet of saints
Who stand at either side. It is eight o'clock
On a sunny April morning, and there is much here
Worthy of observation. First of all,
No one in all the group seems to be speaking.
The Baptist, in a rude garment of hides,
Vaguely unkempt, is looking straight at the viewer
With serious interest, patient and unblinking.

Across from him, relaxed but powerful,
Stands St. Sebastian, who is neither a ruse
To get a young male nude with classic torso
Into an obviously religious painting,
Nor one who suffers his target martyrdom
Languidly or with a masochist's satisfaction.
He experiences a kind of acupuncture
That in its blessedness has set him free
To attend to everything except himself.
Jerome and Francis, the one in his red hat,
The other tonsured, both of them utterly silent,
Cast their eyes downward as in deep reflection.
Perched on a marble dais below the lady
A small seraphic consort of viols and lutes
Prepares to play or actually is playing.
They exhibit furrowed, child-like concentration.
A landscape of extraordinary beauty
Leads out behind the personages to where
A shepherd tends his flock. Far off a ship
Sets sails for the world of commerce. Travelers
Kneel at a wayside shrine near a stone wall.
Game-birds or song-birds strut or take the air
In gliding vectors among cypress spires
By contoured vineyards or groves of olive trees.
A belfry crowns a little knoll behind which
The world recedes into a cobalt blue
Horizon of remote, fine mountain peaks.

   The company, though they have turned their backs
To all of this, are aware of everything.
Beneath their words, but audible, the silver
Liquidities of stream and song-bird fall
In cleansing passages, and the water-wheel
Turns out its measured, periodic creak.
They hear the coughs, the raised voices of children
Joyful in the dark tunnel, everything.
Observe with care their tranquil pensiveness.
They hear all the petitions, all the cries
Reverberating over marble floors,

Floating above still water in dark wells.
All the world's woes, all the world's woven woes,
The warp of ages, they hear and understand,
To which is added a final bitterness:
That their own torments, deaths, renunciations,
Made in the name of love, have served as warrant,
Serve to this very morning as fresh warrant
For the infliction of new atrocities.
All this they know. Nothing is ever lost.
It is the condition of their blessedness
To hear and recall the recurrent cries of pain
And parse them into a discourse that consorts
In strange agreement with the viols and lutes,
Which, with the water and the meadow bells,
And every gathered voice, every *amen,*
Join to compose the sacred conversation.

I

Robert Frost's account of the conception, growth and completion of a poem is jaunty, freewheeling, and very attractive for its air of youthful, picaresque confidence. The poem, he tells us, "begins in delight, it inclines to the impulse, it assumes direction with the first line laid down, it runs a course of lucky events, and ends with a clarification of life—not necessarily a great clarification, such as sects and cults are founded on, but in a momentary stay against confusion. It has denouement. It has an outcome that though unforeseen was predestined from the first image of the original mood—and indeed from the very mood. But it is a trick poem and no poem at all if the best of it was thought of first and saved for the last."

We like that; it sounds right. Pioneering, risky, independent. It has the fine, carefree and unburdened spirit of improvised narrative, a journey almost allegorical because destiny will make sure it comes out all right in the end. We like it because it sounds like a life story in which the will of heaven perfectly accords with the breezy, uncalculating innocence of the hero. This is what inspiration ought to be!

The question it raises, however, is: how much of this is *voluntary self-deception?* Take only one point out of that lively account: the ending must be at once "unforeseen" and "predestined." It's not fair to think of the end first (some brilliant, concluding fanfare) and then try to build up the preparatory ground in front of it. How are we to make sense of this requirement? It seems to have something to do with just how *conscious* the poet really is of the potentials of his raw materials, on the one hand; and, on the other, with how rich and complex those materials may turn out to be. With a short and simple lyric it's a lot harder to avoid knowing what the ending will be than with an extended poem of psychological or narrative complexity. Also, a poem of elaborate formal intricacy would almost guarantee that its author could not have foreseen its ending when he began.

And this may indeed be one way that "form" helps the poet. So preoccupied is he bound to be with the fulfillment of technical requirements that in the beginning of his poem he cannot look very far ahead, and even a short glance forward will show him that he must improvise, reconsider and alter what had first seemed to him his intended direction, if he is to accommodate the demands of his form. Rhyme itself, as Dryden wrote, reins in the luxuriance of the imagination, and gives it government. Form (and there are plenty of formal considerations apart from rhyme) slows the poet in his tracks, makes him examine the few words with which he began, and discover what their potentials might actually be. The effect on him should not be hobbling, but, on the contrary, liberating. He will be invited to discover meanings or implications he had never considered before. In this way the "unforeseen" emerges from the small germ of the beginning, and therefore seems precisely "predestined." In other words, for all of Frost's jauntiness, this is not a doctrine that embraces unrevised and spontaneous utterance.

At the same time, we must not fail to see that the degree to which any poet may be taken by surprise at how his poem is developing may be a factor of just how alert he is, and a poet who is sufficiently slow-witted might revel in an almost constant state of astonishment in regard to his own discoveries. So it is always hard to say just how amazed we are entitled to be about our work.

II

"Meditation" was written in the garden of the Hotel Cipriani in Asolo in northern Italy, where I visited with my family just after a stay of several weeks in Venice. The Venetian sojourn had of course involved going to the Accademia to see the paintings, and again I was struck by the stunning beauty and serenity of those great altarpieces by Bellini and Carpaccio and Cima de Conegliano that are crowded into one astonishing room. One is more breathtaking than the next, and most center upon a throned Madonna; and whether or not any one of them is actually entitled "Sacred Conversation," they closely resemble others that are so titled. When I began writing I didn't know (and didn't find out until after the poem was published) that the *type* of "Sacred Conversation" painting is much more strictly defined than I supposed, and that the actual subject—the subject of the painting, and the putative subject of the conversation—is the Immaculate Conception. Not being aware of this, I construed the subject more broadly, and the painting described in Part III is no particular painting by any artist but rather a conflation of landscape and figures of my own choice, but obviously based on celebrated models. What I find so hypnotic about such paintings is their ability in some uncanny way to assimilate grief and even catastrophe into a view wholly benign and even serene and joyful. Anyway, just after seeing those spectacular paintings we moved to Asolo, which, like Todi or Urbino, affords the view of a landscape so idyllic it might have served any of those painters. And it seemed as if we were living in the midst of a particularly beautiful Renaissance painting, and one, moreover, that had to do with the blessedness of life.

But the poem begins elsewhere, and perhaps its interest lies in its tripartite form. It's based on a set of metaphors or figures that are acoustical or auditory in character, and that move from music and its opposite, cacophony, to an articulate silence; that is, from a perilous oscillation between order and chaos to an intuition of an unapprehended order, a posited one, like the music of the spheres. And there is oscillation also between a real world and an imagined one; or, rather, not oscillation but interpenetration. The imagined world is art, whether as music or painting. But it is a world into which we enter, and even seem to inhabit, however briefly. The poem in its three parts is about the strange way we negotiate our entrance into this world, and the strangeness of that world in which all disharmonies are somehow reconciled. "Facts," wrote Kenneth Clark in *Landscape into Art,* "become art through love. . . . Bellini's landscapes are the supreme instance of facts transfigured through love." The poem is about that mystery.

Human and musical discourse (and their opposites, incoherence and cacophony) begin the poem; and incoherence is identified with solipsism, with whatever it is in our own nature (frailty or self-love) that isolates us and makes nonsense of the rest of the world. Part II moves nearer to the inaudible, and into what might be the archive of departed sound that reaches infinitely back into the past, and at the same time reverberates indefinitely into the future. It serves as a bridge between the immediate present of Part I and the immortality of Part III. It was the last part of the poem to be written, and the most difficult to discover, though once discovered it seems obvious enough.

Gerrit Henry

was born in Baldwin, New York, on May 30, 1950, and "is, thus, a Gemini." He attended Columbia College, where he studied with Kenneth Koch, and graduated with a B.A. in English in 1972. Since then, he has written on theater extensively for the New York Times, on contemporary fine arts for Art in America and ArtNews, and on the New York cultural scene for the New Republic and the London Spectator. His books of poetry include The Lecturer's Aria and The Mirrored Clubs of Hell (Arcade/Little, Brown, 1991). His hobbies include "watching reruns of 'Murder, She Wrote' on USA [cable network], listening to old Cy Coleman jazz tunes on my CD player, and, like all poets, working on a novel."

Cole Porter's Son

When the pills don't work anymore,
And the one that you adore

Is slippery as an eel,
I can guess how you feel.

Don't have a seizure.
Make it a little easier.

When the liquor has turned you green—
You know what I mean.

When the food is making you sick,
And the love that makes you tick

Is getting to your ticker,
Don't lay it on any thicker.

Think of only this:
You're just as hot as piss,

Whoever you happen to be.
When you can't manage to see

What's the use any longer,
I swear you're getting stronger.

When the one you can't do without
Is always getting about

Like a beautiful wolf,
And you think that you have proof,

Think about who you are.
Back when you were a star

Could you know you'd be a comet?
I know someone who'd want it.

Our popular songwriters—Cole Porter, Ira Gershwin, Lorenz Hart, Stephen Sondheim—often make more economical, more evocative, and certainly cleverer use of words than many of our most esteemed modern poets. As a result, pop songs are often more lyrically *enjoyable* than much poetry. They also hold a solution—in rhyme and form—to the abyss of prose that modernism has pushed poetry into. Words and music can still exalt the soul in a day when modernistic poetry sometimes cudgels it. The best Broadway and rock songs—and even some of the old Tin Pan Alley tunes, such as those by Irving Berlin—are intrinsically American forms of poetry, tricky, even gimmicky perhaps, but emotionally affecting.

In my twenties, I wrote poem after poem emulating vintage Broadway lyricists, expressing (with a kink, I hoped) many of the same emotions they exploited—I was in love a lot in my twenties. Still, these were discernibly poems, and not lyrics without music, the way an Alex Katz painting is still discernibly fine art and not a comic strip or an image from the technicolor screen. Katz was, and still is, the artist I felt closest to in goal—to make the popular noble beyond its wildest dreams.

For a while I worked with a young composer fresh out of Columbia (and Charles Wuorinen), writing lyrics to his music and performing our songs in cabarets around the city. But I discovered something disheartening—audiences don't listen to lyrics much. They do not expect to find much talent there, and so they *don't* find it; there's just so much content an audience can feel comfortable with. I have a feeling this wasn't true in the earlier part of the century, before rock music garbled the word. Anyway, in my own work, poetry won out over lyrics, the way sheer painting wins out over pop image in an Alex Katz canvas. "Cole Porter's Son" is both a tribute to and a parody of the deviltry and appeal of pop lyrics. But it also celebrates its being a poem—after all, very few lyricists write in rhymed couplets, and there's little room in song for the kind of blatant off-rhyme with which I ended the poem.

"Son" was written in 1980. These days, pop music still inspires me, though not nearly as much as the ballad form—the traditional *a a b a* scheme. My subject matter now includes weighty things like sex and death and religion and myth, and the rhyme and the form are, I hope, counterbalances to the seriousness of the ideas and emotions expressed. A poet friend even noted a new influence on my work—hymns. I'm getting older. So be it.

Daryl Hine *was born in Burnaby, British Columbia,*

in 1936. After studying classics and philosophy at McGill University in Montreal, he traveled and lived in France, England, Scotland, Italy, and Poland until 1962, when he returned to this continent. He worked for a brief period in New York as a freelance poetry editor, and then earned a Ph.D. in comparative literature at the University of Chicago. In 1967 he joined the faculty of the University of Chicago; he has since taught at Northwestern University and the University of Illinois. From 1968 to 1978 he edited Poetry *and is the editor of an anthology of verse drawn from that magazine since its founding in 1912. He is the author of eight books of poetry; his Selected Poems appeared in 1981. He is also the author of a novel* (The Prince of Darkness and Co., *1961*); *a travel book* (Polish Subtitles, *1962*); *translations of Euripedes'* Alcestis, *Ovid's* Heroides, *and the* Idylls *and* Epigrams *of Theocritus; and a play,* The Death of Seneca. *He lives in Evanston, Illinois.*

Si Monumentum Requiris

Cold holds its own, inside and out,
More than a mere matter of degrees,
As if zero were an absolute.

Closing the old to open a new route,
Snow drifts tacitly through clear-cut trees
Cold holds, its own inside and out.

A baffled sun is struggling to come out
And celebrate the solar mysteries
As if zero were no absolute.

The muffled earth, tough as an old boot
Underneath these frozen fripperies,
Cold, holds its own inside and out.

Winter, an implacable mahout
Riding a white elephant, decrees
Zero, as it were, an absolute.

If you want a monument, look about
You at this classical deep frieze.
Cold holds its own inside and out
As if zero were an absolute.

The given, data, what the tantalizing text is to the translation that more
and more preoccupies me, was, as often enough these days, a phrase
from my diary which, seeming to have a gravity and cadence, a resonance
and ambiguity surpassing those of prose, bred like an amoeba another
phrase, discernible by now as a line, which did not quite rhyme yet did
not quite not, the echo more than consonantal involving kindred vowels
and suggesting certain words with variant pronunciations in American
and Canadian speech: *route, mahout,* even, it is said, *out* and *about.* So
much for meter and rhyme, schemes without which I cannot be both-
ered; with the epigrammatic amoebean character of the lines, these proposed a game, trite and limited, that I had not played for nearly thirty
years: a villanelle. The sixteenth line is of course a translation of the title,
which it dictated: a beast still to be found in some old-fashioned inscrip-
tions.

Edward Hirsch was born in Chicago in 1950.
*He was educated at Grinnell
College and the University of Pennsylvania. He has published four
books of poems,* For the Sleepwalkers *(1981);* Wild Gratitude *(1986),
which won the National Book Critics Circle Award;* The Night Parade
(1989), and Earthly Measures *(1994). His poems and reviews appear
regularly in a wide range of literary magazines—among them the* New
Republic, *the* New Yorker, *and the* New York Times Book Review.
He has received a Guggenheim Fellowship, a fellowship from the Na-

tional Endowment for the Arts, an Ingram Merrill Award, and the Rome Prize from the American Academy of Arts and Letters. He teaches at the University of Houston.

Fast Break
(In Memory of Dennis Turner, 1946–1984)

A hook shot kisses the rim and
hangs there, helplessly, but doesn't drop,

and for once our gangly starting center
boxes out his man and times his jump

perfectly, gathering the orange leather
from the air like a cherished possession

and spinning around to throw a strike
to the outlet who is already shovelling

an underhand pass toward the other guard
scissoring past a flat-footed defender

who looks stunned and nailed to the floor
in the wrong direction, trying to catch sight

of a high, gliding dribble and a man
letting the play develop in front of him

in slow-motion, almost exactly
like a coach's drawing on the blackboard,

both forwards racing down the court
the way that forwards should, fanning out

and filling the lanes in tandem, moving
together as brothers passing the ball

between them without a dribble, without
a single bounce hitting the hardwood

until the guard finally lunges out
and commits to the wrong man

while the power-forward explodes past them
in a fury, taking the ball into the air

by himself now and laying it gently
against the glass for a lay-up,

but losing his balance in the process,
inexplicably falling, hitting the floor

with a wild, headlong motion
for the game he loved like a country

and swivelling back to see an orange blur
floating perfectly through the net.

My taste in sports has always been hopelessly American: football, basketball, baseball—the three games that I played constantly as a child. Sometimes it seems as if my sister and I spent our entire childhoods running pass patterns in the street, or tossing up one-handed set shots in a neighbor's driveway, or throwing each other high, towering fly balls and low grounders that sizzled along the sidewalk in front of our house. All year we waged long imaginary games against awesome opponents— games which we usually won in double overtime or extra innings when our mother called us home. From this distance it seems as if we loved each sport fervently, seasonally, equally.

My friend, Dennis Turner, had no such divided loyalties: he loved basketball with a deep exclusive passion. Basketball was for him the ultimate city game, the only game that genuinely touched his emotional life, a way of staying in touch with his boyhood in Queens. He loved the grace, agility and quickness of the game, and took great pride in understanding its nuances. For years I had wanted to write something about basketball (or football, or baseball—I didn't know precisely what), but after Dennis died I started to feel a real impetus and imperative. Suddenly it seemed to me a worthy ambition to write a poem that could capture a single extended moment in sport, that would not only take basketball as its locale but would also take on the undercurrents of an elegy.

That's how I started replaying games in my memory, going over single plays again and again in my mind, the way that my sister and I had once done as children, the way that my friend and I had sometimes done on Saturday afternoons and Monday nights. At the same time I read everything that I could find about New York City basketball, once more thinking about playgrounds and park leagues, pickup games on warm evenings in musty gyms, amateur tournaments. I began coming across sentences like this one in Pete Axthelm's *The City Game:* "To the uninitiated, the patterns may seem fleeting, elusive, even confusing; but on a city playground, a classic play is frozen in the minds of those who see it—a moment of order and achievement in a turbulent, frustrating existence." At times Axthelm sounds oddly like an urban, streetwise version of Robert Frost, and it occurred to me that some men think about a basketball play the way that I think about a lyric poem—as an imaginative event, an intimate way of focusing and extending a radiant moment, a breakthrough into epiphany, a momentary stay against confusion.

Form is the shape of a poem's understanding, its way of living inside of an idea, the structure of its body. In "Fast Break" I tried to find a form that would create the rhythm and texture of a perfect play, a moment that was simultaneously inside and outside of time. Eventually, I decided upon a single enormous sentence unrolling in long snakelike couplets. My task was to establish a ground rhythm that could both quicken and slow down, rising and falling; and I wanted a form that was simultaneously open and closed, flexible and determined, giving the feeling of a play (and a poem) unfolding toward an inevitable conclusion, developing and taking shape as it progressed, moving organically toward an ideal conclusion. I wanted a language that could recreate the feeling of a fast break perfectly executed, the sense of five men suddenly moving in harmony, realizing together what had once happened separately in their imaginations. And I wanted a poem that could reclaim an instant of fullness and well-being, a moment of radiance propelled forward and given special poignance and momentum by a sudden feeling of loss. The result: a basketball poem, an elegy for a close friend, a lyric aspiring to a triumphant moment of order and achievement, a momentary stay against confusion.

John Hollander was born in New York City in 1929. A Crackling of Thorns, *his first book of poems, was chosen by W. H. Auden as the 1958 volume in the Yale Series of Younger Poets. His other books include* Types of Shape *(1969),* Reflections on Espionage *(1976), and* Harp Lake *(1988), as well as several volumes of criticism.* Selected Poetry *appeared from Knopf in 1993, as did* Tesserae, *a new collection. Hollander edited the Library of America's two-volume anthology* Nineteenth Century American Poetry *(1993). He is A. Bartlett Giamatti Professor of English at Yale University. "Poems cannot be about the world unless they are about themselves first," Hollander has said.*

"Poetry is a use of language in which language is opaque rather than transparent, and in which what is being said about the world immediately becomes part of the world as it comes to be uttered; so the misuses of language, the games played with language, are all part of the essential work of what poetry does."

The poem in fact glosses and explains its own form, or at any rate, its own revisionary claim to "its" "form" (both of these terms being problematic). The twenty-six untitled quatrains are one of a series of fifty-five poems, from two to thirty-four stanzas in length, all written in the spring and summer of 1975, and all addressed to the matter of absence and loss. The very first of these, dated 16 February, was a kind of post-et-anti-Valentine verse, deliberately framed in an old-fashioned *a b b a* four-beat quatrain, announcing an intention to keep at the task of writing:

> There was an end to hearts and rhymes,
> The old occasion rushed on past.
> Now? Unruled pages, and the vast
> Spaces of our unsinging times
>
> Within which these still measured lines
> Shall wander yet, slowly to mark
> A journey in a kind of dark
> In which a distance faintly shines.

But all the subsequent poems fell into the same stanza form (I had not been writing rhymed verse for a good many years), and I soon realized that I was writing in memoriam to part of my life. Some of the sections were dangerously occasional, or literal, but I kept coming back to the question of why, if I was feeling so much strangeness and pain, I kept talking about it in rhymed quatrains like these. Several of the poems engage this question broached all-too-directly by Wordsworth ("In truth, the prison unto which we doom / Ourselves no prison is"), all-too-obliquely by Emerson (the "stairway of surprise" is *not* an escalator)— one begins, for example, "Why rhyme?"; another ends "This succedaneum and prop / May signal truth's infirmities, / But chanting chokes on its own lees, / And rhymed lines know best when to stop." But more than halfway through the sequence, I dealt with the question more directly, "accounting" for the form by allegorizing it in order to expound the meaning that my poems had been making accrue to the form, which in itself "meant" nothing until particular poems written "in" it (and what a misleading form/content distinction *that* preposition sets up, suggesting liquid, bottle or worse) would invent/discover its significance. This was a poem that taught the sequence preceding it where it came from (as a counter to the sequence's own version of lyric's oldest story about itself, that it "comes from" a speaker-writer's feelings), what it had been up to, what it might have been meaning, as far as its "use" of a stanza form was concerned. It explains itself, as part of the sequence, better than any *obiter dicta* on form could. I should only gloss, in the seventh stanza (and for the unbibled), the Aramaic *"Abba,"* which means "father," and perhaps unnecessarily add that the only presence whose name is suppressed in the poem's desperate little literary history of its own obsession is, of course, the dominant one of Tennyson.

Why have I locked myself inside
This narrow cell of four-by-four,
Pacing the shined, reflecting floor
Instead of running free and wide?

Having lost you, I'd rather not
Be forced to find my way as well
In the broad darkness visible
Of prose's desert, vast and hot;

But in the shade of these four walls
Bounce the black ball of my despair
Off each in turn, and spurn the glare
Outside the cool, confining walls.

Why, then, if so ascetic, a
Rich game? Why must I always play
The stanza called *a b b a*
In books of *ars poetica?*

Avoiding hollow chime or cant,
The false narration and invalid
Wails of the modern form of ballad,
Less of a song and more a chant,

Accented crotchets, semi-brave
Measures of resonance will suit
Laying the painfully acute
Finalities beside the grave.

The daughters' measures may surprise,
The Mother Memory can amuse,
But *Abba's* spirit must infuse
The form which will memorialize.

"Memorialize" . . . But who is dead?
The unstressed "and" of "wife and man"?
Its life was measured by the span
As by the act, a word unsaid

That sleeps with memory and John
Hollander's long unpublished poem,
And will yet rise from its mute home
In textual sepulchre anon.

This rhyme of mirrored halves arose
Headless from the ashes of
Phoenix and his constant dove
Intestate else, as Shakespeare shows:

"So they loved as love in twain
Had the essence but in one;
Two distincts, division none:
Number thus in love was slain."

Sidney and Sandys when they gave alms
To Sion's muse, and called upon
Strophes that purled through Helicon,
Used it to paraphrase the Psalms;

Herbert of Cherbury employed
The same form to determine whether
Love could continue on forever
After mere bodies were destroyed,

Writing, *"in her up-lifted face*
Her eyes which did that beauty crown
Were like two starrs that having faln down,
Look up again to find their place."

Our stanza with a great to-do
Warned the seducer to be wary

And thus (trochaically) by Carew
(Or, as the learned say, Carew):

"Stop the chaféd Bore, or play
With the Lyons paw, yet feare
From the Lovers side to teare
Th'Idoll of his soul away."

Thus Marvell's Daphnis, turning down
His never-yielding Chloe's last
Frantic attempt to hold him fast
By finally rucking up her gown:

"Whilst this grief does thee disarm,
All th'Enjoyment of our love
But the ravishment would prove
Of a Body dead while warm."

Filling these decorous and deep
Cups of rhyme, Jonson's "Elegy"
Lay still; draining their melody,
Rossetti dreamed his sister's sleep.

Shores the Virgilian river laves
Crossed with the sounding of the bar
Out in the North Sea, heard afar
Graven in Keatsian beating waves;

Heard by the voice that filled these rooms
With sounds of mourning, cries of hope
Escaped love's fire, in a trope
Of marriage, memory and tombs

Of faith deceased, to which he fled
From touch not taken, half-recalled
Stillborn caresses that appalled
The poet, not the loving dead.

I, too, fill up this suite of rooms,
a bit worn now, with crowds of word,
Hoping that prosody's absurd
Law can reform the thoughts it dooms;

An emblem of love's best and worst:
Marriage (where hand to warm hand clings,
Inner lines, linked by rhyming rings);
Distance (between the last and first),

This quatrain is born free, but then
Handcuffed to a new inner sound,
After what bliss it may have found
Returns to the first rhyme again.

—Not our bilateral symmetry,
But low reflecting high, as on
His fragile double poised, the swan:
What's past mirrored in what will be.

Paul Hoover *was born in Harrisonburg, Virginia,*

in 1946. Educated at Manchester College and the University of Illinois, he is the author of five poetry collections, including The Novel *(New Directions, 1990). His poetry has appeared in three editions of* The Best American Poetry *and in* Up Late. *He edited* Postmodern American Poetry: A Norton Anthology *(1994). In 1988, he published a Vietnam-era novel,* Saigon, Illinois *(Vintage Contemporaries). In 1994, his long prose poem* Viridian *was the basis for a ninety-minute film (of the same title) produced and directed by independent filmmaker Joseph Luis Ramirez. He has received a fellowship from the National Endowment for the Arts and the General Electric Foundation Award for Younger Writers. With his wife, Maxine Chernoff, he edits the literary magazine* New American Writing. *He is the poet-in-residence at Columbia College in Chicago, and divides his time between Chicago and northern California.*

Poems We Can Understand

If a monkey drives a car
down a colonnade facing the sea
and the palm trees to the left are tin
we don't understand it.

We want poems we can understand.
We want a god to lead us,
renaming the flowers and trees,
color-coding the scene,

doing bird calls for guests.
We want poems we can understand,
no sullen drunks making passes
next to an armadillo, no complex nothingness

amounting to a song,
no running in and out of walls
on the dry tongue of a mouse,
no bludgeoness, no girl, no sea that moves

with all deliberate speed, beside itself
and blue as water, inside itself and still,
no lizards on the table becoming absolute hands.
We want poetry we can understand,

the fingerprints on mother's dress,
pain of martyrs, scientists.
Please, no rabbit taking a rabbit
out of a yellow hat, no tattooed back

facing miles of desert, no wind.
We don't understand it.

Sartre wrote in "Why Write?": ". . . whatever the subject, a sort of essential lightness must appear everywhere and remind us that the work is never a natural dictum, but an *exigence* and a *gift*." No matter how serious or heavy the intention of a poem, its form brings to it a sense of play or "essential lightness" that is disarming and inviting. Form is sociable, allowing the reader to acknowledge, to his relief, that the writing before him has been arranged for his delectation.

"Poems We Can Understand," because it was conceived as an argument, required the lightness of form in order to avoid turgidity. I composed by sound, using rhymes when the argument itself, not the line ending, called for them. After the first couple of drafts, I broke the poem into quatrains for the purpose of making a better shape on the page. Once that form was determined, however, I reworked the poem to sharpen each line as sound and as information. The final couplet was chosen for its abruptness; filling out a final quatrain would have spoiled the rhythm. Besides choosing to write an argument, the use of refrain was my only other initial constraint. The polarities (not this, but that) and the anaphora (the reiterated phrases) give a nodding forward movement that drives into the couplet wall at the end.

The poem marks a period when I was trying to move from a poetry consisting exclusively of imagery—I'd been raised to think that "essaying" in poetry is unacceptable—to a poetry of thought and music.

Richard Howard *was born in Cleveland in 1929. He was educated at Columbia University and the Sorbonne. He has published ten books of poetry; for his third,* Untitled Subjects, *he was awarded the Pulitzer Prize in 1970. A distinguished translator of French literature, he has received the PEN Translation Medal, the Ordre National Merite from the French government, and the American Book Award for his translation of Baudelaire's* Les Fleurs du mal. *His comprehensive critical study,* Alone with America: Essays on the Art of Poetry in the United States *(1970) was reissued in an enlarged edition in 1980. He is a chancellor of the Academy of American Poets. He is poetry editor of both the* Paris Review *and the* Western Humanities Review *and served as guest editor of* The Best American Poetry 1995. *He is University Professor of English at the University of Houston.*

At the Monument to Pierre Louÿs
Jardin du Luxembourg

Sage nor Saint nor Soldier—these were not
the sobriquets he fastened onto Fame:
let other men indulge the mummery
endorsed by these obsequious thoroughfares

with such abandon, yard by gravelled yard—
theirs would not be the idols he adored.
What *were* the sacred semblances he chose
to traffic in? And did they cheat his trust?

Inchmeal moss has muddled the design:
a palm? a laurel? or an aureole

as futile as anathemas would be?
The cenotaph *his own estate* bequeathed

(as though forewarned no Popular Demand
would pay a sculptor, specify a plot
and meet the tariff of Perpetual Care)—
the cenotaph! obtrusive as it is,

thwarts all my efforts at decipherment.
Just as well. There is no cause to mind
whatever mutilations have occurred
as though in nothing solider than mud,

to mourn what the successive rain has made
of this "immutable" monstrosity
erected to an undermined career
beginning only when—as History does—

the tale it has to tell attains its end.
Appropriate decay: like "other men"
he lived in search of what he saw as joy,
ecstatic consolations. *There she stands!*

Balancing an urn as effortlessly
as if no more than his very ashes swelled
its brimming load, behind the stele looms
an academic Naiad rather worse

for wear by rising (the intent is clear)
gently from the reeds' enjambment—she
is cold but she is patient, waiting for
the furtive metal of her eyes to fill . . .

Glancing back in haste to catechize
her shoulders where they falter, suddenly
she catches up a hank of molten hair
and wrings it out as if it had become

another green, wet, heavy nenuphar:
she waits for the tune of little drops to fall . . .
Also appropriate: what else remains
of him but *l'odeur de la femme,* page after page?

And even that would soon evaporate
without the fickle traces of three friends
(Valéry desisted, Gide despised,
Debussy meant what he said but managed to die)

—save for such captious camaraderies,
nothing would survive a period taste
but this absurd contraption: brazen Muse
and marble slab on which all syllables

erode but APHRODITE BILITIS—
the rest is . . . silly. Who was Pierre Louÿs?
The real names of the poems in his books,
for all their happy Sapphic hoaxes, are

. . . *and Other Poems.* Night after night he wrote
as if there were a tide to float him on,
nacre enough to laminate his itch—
who was it called him an oyster inside a pearl?

If once and for all he could make chance into choice,
change what he had to love to what he wanted to . . .
Forever hostage to the chiding animal,
he was elided. In his will was no

peace, as he learned whenever a meal came late
or the nearest pissotière was occupied:
the change never ceases, never being complete.
There *is* a tide in the affairs of men,

but apt to strand them high and dry. You haunt
my frequentations of your great
contemporaries like a thirsty ghost . . .
I read you, *mon semblable, mon Pierre!*

During the years I was translating *Les Fleurs du mal,* something of the
Baudelairean patina must have rubbed off, been transferred: poems
written then, of which this one is my delight, show a craving to load
every rift with . . . glue, perhaps—to bind the intervals of resource with
the mortar of commemoration, as it were. And perhaps, too, because I
was so much aware of the discrepancy between the French poet's
achievement and my own doings, it mattered to choose a figure as suc-

cinctly second-rate as Louÿs, one so easily assimilable to my own intentions that the Parnassian truck could withstand the embarrassments of being overpowered, foreshortened by all that was too immense for comfort in the Other Tradition. Gradually the imaginary "monument" became clear—my poem would have to make up for itself in the most lapidary measures and stanzas (stances?) I could manage, if not afford—an iambic pentameter which even the oddity of phrases in French, of titles that were Greek names, could not dissuade from their lugubrious pace. Certain Valerian toyings appeared, as I persisted, to be inevitable: that "cenotaph" should turn into "decipherment," that "mutilations" should become "immutable." For all the shellac, though, what endears the piece to me is that its crazy literary therapeutics are so intimate. The poem comes as close to General Admission as I ever have, and it is only fair, or fond, that it should do so by means of the very practice it a little derides. When all the makings we cobble up as "form" are shown, are *revealed* to be the inside of the outside, rather than the other way around, then surely we have poetry of a representative ardor, an instance of the aspired-to obelisk, another attempt at the shrine.

Colette Inez was born in Brussels, Belgium, in

1931. She came to the United States just before the start of World War II. Her first book of poems, The Woman Who Loved Worms *(Doubleday, 1972) won the Great Lakes College Association First Book Award, launching her career as a poet and teacher. She has since published six more books:* Alive and Taking Names *(Ohio University Press),* Eight Minutes from the Sun *(Saturday Press),* Family Life *and* Getting Under Way, New and Selected Poems *(Story Line Press),* Naming the Moons *(Apple Tree Alley Press of Bucknell University) and* For Reasons of Music *(Ion Books, 1994). She has won many prizes and fellowships, including two fellowships from the National Endowment for the Arts, a Guggenheim Fellowship, and a Rockefeller Foundation Fellowship. For the last ten years, she has taught writing at Columbia University's School of General Studies. She lives in New York City with her husband, a freelance writer, and is at work on a prose memoir,* Notes from an Exiled Daughter.

THE MAKING OF A POEM
Scratch a poet and you'll find affinities. One may be set off by a good bottle of Bordeaux, another by aardvarks or some other eccentricity. I'm hooked on Holiday Inns, or rather, on their dining rooms.

While the chain's motel rooms seem cloned—to hold down a sense of dislocation among traveling salesmen, I'm told—almost anything goes for theme settings in their restaurants. Instance: Cleveland's Holiday Inn features a revival of World War I air wars in its Red Baron Room.

A picturama of Von Richtofen's aerial exploits. Checkerboard Fokkers decimating Allied Spads and Neuports. Smoking coffins for our young lads, spiraling by the score to violent ends as the Red Baron notches yet another Yank in his gunsights.

Bizarre. But there's something to be made of this inspired masochism. Carry it one step forward, and we have:

> A Wehrmacht chain of restaurants,
> our former enemies as kitsch,
> example: Hitler House, The Goebbels Room,
> Eva Braun Chalet, souvenir whips and swastikas
> in multicolored marzipan . . .

I jotted this in my journal in a room whose ceilings and walls were lanced with tracers scoring bull's-eyes behind diners' tables. Amazement gave way to a leap of memory: a friend who found "Love" at the close of a stranger's letter wholly improper. I disagreed, in a passage I attached to the budding poem:

> I never find love at the close of a letter
> offensive.
> Very truly yours bends my ear.
> Very truly yours wants my bankbook
> and remittance.
> Very truly yours writes the world.

What had I done? Coined a few axioms, but why stop there? The poem *could* evolve with a handful of other small homilies for these times. Four, in all, wrote themselves on the facing journal page, a first draft of "Apothegms and Counsels." So did this, a reflection on relative weights:

> If someone says you're too short,
> say diamond rings don't come in cartons.
>
> If someone says you're too large,
> say you're an Amazon at large.
>
> If someone says your breasts are too big,
> say you bought them in Katmandu
> and the fitting rooms were dark.

If someone says your breasts are too small,
say chickpeas are loved in Prague.

How much do I weigh on the sun? On the moon?

I weigh two tons on the sun
I weigh twenty pounds on the moon.
Love makes me weightless.

It soon dawned on me that Teutonic asides and correspondence closings seemed beside the point. So I abandoned them, allowing the second draft of my poem to indulge only in figures of speech for the body. Cutting it back to the purity of its counsels, I also took out numerical values; "tons" on the sun and "pounds" on the moon could stand alone. *I* shifted to an imaginary, feisty and commanding *you* to give the poem universality. And, in a final resolution, a last quatrain was burnished several months later:

Apothegms and Counsels

If someone says you're too short,
say diamond pins don't come in cartons.

If someone says you're too large,
say you're an Amazon at large.

If someone says your breasts are too big,
say you bought them in Katmandu
and the fitting rooms were dark.

Say chickpeas are loved in Prague
if someone says your breasts are too small.

How much do you weigh on the sun? On the moon?

Tons on the sun.
Pounds on the moon.
Love makes you weightless.

If someone says you're too far out,
say Doppler Effect,
that you're writing a history of light
for the children of Pythagoras.

Phyllis Janowitz

was born in Manhattan, at Knickerbocker Hospital, "in the Twentieth Century." Her first book of poetry, Rites of Strangers, *was chosen as the first selection in the Associated Writing Program's book competition judged by Elizabeth Bishop in 1978; her second, selected by Maxine Kumin for Princeton University Press in 1982, was nominated for the National Book Critics Circle Award.* Visiting Rites *was named one of the notable books of 1982 by the* New York Times Book Review. *Her most recent book of poems is* Temporary Dwellings *(University of Pittsburgh Press, 1988). She has been an Alfred Hodder Fellow in the Humanities at Princeton University, a fellow of the Bunting Institute, and the recipient of two National Endowment for the Arts awards in poetry. She is a professor of English at Cornell University and lives in Ithaca, New York.*

Change

Certain Americans refuse to return
To their country or county of origin
Fearing their roots will pull them

Back into the soil, fearing the land
Will cover them over, bright green
Hairs like plastic grass in an Easter

Basket will sprout on their private plots.
Where are our roots, Gussie's and mine?
Surely near some huge coastal mecca

Mart, market, mall, bazaar, *sook.*
Gussie says, "Mother, perhaps we purchased
Too much? I'm sorry about the checks."

Arms laden with parcels we take
A taxi home. Our feet ache.
The meter ticks: four   five   six.

We hear only the roll of breaking waves.
Gussie over-tips. My habitual glum
Incantation begins: "Once again it's

Plain you have no respect for the slim
Thumbprints, the fibroblasts of skin
Even small change is weighted with."

Gussie hushes up ferociously.
When I received my final decree
My father abstained from sustenance

For a week. "What will become of Gussie?"
He wept. No way for me to reply,
Remembering how he'd walk sixty

City blocks to save a subway fare.
To ride cost a nickel them. Now
In our fashion, Gussie and I, warbling

Mermaids, comb the snarls from our
Raveled days. Sometimes we bring home
Gifts for those who wait, round

Soap on a rope, seals carved from stone,
Seashells—each night fingering
Findings like fat beads on strings.

Tonight we will sleep on the hefty
Laps of angels. Tomorrow we will catch
A ride back to each store, the way
Fortunate starfish return with the tide.

Even chaos has a form. Melted ice cream has the form of melted ice cream. Therefore we cannot speak of formlessness. There is no such beast. To try to construct one is to try to make a snowball out of dry sand. There are merely approaches to perfect symmetry, which is vastly different from perfect form, and not necessarily desirable at all.

"Change" delivered its lines to me one day while I was in the kitchen watching soap bubbles in the dishwater coalesce and disperse, each bubble a miniature galaxy in the cosmic sink. The idea of flux in recurrence came to me then: how one of the most life-sustaining molecules, water, arranges itself consistently into two parts hydrogen to one part oxygen, whether pond, stream, or sea. Yet a microscopic change may result in a totally different compound, as the molecule becomes "heavy water," or deuterium oxide, with the addition of another hydrogen atom.

I decided to write a poem about a family constellation in a changing social order. The poem would have a regularity expressed in visual form and would consist of stanzas of three rather lengthy lines, giving a nod in the direction of terza rima, but with internal rather than end-rhymed lines. After the poem was written in longhand I took it to the typewriter, where it altered its shape when assaulted by the molecules in the keys. At that point I felt I had to push the material around somewhat, but in its DNA direction of growth, to help it achieve its cultural potential, and yet not to interfere so much that the poem became diverted out of its primitive inclinations and uncertainties.

The finished version retained the triplet stanzaic form, but the lines had become much shorter, and a quatrain seemed necessary at the end to add a weight and strength, as the trunk of a tree thickens at ground level. "Change" arrived at a point similar to where it had started out; there was a repetition, yet the beginning and end were not the same. Of course, any poem must have a beginning, a middle and an end—a premise rooted in biological necessity. The first word is its beginning; if there are no more words, then the first word is also the middle and the end. The entire completed structure is held together by a kind of electromagnetic glue. This glue is called "form."

Events take place in a person's life which are so beautiful or terrible that they must be repeated or inflicted on others; this repetition or infliction is also a kind of form. The form of a poem begins in the body of the poet; his or her entire genetic conformation and total sums of experience are always involved in the construction. We can go further and say that the force that moves the planets around the sun and the energy the poet uses to set down the word-particles on the paper are the same thing. When the universe ends, the poem will go with it. The poem may last several trillion years but not forever. The last blips of light it emits will traverse an empty space as the cosmos collapses into silence.

Lawrence Joseph *was born in Detroit in 1948. His grandparents were Lebanese and Syrian Catholic emigrants. He was educated at the University of Michigan, where he received the Hopwood Award for Poetry; Cambridge University, where he took degrees in English language and literature; and the University of Michigan Law School. His books of*

That's All

I work and I remember. I conceive
a river of cracked hands above Manhattan.

No spirit leaped with me in the womb.
No prophet explains why Korean women

thread Atomic Machinery's machines
behind massive, empty criminal tombs.

Why do I make my fire my heart's blood,
two or three ideas thought through

to their conclusions, make my air
dirty the rain around towers of iron,

a brown moon, the whole world?
My power becomes my sorrow.

Truth? My lies are sometimes true.
Firsthand, I now see the God

whose witness is revealed in tongues
before the Exchange on Broad Street

and the transfer of 2,675,000,000 dollars
by tender offer are acts of the mind,

and the calculated truths of First
National City Bank. Too often

I think about third cousins in the Shouf.
I also often think about the fact that

in 1926, after Céline visited
the Ford Rouge foundry and wrote

his treatise on the use of physically
inferior production line workers,

an officially categorized "displaced person"
tied a handkerchief around his face

to breathe the smells and the heat
in a manner so as not to destroy

his lungs and brain for four years
until he was laid off. I don't

meditate on hope and despair.
I don't deny the court that rules

my race is Jewish or Abyssinian.
In good times I transform myself

into the sun's great weight, in bad times
I make myself like smoke on flat wastes.

I don't know why I choose who I am:
I work and I remember, that's all.

I began "That's All" in late 1982, two and a half years after I moved to
New York City from Detroit. I wanted to write a poem that incorporated
various aspects of both cities and of the Shouf mountains in Lebanon
(from which my grandfather emigrated, and which was immersed at the
time in fierce warfare). I wanted to make emblematic images of Detroit,
New York and Lebanon: Detroit, as an expression of labor; New York
City, as an expression of finance capital; Lebanon, as an expression of
religious violence. I also wanted to create a person—the *I* of the poem—
who reacted to and was part of these worlds.

I needed a form that would hold the poem's multiple dimensions. I
also wanted the poem—as I want all of my poetry—to achieve a sense of
control, balance, and lucidity: a classical *claritas*. I decided to use an
open form—a juxtapositional and somewhat disjunctive structure expressed, stanzaically, in couplets and, metrically, through a variable pentameter line. I chose couplets because they require clarity of image or
statement to work at all. I chose a variable pentameter line for its declar-
ative potential. When I work this line, I imagine a ten-syllable line
(which is sometimes iambic pentameter) within which I vary the number
and quality of feet in order to modulate and effectuate the line's mean-

ing. Weldon Kees uses this line in many of the poems in his last collection, *Poems 1947–1954*. John Berryman also uses it in his most dazzling technical achievement, *Love & Fame*. Acting within a couplet structure, it can create not only an aphoristic, moral, and ironic tone but also a sense of interior formal balance.

The poem's final movement fuses the poem's "places" and the *I* within them. The last couplet—"I don't know why I choose who I am: / I work and I remember, that's all"—is a patently moral conclusion, expressed with restraint. Its formal lineage is classical.

Donald Justice was born in Miami, Florida, in 1925. He studied piano with the composer Carl Ruggles at the University of Miami. After receiving his master's degree from North Carolina, he studied poetry with Yvor Winters at Stanford and went on to take his Ph.D. from the University of Iowa in 1954. He taught at the Iowa Writers' Workshop from 1957 to 1982. Justice's Selected Poems (1979) won the Pulitzer Prize. His other books include The Summer Anniversaries (1960), Night Light (1967), Departures (1973), The Sunset Maker (1987) and A Donald Justice Reader (1992). He recently moved from Florida (where he taught for a time at the University of Florida, Gainesville) back to Iowa City. He has won the Bollingen Prize. "I've written some poems in a day—not very often," Justice told an interviewer. "Other times I've worked over the notes for a poem for years. The poem isn't necessarily any better for that, of course. If I could write poems the way I dream of writing poems, I would dash off a poem in an afternoon. Then probably take the rest of the week off. There simply shouldn't be too many poems."

Pantoum of the Great Depression

Our lives avoided tragedy
Simply by going on and on,
Without end and with little apparent meaning.
Oh, there were storms and small catastrophes.

Simply by going on and on
We managed. No need for the heroic.
Oh, there were storms and small catastrophes.
I don't remember all the particulars.

We managed. No need for the heroic.
There were the usual celebrations, the usual sorrows.
I don't remember all the particulars.
Across the fence, the neighbors were our chorus.

There were the usual celebrations, the usual sorrows.
Thank God no one said anything in verse.
The neighbors were our only chorus,
And if we suffered we kept quiet about it.

At no time did anyone say anything in verse.
It was the ordinary pities and fears consumed us,
And if we suffered we kept quiet about it.
No audience would ever know our story.

It was the ordinary pities and fears consumed us.
We gathered on porches; the moon rose; we were poor.
What audience would ever know our story?
Beyond our windows shone the actual world.

We gathered on porches; the moon rose; we were poor.
And time went by, drawn by slow horses.
Somewhere beyond our windows shone the world;
But the Great Depression had entered our souls like fog.

And time went by, drawn by slow horses.
We did not ourselves know what the end was.
The Great Depression had entered our souls like fog.
We had our flaws, perhaps a few private virtues.

But we did not ourselves know what the end was.
People like us simply go on.
We have our flaws, perhaps a few private virtues,
But it is by blind chance only that we avoid tragedy.

And there is no plot in that; it is devoid of poetry.

Partly because of the beautiful Baudelaire pantoum, "Harmonie de soir," I had for a long time wished to try my hand at this form. In any case, I have a weakness for forms involving repetition, and the pantoum is an almost absurdly extreme instance of the type. (It is said to be a Malaysian form, and there *is* a Malaysian form with this name, but this is not it; this is French—Hugo, Leconte de Lisle, Baudelaire.) There is almost inevitably some of what poets like to call music in this kind of repetition, but my thought was to try to get at the musical, if I could, by steadfastly ignoring the obviously lyrical and putting down instead a mere series of proselike sentences, one after the other, only occasionally linking them syntactically in what one might suppose to be the expected and approved manner. This would be more like something built from a child's set of blocks or perhaps the broad strokes of a brush loaded with various colors laid down side by side.

I imagine it is perfectly obvious that the argument of the poem is based on some of the points Aristotle makes in the *Poetics*.

Finally, let me say that I was interested all along in giving some of the truth of those times, and this interest was the foundation of all formal considerations.

Richard Kenney *was born in Glens Falls, New York, in 1948. He graduated from Dartmouth College in 1970. James Merrill chose his first book of poems,* The Evolution of the Flightless Bird, *in 1984, for the Yale Series of Younger Poets. It was followed in 1985 by* Orrery *and in 1993 by* The Invention of the Zero. *Kenney has received grants from the MacArthur and Guggenheim Foundations, the Rome Prize in literature, and a Lannan Literary Award. He currently teaches at the University of Washington in Seattle and lives in Port Townsend with his wife and two sons.*

from "The Encantadas"

One might as well conceive this story in the cirrose
streamings of volcanic dust across a solar
wind four billion years ago—ground zero,
so to speak, the first shrieking cautery
of earth. One has to start a story someplace; space
would do. The romance of our insularity
is nothing new—
                But this anticipates
as well—imagine, then, that gaseous catarrh
all lit like Eniwetok in the white smelter

of the mind's eye, and stirred, turned, tipped
out, vitreous and blazing, so: a scattering
of star-stuff from the far antipodes
of time, *tic-toc*—
           The mantle first, the elder
mountain chains and continents, Pangaea's
cracked shell—and then the islands, *ssspink ssspink*
ssspink into the sea . . . They shone like pan-gold
bright seeds broad-cast across the Great Arc-Welder's
dream! Well done. With all the sparks and spangles
of His lapidary work still guttering
in place, God smiled, imagined Papeete, Pago-
Pago populous—and knocked his calabash
against his palm six hundred miles off Ecuador,
and turned his face. And what a purgatory
hissed behind his back! An arc of crater-
scrapings, cinders, pig-lead slags and smelter ash
all splash into a black square on the Mercator
projection of the mind!
           It was an Arcady
in broken black and white, a shattered parquet
floor cartographers took centuries to fix.
Begin again: imagine rocks rattling like a fist
of buckshot down a coal-chute, say, some baker's
dozen undiscovered moons of Mercury
that funnelled down the wrong end of a Buccaneer's
brass telescope and tore his patch and lodged deep
down some dread dream there amidst the profound
  breakage
of a dark mind . . .
           Sometimes I see it in my own sleep
still, by the lit candelabrum of a Bofors gun: canaries
sputtering the poisoned air in a nightmare's dark
mine-shaft, the flickering of yellow flames.
An archipelago. And see again by arc-
light late at night of a thousand cigarettes coughed out
over yet another long, savage, debilitating
siege at chess—

But this anticipates the flim-
flam war I mean, in my own good time, to tell about.

A Creation scene—in this case, of the Galapagos archipelago, where the
formless void is only lightly cobbled over, and the poem's more or less
apocalyptic tale, about to be told, is set.

First, a point of common sense, commonly trampled. I think there's
a noteworthy difference between "form" as conceived prospectively,
with an eye to composition, and the retrospective discovery or proof of
"form" in a work already drafted. In the limited sense, "forms" are taken
as practical tricks of the joiner's trade. In the loftier sense, insofar as
language is the formal drapery thought wears, one can't help finding
"form" in it. This is governing "Design" vs. "The Road Not Taken";
making to measure vs. inventive critique. There may be room for both
exercises in the same word, but a curtain—the poem, say—hangs between. Without entangling grand questions of intention, creative revision, the entire nature-of-Art tar baby, I'd only note the priority of any
maker's impulse, e.g., "Four and twenty blackbirds in a fifty-inch tin,"
and suggest it's not usefully confused with what's said over cigars when
the dish is cleared, and the chirping dies away.

So, trying not to exhale too much smoke over what subtler, inadver-
tent rhythms may have insinuated themselves through these lines, I'll say
that the formal concerns I started with were the two usual ones. The
meter is iambic hexameter, with shorter pentameter lines scattered
through. The rhyming may seem less straightforward, though the scheme
is simple: each end-rhyme rings on another, no more than four away.
Farther than that, the echo seems to fade. The rhymes are slant, consonant, involving stressed or unstressed syllables. This permits a kind of
cascade, where certain echoes evolve, so to speak, in a branching way,
down the side of the page. Though not always so complex, the technique
allows three separate chains, of varying length, to be braided together
over a considerable distance. Here *catarrh* chimes on *scattering,* disappears under the short *Pangaea/ssspink/pan-gold/spangles/Pago* series,
resurfaces at *guttering,* and rings on through six more changes. By that
time it's turned to *parquet,* which wouldn't induce the slightest sympathetic tremor in *Ecuador,* above. Or consider *Buccaneer's,* which hears
baker's perfectly well (*breakage* hears that, too, though they don't each
other, much); *canaries* echoes on the fourth line down. *Canoe race* might
have followed, or *Cunard,* or (by syllabic chicanery) *Eerie,* though with
the Canal so far from the Pacific, that would seem a canard.

Art rings off *canard* all right, except they're both rejected on logical grounds. Such rejections litter the way to a poem, and illustrate the first of two practical pleasures I take in rhyme. One, in the hearing, is obvious; the other, in the making, has to do with a kind of random or irrational search, a momentary crippling of the intellect, looking for words according to sound rather than sense. It's a practical tool for finding what you don't know you're looking for, as the expression goes—what sometimes comes to perfect sense.

A final quixotic swipe at the tar baby—*constraint,* the liberating manacles of formal poetry, etc.:

⚘ Poetry is a way of thinking, by the slant, analogical laws of metaphor. It's no accident that certain forms have evolved over time to streamline the process. They aren't geometric ornament, they're forms of thought.

⚘ Related so, over time, the thoughts and forms tease one another into existence. Imagine great narrative—Shakespeare—steeplechase—a fluid course occasionally stretched through moments of high lyric intensity. There was a time, earlier in the tradition, when the world was full of flatworms, when such miracles were as impossible as their imagining. The muscularity and amplitude and grace of the long iambic line, a gift of the literature, superbly adapt it to this kind of work. There are other kinds of work; birds fly, fish swim. Out far, in deep, poets wear feathers and scales they never invented, no matter what they say. In this case, the husbandry of successful forms since the first organic snort has led over long tradition to the whipped mules and plug dromedaries most of us ride, and the occasional Pegasus, too.

⚘ Again, a question of retrospect and prospect, reading vs. composition, serendipity and plan. It's not so much that the forms are fine to behold as that they help us to think and write. Whole histories reel out (witness tennis) at the shackling of liberty and desire. Frost's "playing without the net" seems to me as often misunderstood as his "Road Not Taken." With the highly evolved rules of tennis in mind, he wasn't speaking altogether of "the fascination of what's difficult," but of freedom from the natural urge to try the game with three serves, or oblong balls, or matched pistols.

⚘ To say it's often a shapely world, and that formal expectations are a measure of that, takes me out of my intellectual depth, but I think so.

John Koethe *was born in San Diego in 1945. His early interests were mathematics and physics, but in college at Princeton University he decided to major in philosophy and began writing poetry seriously. He went on to obtain a*

doctorate in philosophy at Harvard University. His first book of poems,
Blue Vents, *was published in 1968; his second book,* Domes *(Columbia University Press, 1973) received the Frank O'Hara Award for Poetry. His most recent book is* The Late Wisconsin Spring *(Princeton University Press, 1984). He has received a fellowship from the Guggenheim Foundation, the Bernard F. Connors Award for a long poem from the* Paris Review, *an award from* Southwest Review, *and a Milwaukee Country Artists Fellowship. He is a professor of philosophy at the University of Wisconsin, Milwaukee, and has published papers on Wittgenstein, philosophy of language, metaphysics, and epistemology in* Philosophical Review, Nous, Synthese, *and other journals. He has written on poetry and literary theory for* Critical Inquiry, Parnassus, Poetry, *and for various collections. He has one son, who is currently an undergraduate at Oberlin College.*

The Substitute for Time

How things bind and blend themselves together!
—Ruskin, *Praeterita*

I came back at last to my own house.
Gradually the clear, uninhabited breath
That had sprung up where the spent soul disappeared
Curved in around me, and then it too slowly disappeared.
And I have been living here ever since,
In the scope of my single mind, the confines of a heart
Which is without confinment, in a final pause
Before the threshold of the future and the warm,
Inexhaustible silence at the center of the lost world.
Now the days are sweeter than they used to be,

The memories come more quickly, and the world at twilight,
The world I live in now, is the world I dreamed about
So many years ago, and now I have.
How far it feels from that infatuation with the childish
Dream of passing through a vibrant death into my real life!
How thin time seems, how late the fragrance
Bursting from the captured moments of my childhood
Into the warm evening air that still surrounds me here.
And how the names still throb into my mind, and how my heart
    dissolves
Into a trembling, luminous confusion of bright tears.

For the texture of this life is like a field of stars
In which the past is hidden in a tracery
Looming high above our lives, a tangle of bright moments
Vibrating like a cloud of fireflies in the warm summer air.
And the glow of each one is a lifetime waning,
Spending itself in the temporary consolations of a mind
Beyond any possibility of happiness, that hovers in the air
A little while and then descends into itself
And the liberation of the clear white sky inside
Where the names float like birds, and all desire dies,
And the life we longed for finds us at the end.

"The Substitute for Time" was the third of a "private" sequence of three poems I wrote two years ago. I intended each poem to stand by itself, rather than figure as part of a group, but I also expected each to reflect on the others in ways which—while no doubt purely personal and idiosyncratic—might, I hoped, invest the writing with the sense of a subject matter just out of reach, or of the memory of some obscure experience just beyond the borders of the page. I was also reading Ruskin at the time and was quite taken with the sort of unembarrassed grandiloquence you find in him, which is supposed to be so objectionable in modern poetry; and being of a contrary nature myself, I wanted to incorporate a different version of that in the poem, too. The form I used was largely determined by the fact that I had been carrying line twenty-one around for some time, intending to use it in a poem as a detached, isolated line between stanzas, forming a bridge between some first-person musings and a more distanced, romantic ending written in the third. I'd been carrying around the last three lines as well, and didn't want the whole poem to be too long; and so an arrangement of three ten-line stanzas with the bridge between the second and the third struck me as just about right. The poem more or less wrote itself. The previous poem ("One Light") supplied the private subject matter and anchored the anaphoric references; the naive style supplied the repetitions, flat-footed grammatical constructions and exclamations; and Ruskin supplied the fireflies.

Yusef Komunyakaa was born in 1947
in Bogalusa, Louisiana. In 1969 and 1970 he served with the United States Army in Vietnam. He writes about the war in his book Dien Cai Dau (Wesleyan,

1988). "The morning cleared again, / except for a distant mortar / &
somewhere choppers taking off. / I slid the wallet into his pocket / &
turned him over, so he wouldn't be / kissing the ground." Since 1985,
Komunyakaa has taught creative writing and literature at Indiana Uni-
versity. He was the 1992 Holloway Lecturer at the University of Cali-
fornia, Berkeley, and spent a portion of 1995 in Australia. His latest
book, Neon Vernacular, *was awarded the 1994 Pulitzer Prize as well as*
the Kingsley Tufts Award. He was also the recipient of the 1994 Wil-
liam Faulkner Prize (Université de Rennes). He spent the 1994–95 aca-
demic year in Australia.

Trueblood's Blues

They're on the edge
    of their seats, nodding
        heads up & down.

You know how the devil
    tortures the soul?
        He keeps them waiting.

Fat meat . . . Broadnax's wife
    steps out of the grandfather clock
        for the seventeenth time

& throws herself into Trueblood's arms.
    The bedroom fills with feathers
        again. He's Caliban,

savoring the punishment
    of their eyes like the last
        drops of a strong drink.

Yellowjackets blooming on a jaybird—
    this always grabs their minds. Yes,
        now, nothing can stop Zeus

in the astonishment of falling
    feathers. The dream woman's
        forbidden scent is deep

as his own. He craves
    the hex & lash, but his enemies
        reward his downfall with time,

cash, & plugs of tobacco.
   Norton, the philanthropist,
        meditates on his daughter

till she stands nude
   before him. He peels open a red
        Moroccan-leather wallet

& extracts a hundred-dollar bill,
   erecting his monument
        to someone "more delicate

than the wildest dream
   of a poet." Standing
        beside this sharecropper,

he pays for the look in her eyes
   before she started to fade
        in those ice-capped

Alps. But each sunrise
   the same question begs
        the wound raw again.

Trueblood is a Southern sharecropper (who impregnated his teenaged daughter one cold night when she slept between her mother and father) in Ralph Ellison's *Invisible Man.* This character is a classic storyteller and bluesy confessor and has been accepted into what we can call The Brotherhood of the Ultimate Taboo: these white Southerners, farmers and laborers, the equivalent of today's rednecks, are the "they" in the poem's first line. In essence, they have been willing to let Trueblood escape punishment for a certain crime: his attraction to Fat Meat, Broadnax's wife. In his dream, she seduces him by walking nude out of the grandfather clock. She makes him betray himself. By copulating with this dream image, she has led him to violate his own flesh and blood. His other crime is that he realizes (after waking from the dream-trance) that he is having sex with his daughter; but he doesn't stop until orgasm. The daughter is also guilty.

In *Invisible Man,* the word "Daddy" underlines her guilt. Guilt is what also cements the relationship between Trueblood and the white men he confesses to. He has ventured to the most hostile territory to tell or retell his story. In fact, his confession is profane, which explains the name Caliban in the poem: "You taught me language," says Caliban to Prospero in *The Tempest,* "and my profit on't is I know how to curse." His confession is a scream, a cry for help, a blues he must sing to his enemy because they themselves have had similar thoughts and personal histories. The blacks are ashamed of him (especially those at the college). They want him banished and run out of town, and it seems that the whites want him to stick around as evidence for their ideas about so-called black inferiority. Trueblood knows that the white men are using him against himself: this is the agony and payment for his crime (he wanted his wife to beat him). Is incest a crime of poor whites and rural blacks? No. When Norton, a wealthy Northerner who supports the black college, pays him to tell his incest story, we learn that this rich man has been frightened by the same terror inside himself when he speaks of his own daughter. Trueblood, a black man who has sung the old spiri-tuals, now sings a relentless blues that he hopes can save him from himself. By using the three lines with staggered indentations, I discov-ered that I could incorporate information that enhances the text without undermining the poem's fluidity and music.

Ann Lauterbach *was born and raised in Manhattan. She went to the High School of Music and Art and majored in painting. She graduated from the University of Wisconsin, Madison, and received a Woodrow Wilson Fellowship to Columbia University. She realized, however, that poetry and the academy were not compatible, so she dropped out and began to work in publishing. She made a three-week journey to Europe (Dublin-London-Paris) which turned into a seven-year sojourn in Lon-don, where she worked as an editor and teacher and as director of the literature program at the Institute for Contemporary Arts. She returned to New York in 1973, where she worked primarily in art galleries, wrote occasional art criticism, and continued to write poems. She began teaching at Brooklyn College in the early 1980s, and has since taught in the writing programs at Columbia University, Princeton University, the Iowa Writers' Workshop, and Bard College, where she became head of the writing faculty in the M.F.A. program in 1992. She was appointed professor at City College in 1990 and to the faculty at the graduate cen-ter in 1994. Her books include* Before Recollection *(Princeton Uni-versity Press, 1987),* Clamor *(Viking-Penguin, 1991), and* And For Example *(Viking-Penguin, 1994). She received a Guggenheim Fellow-ship in 1986 and a fellowship from the John D. and Catherine T.*

MacArthur Foundation in 1993. She is a contributing editor of Conjunctions *magazine.*

Psyche's Dream

If dreams could dream, beyond the canon of landscapes
already saved from decorum, including mute
illicit girls cowering under eaves
where the books are stacked and which they
pillage, hoping to find not events but response

If dreams could dream, free from the damp crypt
and from the bridge where she went
to watch the spill and the tree
standing on its head, huge and rootless
(of which the wasp is a cruel illustration

Although its sting is not), the decay
now spread into the gardens, their beds
tethered to weeds and to all other intrusions;
then the perishing house, lost from view
so she must, and you, look out to see
not it but an image of it, would be

nowhere and would not resemble, but would languish
on the other side of place where the winged boy
touches her ear far from anywhere
but gathered like evening around her waist
so that within each dream is another, remote
and mocking and a version of his mouth on her mouth.

Except for those rare instances when I decide to attempt a formal poem with a traditional structure, I have come to think of form as concomitant to composition: my impulses and intentions to make a poem are acted upon by the linguistic necessities and energies generated by the poem itself. The latter may determine length of line, stanzaic arrangement, masculine or feminine endings, rhyme, and so forth—all the usual formal choices. This tandem method usually entails many drafts, during the course of which both the poem's ultimate subject and its form become evident. Often, when I begin, I "have" only rudimentary parts (an image, a phrase), as well as a general sense of a cohering feeling or idea. If this central kernel is strong enough, it will order the several parts into a successful form. If not, the result will be labored and unbalanced.

In the case of *Psyche* I had, initially, two basic ingredients: the phrase "if dreams could dream," which came to me as I was trying to characterize the emotional aura of an actual dream whose impact had been so exquisite, erotic and sublime, that it seemed like a dream within a dream; and secondly, a recent visit with my aunt Priscilla to my grandmother's house in Chappaqua which was about to be sold. (My mother and aunt grew up in this house; I spent many childhood holidays there.) During this final visit, we found stacks of old books from my aunt's, and my mother's, childhood library. Writing the poem, I became aware of how the house, the dream and the books shared a common potency: each provoked an intense, recollected response. As I was struggling with this Proustian notion, I looked up and saw, on my bookcase, a postcard image of François Gerard's hauntingly lovely painting *L'Amour et Pysche*. I was immediately struck by how perfectly this image seemed to capture the dream-within-dream landscape the poem needed, joining the mythic quality of childhood with the sensual vitality of my adult dream. In a sense, the lost house is redeemed or supplanted by the image of Eros and Psyche embracing.

Once I had this last, fortuitously found image, the poem began to form. Since I had begun with the phrase "if dreams could dream," I saw that I could extend the "if" clause, gathering information and suspense. I wanted a breathless, careering effect, mimetic of dream but touching, also, on obsession and loss of control endemic to recollected childhood, with all its unfulfilled "ifs." I liked the idea of stretching the syntax to break-point, holding back the linguistically inevitable "then," with all its temporal, causal logic—the logic of loss—so that, in the final stanza, "nowhere" becomes a curious respite, an escape out of one world (the unconscious, mined world of childhood) into the liberated, charged landscape of maturity. It was not until late in the process that I realized that this progression replicated Psyche's journey from unconscious lover to enlightened woman. But since I see enlightenment as perilous in its own way, the final kiss is mitigated by "remote and mocking," bringing the poem full circle, back to dream.

David Lehman *was born in New York City in 1948. After graduating from Columbia College, he attended Cambridge University in England as a Kel-*

lett Fellow. He initiated The Best American Poetry *in 1988 and serves as the series editor of this annual anthology. His most recent book of poems is* Valentine Place *(Scribner, 1996). His prose books include* Signs of the Times: Deconstruction and the Fall of Paul de Man *(Poseidon, 1991).* The Big Question *(1995) is the second of his critical books to appear in the University of Michigan Press's Poets on Poetry Series. He is on the core faculty of the low-residency graduate writing program at Bennington College and teaches at Columbia and the New School for Social Research. He was the Elliston Poet at the University of Cincinnati in 1995. "A poet deals in fictions just as a novelist does," he has said. "The sophisticated reader knows that the 'I' in a story is someone other than the author. Why shouldn't poets enjoy similar freedoms and employ similar strategies?" He divides his time between Ithaca, New York, and New York City.*

Amnesia
for Tom Disch

Neither the actors nor the audience knew what was coming next.
That's when the assassination must have taken place.
The car pulled up and the driver said "get in."
"Wolves don't criticize sheep," Cage grinned. "They eat them."

That's when the assassination must have taken place.
The wedding dress in the window had vanished.
"Wolves don't criticize sheep," Cage grinned. "They eat them."
This announcement will not be repeated.

The wedding dress in the window had vanished
At dawn, the perfect time for an execution.
This announcement will not be repeated:
The only victory in love is retreat. So we retreated.

At dawn, the perfect time for an execution,
All the suspects were wearing identical blue uniforms.
The only victory in love is retreat, so we retreated;
To one madness we must oppose another.

All the suspects were wearing identical blue uniforms
Because painting conveys the image of its time.
To one madness we must oppose another,
But we don't suppose it will heal people or anything like that.

Because painting conveys the image of its time,
When destiny appears, wearing a badly brushed top hat,
We don't suppose it will heal people or anything like that.
—The tape erased itself. It was time to begin.

When destiny appeared, wearing a badly brushed top hat,
Neither the actors nor the audience knew what was coming next.
The tape erased itself. It was time to begin.
The car pulled up and the driver said "get in."

The more constrictive the form, the likelier it is that a poem cast in that form will gloss itself. High-school readers, who may never have heard of a villanelle, will have no trouble discerning the pattern of insistence in Dylan Thomas's "Do Not Go Gentle into That Good Night." The author of a pantoum like "Amnesia" may thus be reasonably confident that his poem will divulge its form and illustrate its rules and regulations at least as well as a prose explanation could.

In a form built around regularly scheduled repetitions, the trick is to conform to the pattern while at the same time offering some measure of resistance to it. Repetition is not exclusively a device for providing emphasis; repetition, in an ever-shifting context, equals variation. You can't walk into the same river twice, and by the same logic, a line—repeated verbatim or with a slight change in punctuation or emphasis—will be both itself and something else the second time around. "This announcement will not be repeated" becomes, when repeated, a conundrum lifted to the second power.

The poem's title is its governing element. I wanted "Amnesia" to dramatize that interesting condition rather than to comment on it, and I thought that the pantoum structure was oddly appropriate for the task. Oddly, because one ordinarily thinks of repetition as an aid to memory—and yet I was certain it could suggest, in a somewhat sinister way, the action of a tape erasing itself. Or does the constant stop-and-start effect more closely approximate the action of a tape being rewound and played, as someone searches through it for a forgotten, misplaced fragment of speech? In any case, the repetitions in "Amnesia" create expectations that, even when fulfilled, leave us with the perplexed feeling that the unexpected is upon us. It is impossible to say what's "coming next." It is always "time to begin," since the past doesn't exist. Everything happens according to some sort of logic, yet the logic itself is a little terrifying—an effect reinforced, I hope, by the several rhymes in the poem. The memory of the poem's unnamed and disembodied hero—all we have of him is his vocal signature—functions like a blank check that anyone can cash in, for any amount one chooses.

Brad Leithauser *was born in Detroit in 1953.*

His father was an attorney and his mother a cancer researcher and later an English professor. He graduated from Harvard University in 1975 and from Harvard Law School in 1980. Shortly after that second graduation, he married Mary Jo Salter, and they moved to Japan. During the first fourteen years of their marriage, they spent eight years overseas: three in Japan, two in France, and one each in England, Italy, and Iceland. He published his first book of poems, Hundreds of Fireflies, *in 1982, and his first novel,* Equal Distance, *in 1985. He has published three novels, three books of poems, and a book of essays entitled* Penchants and Places *(1995). All of these volumes were published by Knopf. He also edited* The Norton Book of Ghost Stories, *which appeared in 1994.*

Post-Coitum Tristesse: A Sonnet

Why
do
you
sigh,
roar,
fall,
all
for

some
hum-
drum
come,
—mm?
Hm . . .

To speak at any length of a poem consisting of a mere thirteen words, two of them vowel-less, throaty interjections, is to risk absurdity in its most pompous dress. I shall be brief.

This "sonnet" owes its genesis to an afternoon of aimless wordplay, during which I came up with the deservedly abandoned phrase "home-grown humdinger." When this became "humdrum humdinger," and then "some humdrum humdinger," I was nearly to "some humdrum come"—which I perceived could be used as a skeletal quatrain.

I'm fond of those mongrelized rhymes that make use of what might be called "noise words"—as where Eliot links "drop" with "ker-flip, ker-flop" or Bishop connects "shook" to "chook-chook." And once I'd partnered "hm" and "mm"—both intended to off-rhyme with my quatrain—I had the sestet of a sonnet.

Although always skeptical and impatient when I hear a poet announce that a poem wrote itself, I can in all candor say that to work in one-syllable lines which must conform to a strict rhyme scheme is to see one's options reduced to almost nothing. So—the demands of form then wrote the octet; I really had very little choice or leeway in the matter.

William Logan *was born in Boston in 1950. He graduated from Yale University and received his M.F.A. in poetry from the University of Iowa. He is the author of four volumes of poetry:* Sad-Faced Men *(1982),* Difficulty *(1985),* Sullen Weedy Lakes *(1988), and* Vain Empires *(1995). He has also published a collection of essays and reviews,* Reputations of the Tongue *(1996). He has received the Peter I. B. Lavan Younger Poets Award from the Academy of American Poets and the Citation for Excellence in Reviewing from the National Book Critics Circle. He lives in Cambridge, England, and Gainesville, Florida, where he teaches and directs the creative writing program at the University of Florida.*

The Lost Birds of Venice

The hotel entrance was painted green—faux marble.
Our rooms perched on a dead-end street
and backed on a dead canal.
Our walls were spotted as if with moldy roses.

Pigeons warred in arcs across the great piazza,
scolding, in their ragged voices,
the four bronze chargers
who peered down shyly, like carousel horses,

from the balcony of San Marco
("a warty bug out for a stroll," suggested Twain).
Where were the fevered songbirds of Venice?
Wing chairs perched in the echoing palazzo.

Gilt frames were layered with gondolas,
with preposterous mob-capped doges,
the glass-cheeked pages and jealous senators,
the minor bribed officials,

and, as an afterthought,
nothing scarred into an afterthought of sky.
A boy lounging in a gondola,
slightly removed from the procession on Ascension Day,

bored, at ease with youth, with a mild
unafflicted plunder of possibility,
without thought of the black-cloaked sailors,
the quiet removal to one of the outer islands,

stared into the choppy lagoon,
where the waves—wavelets, really—
were whited in like wood shavings.
Inverted V's!

As if the lost birds of Venice
had tired of flying, flying forever,
and plunged in on the melted wings of Icarus,
glad that they must die.

Why is it so attractive, this breaking of free verse into couplets, tercets, quatrains, and other regular units? In regularization free verse recoups some force from form. These artificial couplets and quatrains, whenever they entered American poetry, have now become accepted arrangements, though I've rarely seen them recognized or commented on. It is almost as if the need for form that by common practice had been acknowledged had by common silence been denied.

Does function follow form, or form follow function? Cutting off or relegating units of experience emphasizes the forward drive of the poem—it is no longer one damned line after another when every quatrain can be bypassed like a mileage marker. Reminders of passage—rhyme provides those, and to a diminished degree so does this artificial breakage. Call it breaking and entering, since the solid, blank walls of verse are compromised by a few breathing spaces. Further, these interstices or divisions induce drag, slowing down the movement, or at least the movement through space (which is how a page is read—reading aloud is reading in time).

Regular stanzas achieve a precision helter-skelter ones do not. For myself, these false quatrains absorb some of the restrained grandeur of real ones. Purely psychological, perhaps, yet the same poem reads differently when composed by threes and twos, and not simply because different lines benefit from falling first or last in a stanza. A young poet said he preferred tercets because every line was either a beginning, a middle, or an end.

Three sentences, spread out over eight quatrains, live only irregularly in meter—but this is perhaps no more than to provide partial retrospective order to one of the most tangled cities in the world.

J. D. McClatchy was born in Bryn Mawr,

Pennsylvania, in 1945. He is the author of three books of poems, Scenes from Another Life (1981), Stars Principal (1986), and The Rest of the Way (1990), and a collection of essays, White Paper (1989). He has edited many other books—such as Poets on Painters: Essays on the Art of Painting by Twentieth-Century Poets (University of California Press, 1988)—and has written opera libretti for several composers. He is the editor of the Yale Review and lives in Connecticut.

The Method

When you're away I sleep a lot,
Seem to pee more often, eat
Small meals (no salad), listen
To German symphonies and . . . listen.

Sympathy, more often than not,
Is self-pity refined to Fire
And German Symphonies. *Nun lesen.*
Read a book. Write "The Method."

Or is self-pity, refined, two fires
Seen as one? Instructions collapse:
Write the book. (Read: a method.)
The hearth's easy, embered expense,

Seen as one instruction, collapses
In the blue intensity of a match.
The heart's lazy: remembrance spent
Forgetting. Love, break a stick.

In the blue intensity of as much
It is bound to catch—the far away—
Forgetting love. Break a stick.
The flames are a reward, of sorts.

They're bound to reach that far away.
The book says so. And who can't say
The flames are his reward? Of course
They are dying. Still, they scorch

The book. Say so, and—two can play—
Fires kindle *(smack!)* their own display.
They are dying, still. How they scorched
When I put this light to time.

Kindled fires smack of their own display.
Of smaller denials, no saying. Listen:
Where I put this light, it's time,
When you're away, asleep, or lost.

The first born, like any first draft, is closely watched for signs and
wonders. Just last year my mother sent me the baby book in which, forty
years ago, she had recorded the statistics of my arrival and progress. Two
items especially interest me. Asked when I first memorized a poem, she
entered "3 yrs." And some pages later, asked to list my "favorite outdoor
play apparatus and activities" at age three, she struck a line through
"outdoor" (ever the inner, or at least the indoor life!) and answered
"Books, records, puzzles." It can't be accidental, either the coincidence
of poem and puzzle, or the fact that a fascination with them—and with
books and records, with the whole literary life, let's say—starts so early
on. *Poeta nascitur?* Not exactly, but it does seem clear that a preference

for form is temperamental, a part of one's character before any formal steps are taken.

The doctors tell us other connections are made at the same age. No accident either, then, that poems whose energies feed on controlled, obsessive repetitions—sestina or canzone, the villanelle or a pantoum like "The Method"—have a kind of totemic status in contemporary poetry. Repetition is neurotic, and neurosis lends itself as the subject matter for most of these poems—or at least the domestic brands of neurosis: guilt, *ennui,* pain, loss, betrayal, bewilderment. Certainly this pantoum, set before a sort of magic fire which guards the absent beloved, worries its subject. It's a poem about listening, and so it asks the reader, at the end of the first stanza, in effect to listen to the poem echo itself, plaintively. Myself, I'm fond of smudged forms. I almost wanted to call the poem *"Pantoum Négligé,"* after Verlaine's of that title. But I have not wanted to appear casual or negligent when varying the repeated lines; instead, it's meant to seem symptomatic, a further worrying. Anything looked at too long, too closely, flickers. The advantage of any strong form is that it can sustain—indeed, encourages—this kind of *methodical* play.

Heather McHugh *was born in San Diego in 1948. She was raised in Virginia and educated at Harvard University. For the past decade she has served as Milliman Writer at the University of Washington; she is also a core faculty member of the M.F.A. program at Warren Wilson College and a frequent visitor at the University of Iowa Writers' Workshop. Five collections of her poetry have appeared since her first book,* Dangers, *which was published by Houghton Mifflin in 1977. The two most recent are* Hinge and Sign: Poems, 1968–1993 *(Wesleyan/ University Press of New England, 1994)—which was short-listed for the 1994 National Book Award in poetry—and* Broken English: Poetry and Partiality *(Wesleyan/University Press of New England, 1993). McHugh's translations of poems by Jean Follain was published by Princeton University Press in 1979; with her husband, Niko Boris McHugh, she has translated book-length collections of poems by Blaga Dimitrova and Paul Celan. Over the years McHugh has won grants from the National Endowment for the Arts, the Guggenheim Foundation, the Lila Wallace–Reader's Digest Fellowship Program, and the Woodrow Wilson Foundation.*

Nihil Privativum in the House of Ken

It's not one of the realer nothings, only something missing.
Kant's example (is example thin by definition?) goes like this:
the cold and shade are really just
gone sun. For eyes and hair
read looks and strokes. The tease
gets out of hand, and under hat.
For love of god, we had a devil. For eyes and hair
she had the blinkable, the tossable.
But Ken could think (at least) of blades
applied to a too-long barrel.
I'm not sure any longer life is
something you could take, or take away.

You couldn't breathe for all the kissing.
What is getting hectic, having lost its onlyness:
and how is not serenity, but lust.
I point the bone out with my finger: there!
The dog, obliging, licks my hand (despite my years of effort she's
learned nothing, thinks the dog, and only one nothing, at that).
As for the wife of Mr. Ken, there is no possible
repose for her repeating pose. The unregenerate cannot be made
degenerate. (Pin-holes in a stock-pot overturned. My heavens!)
Yes. But is it sterile?
Stuck there, literal, all night, a girl could freeze—

                                          and a day

and a night are number seven.

At best, a poem leaps out of its form; it's not to be caught or nailed there.
Far from being the container or fixer of meaning, form is rather more
like the field of force through which—by which—a meaning moves (a
moving means). The poem's form is where resemblance and distinction
intertwine. It's where you can't tell something. Dancer from dance, for
example. (One oddity of *The American Heritage Dictionary,* Second
College Edition, is that the photo it offers to illustrate "clapboard" and
the photo it offers to illustrate "entwine" are identical: the picture is of
something climbing across something nailed.) We see what we think of,
not what we see *with:* this poem's stanzas rhyme, but the rhymes operate
over such distances a reader may well miss the counter-sunken signs.

Maybe because I'm disposed to sappiness, I'm contrarily nourished—by the propensity, in artistic form, to fire and air, that drier stuff the Greeks said souls were *really* made of. The mirror full of tears is not the true home (only the trappings) of the poetic. Even at my sentimental worst, I remain convinced both that there's something language can teach us about itself (without us), and that there's something we can teach ourselves about ourselves (without it). A poem escapes both the foregone and the afterthought: the form means to mark (and remark) the poem's vanishing act.

How much of the mind's magic is magician-trickery? The house of Ken has a tree of knowledge, bought at Pot N' Pay. Though I love Kant's thoughtful choreographies (the four nothings are more beautiful to me than the four Zoas), still I'm skeptical about our "abouts": we have only mind to know mind with, Ambrose Bierce reminds us. I find it less and less likely we can clearly think *about* life from within it; that's why in "Nihil Privativum" such deictic comedies are enacted, somewhere between dog and heaven. Said one Zen sage, "A finger is needed to point to the moon, but woe unto him who takes the finger for the moon." Still we count.

The myth of the emotionally expressive (strong emotion as deep emotion) forgets how depth can be *com*pressive. One very recent poem of mine goes, in its entirety:

> *Shame*
>
> has me:
> am she.

In its tightness I knotted a number of forms. *As, am, me, he, she, sham,* and *same* all figure in its name. The differences between "am" and "(h)as," between "me" and "(s)he" are matched by identities; there's *nomen* in this poem, and the problem of pronominality. As soon as I say "I," a certain duplicity comes into play (and a certain play into duplicity). Shame and self-consciousness arise in a shift from the genderless first toward the gendered third-person pronoun. The predicate, peculiar, registers a split (from *idios* to *alius,* perhaps). The composition is, among other things, anagrammatical (I discarded as incidental such virtuoso variations as "a mesh" and "same H," lines with their own networks of felicitous slippage—one toward drink-distortion and one toward actual self-signature). But anagram may seem less the point, on first reading, than the poem's will to concision: its single five-word sentence contains a title and two rhymed trochaic lines; these lines comprise two verbs and two pronouns, missing their thirds. Or should I say "seconds"? The second person is the only person not represented here—shame shears us off from a thousand thous—and we also miss the pronoun that would fall between "me" and "she" in the syntax of the poem, as subject for "am": *that* pronoun would be a self restored to the nominative, freed from the accusative. Thus, even grammar brings us (back) to shame—but only if we know it.

In the history of a language's changes, some shifts of emphasis may animate, and some may deaden. The changes tell us where imagination is being extended, and where it's being lost, over time. *Eidesis* (knowledge) came from *eidos* (form or shape), but the eidetic today, though vivid, is unreal. I find dispiriting our popular (and pedagogical) devaluations of rhetoric and form: the word *form* itself has come to mean vacant display, something you go through when your heart's not in it. Americans entertain formalities as insignificances not signs, niceties as decorations not precisions. *Quaint* once meant exact; today it's cute. *Cute* once meant sharp; today it's got a sentimental wash about it. Concentration on (and in) aesthetic structures is considered reductive, rather than revealing, of poetic passion. The fallacy keeps cropping up, however eloquently poets disabuse us of it. John Donne's "triple fool" was a fool first for loving, he says, and then a fool for saying so (the poem's nothing if it's not reflexive). Thinking to rid himself of love's bitterness, the lover tries to channel it through forms. But he finds out "grief brought to numbers" isn't, after all, "allay'd"; the metrics wind up making the song memorable, then others take it up, and the hapless poet has to hear his folly sung over and over. "Brought to numbers" comes to mean "brought home to many," where at first it seemed to mean only "metrically contained or diminished." Unless we know and note the way the medium moves, the way it betrays itself, the way it says what we don't mean (not only what we do)—unless, that is, we care about form—we miss not only where a meaning moves, but where a meaning matters.

Michael Malinowitz *was born in New*
York City in 1951
and grew up on Manhattan's Lower East Side. He received a B.A. in literature from the American University in Washington, D.C., and an M.F.A. in poetry from Brooklyn College. He has studied creative writing with (chronologically) Laurence Raab, Henry Taylor, Colette Inez, John Ashbery, Jill Hoffman, and Gilbert Sorrentino. His book of poems,

Michael's Ear, *was published in* 1993 *by Groundwater Press. He lives in Greenwich Village with his wife, the writer Evelyn Horowitz, and is a senior vice president for a prominent sales promotion company on Long Island.*

Glose

Now I wear my named pants;
I am her violin.
Are the casual designs chants
And the assumptions like tin?

Partially, under the nails
Of my hands your discrete
Music; abrasive.
Carols of the fragrance
For the bruise, named after
A president's cants.
You loved better than that.
Maximilian, my secretary,
Confesses in a dark dance:
Now I wear my named pants.

These infidelities make me nauseous.
How piano.
Yet they do, really, love
Me, and I, them.
Or is that what my sister's tits
Showed? In the foreground a sin
Heard the succession of an alternative
Woman. "Ugly things aren't keener,"
She reveals with a win;
I am her violin.

How solar of her,
How math we played it,
But were kicked off stage.
About to go home, the scholars
Are former girls with thick eyebrows
Diagramming the romance of ants.
The end

Could be the indemnity
The bible is; stoney rants.
Are the casual designs chants?

Like drumming, thus, soldiers.
My viola doubled just ran.
Into orange goes man,
Together in escrow by the sea
With a lot of sure support.
That is where I have been,
While it was possible, all
Right for this time and particular
Place. I put on my cuff links and pin
And the assumptions like tin.

My wife, who teaches creative writing in high school, brought home a student's poem written in the glose form. I was amazed, challenged, and compelled by it. I have always thought of form as the thread by which my poetic pants were tied together. To alter the metaphor, it is what flossing might be to tooth-brushing: the plying of inveterate regimentations making the rules palpable.

Writing a glose enabled me to feel both under and out of control. As a poet who does not cavil whatever to "creative play" (I'll even go so far as to call "trial and error" a workable solution to one's esteemed poetic problems), I suddenly felt a thrust of freedom. What I usually experience as impositions and intrusions—rhyme, logic and other rudimentaries—seemed anything but. If the meaning of a poem inheres in the writing of it, one can't really choose a more flattering demand than the glose.

Harry Mathews *was born in New York in 1930. He settled in Europe after graduating from college and has lived there ever since, in Spain, Germany, Italy, and above all France. His first poems were published in 1956, and his first novel,* The Conversions, *in 1962;* The Journalist, *his fifth, appeared in 1994. Other recent books are* A Mid-Season Sky: Poems 1954–1991 *(1992) and* Immeasurable Distances: The Collected Essays *(1991). At present he is preparing, in collaboration with Lynn*

Crawford and Alastair Brotchie, An Oulipo Compendium, *a critical anthology of work by (or inspired by) the Ouvroir de Littérature Potentielle, to be published by Atlas Press in the spring of 1996. He divides
his time between Paris and the United States.*

Condition of Desire

Some starry head . . . not
present, I know. In other places, will there
   be no stars? Can I know?
But the quickness of this spasm, a longing
   to act now, to be there:
I love someone. The thought is with me as if
   it allowed no choice.
Why is this thought not always with me? Can
   a force disrupt love?
I look around to say how I feel, and I can't if
   no person is present,
or none that I can see. What possible force
   misleads love and me?
It is intolerable having nobody present,
   I want to start to cry.
The moment is short, that's clear; I still ask
   what force disrupts
Love? Can a thought have no object? I move on.
   I know he's not coming.
There is no prize. A lady offers offerings,
   old chrysanthemums.
I stand by a slab among stone slabs; beyond,
   zero's immutability.

STARTING POINTS

1. A general question: Since poetry often concerns itself with the
   passage of time, both as subject and method, is it possible to
   write a poem from which memory is absent? Not literally (without memory we could not finish a sentence or decipher a word
   like "chrysanthemum") but as a motive in discourse.

2. A situation of personal loss and the desire to express it.

PROCEDURES

1. No statement refers to a time preceding it.

2. A classic poem of loss and grief is the source of what the poem says (or says it says).

3. The poem is metrically regular: alternating verses of seventeen and thirty-four (2 × 17) letters. (For puzzle-solvers: there are seventeen letters in the name of the author of the source-poem. The average length of all the lines in the poem is thirty-four letters.)

RESULTS

The theoretical pretext—the exclusion of memory—became the subject of the poem.

William Matthews *was born in Cincinnati in 1942. He received his B.A. from Yale University and his M.A. at the University of North Carolina at Chapel Hill. He has taught at colleges across the country; for the past ten years he has been professor of English at the City College of New York. His most recent books are a collection of poems,* Time and Money *(Houghton Mifflin, 1995), and a volume of translations,* The Mortal City: 100 Epigrams from Martial *(Ohio Review Press).*

Merida, 1969
for Russell Banks

We sat in the courtyard
like landlords and dispatched
teak-colored Manolo
at intervals for Carta Blanca,
and propped idiomatically
little wedges of lime on top
of the bottles like party hats.
O tristes tropiques. Our pretty
wives were sad and so were we.

So this is how one lives when he
is sad, we almost said out loud.
Manolo, we cried, and his tough
feet came skittering across
the blue, rain-streaked tiles.

Travel turned out to be no
anodyne, for we went home.
It was a sort of metaphor,
we now agree, a training
in loss. For if we'd been happy
then, as now we often are,
we'd have sat there in Merida
with its skyline of churchspires
and windmills, the latter
looking like big tin dande-
lions from which the fluff
had just been blown by wind
they couldn't hold, and we'd cry
Manolo, and beer would arrive.

I was first stirred to write "Merida, 1969," by looking at a watercolor of
Merida used as the cover illustration for Elizabeth Bishop's *The Complete Poems 1927–1979.* Miss Bishop herself did the drawing. I had been
in Merida some fifteen years ago; an old friend, the novelist Russell
Banks, and I had spent a week there with our wives, now our ex-wives.
And Banks was about to arrive in Maine, where I wrote the poem, for a
visit, and so I had been thinking about friendship, its duration, the
mutual stories friends invent and revise. And since Banks had recently
remarried and I would soon remarry, I was prickly, sentimental, skeptical, alert. In short I was about to start work on a poem, and had a welter
of musings, memories, notions, confusions, etc., to work with.

Miss Bishop's drawing is dated (1942) and perhaps that's why my
title includes a date, though I may in any case have wanted to set the time
and place quickly in the title. Probably there were in draft some lines
that I had to write and reject before I found my first line; I no longer
have any version of the poem but the one given here.

One thing I know about the form the poem took is that I didn't
decide on it before I started work, as I sometimes do, nor did I assume
the poem would find a form on behalf of its own urgencies, as I some-

times do. What I must have wanted was for the poem to hint at some possibilities from which I could choose some constraints, but not until I was a little way into the poem and could sense what manner of resistance (4 ohms? 8 ohms?) might serve it best.

What I wound up with was a sort of mirrored diptych, two fourteen-line stanzas, one recounting 1969 and one about knowledge in the present, one narrative and one reflective, each one using some of the same incidents and atmosphere. There would be an implied contrast, naturally enough. How much has changed in the interval? How much have we learned? If we knew then what we know now . . . ?

Of course the preceding paragraph is written with hindsight, rather than with the attentive bumbling and diligent indolence that accompany composition. What I remember about writing the poem is that somewhere about five or six lines along I sensed, the way people suddenly know what it is they would like to eat for lunch, that I'd like the stanza to be fourteen lines, that in the blank space between the two stanzas—yes, there should be two stanzas—there would be an invisible hinge, and that the poem could propose by such a form an implied relationship between the past and the present that the poem could question and doubt.

Probably Frost's "The Road Not Taken" is a sort of model for my poem, though on a sufficiently unconscious level that I had no thought of it nor of Frost while I was writing. We all remember the ending of that poem:

> I shall be telling this with a sigh
> Somewhere ages and ages hence:
> Two roads diverged in a wood, and I—
> I took the one less traveled by,
> And that has made all the difference.

We sometimes forget how differently the poem's speaker describes the two roads at the time he actually chose one of them.

> . . . long I stood
> And looked down one as far as I could
> To where it bent in the undergrowth;
>
> Then took the other, as just as fair,
> And having perhaps the better claim,
> Because it was grassy and wanted wear;
> Though as for that the passing there
> Had worn them really about the same,

And both that morning equally lay
In leaves no step had trodden black.
Oh, I kept the first for another day!
Yet knowing how way leads on to way,
I doubted if I should ever come back.

The roads beckoned about the same, but later, when the pleasure of telling the story was part of the story's truth, and there was much intervening life to explain, we could hear the poem's speaker veer off again, this time away from incident and toward shapeliness.

Two roads diverged in a wood, and I—
I took the one less traveled by,
And that has made all the difference.

"And I," he says, pausing for dramatic effect and then giving his little anecdote a neat and summary dramatic effect that's in the story but not in the original event. Though of course by this stage in the life of the story each exists somewhat for the sake of the other.

My friend, an able writer of stories, was coming to visit, and one of the things I was mulling was how stories work.

Fourteen lines was no accident. I've written a number of pale sonnets, unrhymed and in a trimeter or tetrameter line that hovers somewhere between so-called free verse and metrically regular verse. It's a territory I've been attracted to by noticing how the two modes, so often poised against each other in neat and false opposition, want to be each other. Be that as it may, I've had happy experience with fourteen-line poems, and so poising two stanzas that length against each other, in ways I had yet to work out, satisfied both my need for familiarity and my need for surprise. With luck, then, the poem had a form to become, and I had both the comforts and challenges of an apt form. . . .

How well this all turned out the reader may judge. The two friends in my poem seem to behave about the same under either disposition— the narrative past, in the first stanza, or the past as understood along all the intervening time, in the second. In this second and hypothetical life, they may or may not be wiser, but they are happier, and manifest their happiness, as they did in 1969, by sending for beer. And why not? How often do we get a chance to vacation like this? Won't it all seem like a dream in, say, fifteen years?

The equality of the two behaviors is at least made easier—and perhaps made possible, for all I know now, long after I wrote the poem—by the discovery of the form.

What else should I say about the form? Content is often unsettling or painful in poems, but form is play, a residue of the fun the poet had while working. Of course, like form and content, pain and fun want to be each other. . . .

James Merrill was born in New York City in 1926. He received his B.A. from Amherst College in 1947 and published his First Poems in 1951. His books received two National Book Awards, the Pulitzer Prize, and the Bollingen Prize. The epic poem begun in Divine Comedies (1976) and extended in two subsequent volumes was published in its entirety as The Changing Light at Sandover (1983), which won the National Book Critics Circle Award. His most recent books of poetry are Late Settings (Atheneum, 1985), The Inner Room (Knopf, 1988), and A Scattering of Salts (Knopf, 1995). A Different Person, a memoir about the years he spent in Europe in the early 1950s, appeared from Knopf in 1993. "Freedom to be oneself is all very well," he wrote. "The greater freedom is not to be oneself." He established the Ingram Merrill Foundation, which gives grants to writers and artists. He died suddenly on February 6, 1995, in Tucson, Arizona.

Snapshot of Adam

By flash in sunshine "to reduce contrast"
He grins back from the green deck chair,
Stripped, easy at last, bush tangle rhyming
With beard and windblown hair;
Coke sweating, forearm tanned to oak,
Scar's lightning hid by flat milk-blaze of belly
—But all grown, in the sliding glass
Beyond him, unsubstantial. Here I dwell,

Finger on shutter, amid my clay
Or marble ghosts; treetops in silhouette;
And day, his day, its vivid shining stuff
Negated to matte slate
A riddle's chalked on: Name the threat
Posed never long or nakedly enough.

Imprinted over centuries upon the sestet of a sonnet is a change of mood or direction. The example at hand modulates from solid to flat; Adam to his maker; the opener (if only of a Coke) to the camera's shutter, etc. Rather than plan ahead as the eighth line approaches, I'm apt to recall a moment at the Kabuki in Tokyo decades ago. A long ramp (the *hamamichi* or "flower way") cuts through the public to join the stage at right angles. This transitional point challenges the actor who crosses it. That day we had seen Benten the Thief at work plundering a house from top to bottom. Frightened, furtive, eyes darting, sleeves full of loot, he ran from the scene, set foot upon the ramp, paused, straightened, tidied his clothing, stuck out his chest. An imaginary thoroughfare took shape around utter probity, now striding out of sight to loud cheers.

W. S. Merwin was born in New York City in 1927 and grew up in New Jersey and Pennsylvania. A Princeton graduate, he worked as a tutor in France, Portugal, and Majorca, and has translated from the French, Spanish, Latin, and Portuguese. A Mask for Janus, *his first book of poems, was chosen by W. H. Auden as the 1952 volume in the Yale Series of Younger Poets. His subsequent books include* The Moving Target *(1963),* The Lice *(1967),* The Carrier of Ladders *(1970),* Writings to an Unfinished Accompaniment *(1973),* The Rain in the Trees *(1988), and* Travels *(1993). He has completed a new collection,* The Vixen. *He has been the recipient of a PEN Translation Medal, the Fellowship of the Academy of American Poets, the Bollingen Prize, and (for* The Carrier of the Ladders) *the Pulitzer Prize. In 1994 he was named the first recipient of the six-figure Tanning Award bestowed by the Academy of American Poets, and in 1995 he won a three-year writer's award from the Lila Wallace–Reader's Digest Fund. He lives in Haiku, Hawaii, and devotes much of his time to environmental causes. Merwin once likened a poem to "an echo except that it is repeating no sound."*

Ancestral Voices

In the old dark the late dark the still deep shadow
    that had travelled silently along itself all night
while the small stars of spring were yet to be seen and the few
    lamps burned by themselves with no expectations

far down through the valley then suddenly the voice
   of the blackbird came believing in the habit
of the light until the torn shadows of the ridges
   that had gone out one behind the other into the darkness
began appearing again still asleep surfacing in their
   dream and the stars all at once were gone and instead the song
of the blackbird flashed through the unlit boughs and far
   out in the oaks a nightingale went on echoing
itself drawing out its own invisible starlight
   these voices were lifted here long long before the first
of our kind had come to be able to listen
   and with the faint light in the dew of the infant
leaves the goldfinches flew out from their nest in the brambles
   they had chosen all their colors for this day and they sang
of themselves which was what they had wakened to remember

I'm not sure I can say much that would be to the point about the form of the poem—whatever, indeed, one takes that word to mean. The absence of punctuation, which has been characteristic of my poems since the early 1960s, stems in great part from the conviction that punctuation is predominantly a mark of allegiance to the protocols of prose and of the printed word. Doing without it, in my mind, maintains a living line to the spoken word and its intonations and motions, which do the work of punctuation themselves. The lack of punctuation is itself a formal matter, and with it—a further formal condition—is the aspiration, at least in most of the poems, to make it possible to read them in each case as a single sentence, whether one actually does so or not. Another argument, or reason, for these conditions is that they should make *hearing* the poems more than ever an imperative, and should make them come clearer when they are heard.

    The form of the poems in the group comprising "Ancestral Voices" was not a matter of theory or calculation. I am not, in the main, a theorist. The first poem in the series, "Fox Sleep," came to me in this form and the others led on from it. The poems have a number of things in common, I think, and one of them is a preoccupation with the past and our relation to it. That makes it appropriate, I think, that the lines with their alternate indentations and altering lengths may suggest, to some, the Latin elegy.

Susan Mitchell

grew up in New York City and was educated at Wellesley College, Georgetown University, and Columbia University. She is the author of two books of poems, The Water inside the Water *(1983) and* Rapture *(1993), both from HarperCollins.* Rapture *won the Kingsley Tufts Award. She has received fellowships from the Guggenheim Foundation, the Lannan Foundation, and the National Endowment for the Arts. Her work was chosen for* The Best American Essays 1988 *and for four volumes of* The Best American Poetry. *She is the Mary Blossom Lee Professor of Creative Writing at Florida Atlantic University, in Boca Raton, Florida, where she lives.*

Venice

Furtive, that's the version I want.
With eyes averted. Downcast, a little sly.
It's where it's looking, that's
where I want us—
in a harbor where we in our gondola
stare up and up at the enormous
freighters rusting the Adriatic, the ocean
oiled and ropey, scary even,
the way the waters seem higher than
our boat, about to topple onto.
Did I forget to say it's night, we're
seeing by artificial light how small
fists of snow are falling from. So easy
to say *the sky,* but that
would be wrong. We could puzzle over
how to say this. Or we could kiss.
Let's kiss, standing up in
scary, its huge hood lowering,
cover of darkness down
which the crusaders with lances and crosses
high held in a once upon a time still
tarnishing, still audible version
of a version of a version.
There's a vertigo to history different
from the vertigo of sex.

The children sold into slavery, into brothels.
The sores. The futility of crying and the futility
of stories that gradually wash up
on other shores. To what purpose all this
telling, version by version
deteriorating like silk, the patterns
no longer recognizable: ripple by ripple, the lush
lappings as if certain words, *pieta*
or *sofferenza* were enough.
I had wanted to sight-see, to be taken slowly
by gondola, canal by canal where Byron
where shadows on stilts or like inverted
bells somberly under the arches
swaying and Goethe who stood on the foamy
crescendos and saw the *chiaro*
nell' chiaro and bibelots
of old and charming, the glimmers
well-worn where the moon
all its chandeliers and stairways let down
into the sea-black sea. To stand
on the outstretched lip of
what might be called a romantic evening,
though already that version is
starting to bore me. It's not a question
of what's true or not true, it's more
a matter of what I want to hear.
Which is why we are standing in a boat
perilously small and stiffening
our necks to size the hugeness
of prows—barnacle-studded, iron clad, steely
beaked, with involucral bracts, with
scale on scale, a rust of buds.
Yes, that's how I want us, our love
pressed mouth to mouth
with history, and if with a partition,
then something thin
as lingerie.
I don't want us anaesthetized, I want
us terrified and tied to it.

I used to think *it* was teeming, alive
with voices, flashings, with
music in which the dark lit candles.
I tried to reach any way
I could, rung by rung
or with sex shouldering me all the way.
Well, now I think otherwise.
More of a wall or impasse, more of—nothing.
Which isn't to say I'm not moved.
What tumbles through is icy and swift
and doesn't stop. I want us pressed
to that when you shove into me.
No candles. Not even darkness.

Form is like a psychotic or a hysteric—it acts out. It gestures. It mimes.
Form is the poem's unconscious, its preverbal patterning of desires and
impulses that I become aware of only gradually in the process of writing
and rewriting. Yes, I really think, form precedes language. Does that
make me a Platonist? First, the crescendos and diminuendos, the stac-
catos and legatos: a nonverbal sputter and glide. Does that make me a
composer?

In "Venice," form is subversive, sly, furtive: it diverts and undercuts
the speaker's romantic yearnings. Sentences are broken off, phrases left
incomplete. The big crescendo of longing that begins, "I had wanted to
sight-see, to be taken slowly / by gondola, canal by canal where Byron /
where shadows on stilts or like inverted / bells somberly under the
arches" starts to break up the way a wave rushing toward shore breaks
up. The more the sentence extends itself, the more it remains fragmented, unfinished. Its very structure acts out a kind of romantic desire
that cannot be satisfied.

When I first tried to comment on the form of "Venice," I ended up
writing another poem, a poem in which walls figured as an important
image. But since that poem took on a life of its own, it does not seem fair
to use it as a gloss. I do, though, have something to say about walls in
regard to the form of "Venice." When I was making the poem, I was very
aware of syntax because so many of the sentences are chipped and
broken. I felt as if I were trying to fit together large stones that had
spaces between them. I did not want the stones to fit snug. I did not want
to use mortar. I wanted the spaces to show. I wanted the missing to
be felt and experienced as part of the structure. So the sentences in

"Venice" act out. They pretend to give, but then they take back. They pretend to go in one direction, only to swerve: "Did I forget to say it's night, we're / seeing by artificial light how small / fists of snow are falling from. So easy / to say *the sky,* but that / would be wrong. We could puzzle over / how to say this. Or we could kiss." The speaker never says what the snow is falling from. The kiss takes over, only to be overtaken in turn by history and terror—and nothingness. But the nothingness that the speaker finally voices in the poem's concluding lines has been articulated all along, acted out by the poem's form, in particular, its syntax— those sentences that do not finish, that yank away, that keep reminding the reader of the something that is not there: "I want us pressed / to that when you shove into me. / No candles. Not even darkness."

Robert Morgan *was born in Hendersonville, North Carolina, in 1944. He grew up on the family farm in nearby Zirconia. After graduating from the University of North Carolina, he worked as a house painter, free-lance writer, farmer, and salesman, before joining the English department at Cornell University in 1971. He has published nine books of poetry, most recently* Sigodlin *(1990), and* Green River: New and Selected Poems *(1991). He has also published three books of fiction, including* The Hinterlands *(1994), and the collection* Good Measure: Essays, Interviews, and Notes on Poetry *(1993). A new novel will be published by Algonquin Press in 1996. He lives in an old farmhouse in Freeville, New York, with his wife, Nancy, and his younger daughter, Katie.*

Grandma's Bureau

Shivering and hoping no one
would come from the heated rooms, I
handled the great black comb fine as
the sieve of a whale's mouth, and dared
not look at the coffin-wardrobe.
My finger bulldozed dust on wood
and left a half-moon of lint at
the end of its trail. The steel brush

held a few gray strands among its
thousand stingers. My breath summoned
a ghost to the heavy pane of
the tortoiseshell mirror. More than
all I loved to slide the hatpins
like adjustable rods in the
plum-shaped cushion. They pushed out and
in like throttles and chokes of some
delicate engine. There was a
mystery to such thin strength; I
knew without asking I wouldn't be
allowed such deadly probes and heart-
picks. Some were long as witch's wands
with fat pearl heads. They slid in the
cushion as through waxy flesh.
I extracted a cold sliver
excalibur and ran it on
my wrist and stabbed at the mirror,
then froze, listening for her steps.

GOOD MEASURE

The formal decisions made while writing a poem are usually forgotten soon as enacted. It is only the poem we want to remember, whether written in one or fifty drafts. So many choices in composition are made unconsciously, almost by reflex, and many of the happiest touches in a poem are accidents, gifts of the gods of chance. All poets are hopeless gamblers.

"Grandma's Bureau" represents much of the work I have been doing recently. The versification is the simplest I know, an eight-syllable line with no regular meter, no counting of stresses. It is almost-free verse broken into an arbitrary length, based vaguely on four-beat common meter: a kind of humble blank verse. I like this form because it leaves the musical cadence almost entirely free to follow the content, the narrative line, the local dynamics of the sentence, yet has some of the surface tension of regularity, the expectation of repetition, with the fulfillment and surprises of advancement across an uneven terrain.

My greatest difficulty here, in fitting the sentences into lines, has been avoiding too many articles and conjunctions at the ends of lines. A few final *the*s and *and*s create a run-on effect that helps the narration; too many seem like half-justified prose. When I can, I like to retain the autonomy of each line, making it an increment of energy, a self-sufficient image or forwarding of thought, earning its own way. (Or as I used to say, "Make something happen in every line.") It was while reading *The Four Quartets* in 1964 that I realized Eliot made his poems of vigorous and luxuriant sentences carved into lines, into time. Simultaneously I saw that the music of poetry was not of the metronome, but could be as free as Webern or Stravinsky. A truism now, but an enabling recognition then. Suddenly it seemed possible to write in lines and say something, more than in prose, and I began to hammer out my first rough verses.

Giving good measure means that we always deliver more than is expected, more than is required by our contract with the reader. It is the unexpected abundance that delights most, the bonus that could not have been foreseen. Besides good faith, the good measure of the voice gives assurance and reassurance, control, accuracy, direction. Its music turns and enlivens time. The good measure of poetry is the finding of the true response, the appropriate gesture that fits word and experience into a whole. Poetry measures in essential heartbeat the enactment of knowledge through the saying out. The stave is tailored to experience, and sets experience. A poem unexpectedly confides the significant secret.

It is the willingness to address the elementary and elemental that makes a voice interesting. A random fact triggers the memory of the telling detail. Once we become cubists of memory, seeing the familiar from several unexpected angles at once, the music seems to go right of its own accord.

In the body of the poem, lineation is part flesh and part skeleton, as form is the towpath along which the burden of content, floating on the formless, is pulled. All language is both mental and sacramental, is not "real" but is the working of lip and tongue to subvert the "real." Poems empearl irritating facts until they become opalescent spheres of moment, not so much résumés of history as of human faculties working with pain. Every poem is necessarily a fragment empowered by its implicitness. We sing to charm the snake in our spines, to make it sway with the pulse of the world, balancing the weight of consciousness on the topmost vertebra.

Dave Morice was born in 1946. His book Poetry
Comics: A Cartooniverse of Poems
(Simon and Schuster, 1982) consisted of poems by Shakespeare, Donne, Herbert, Herrick, Keats, Tennyson, Browning, Dickinson, Whitman,

Williams, et al., rendered as comic strips. He holds an M.F.A. from the University of Iowa Writers' Workshop and an M.A. in library science and is now working on his Ph.D. in education at the University of Iowa, where he teaches children's literature. Costumed as Dr. Alphabet, with white top hat, cane, and clothes spangled with colorful letters, he has written fifty poetry marathons in the United States and England, including one thousand poems in twelve hours, a mile-long poem, and a poem across the Delaware River. His books of poetry include Quicksand through the Hourglass *(Toothpaste Press, 1979). Recent publications include* The Adventures of Dr. Alphabet: 104 Unusual Ways to Write Poetry in the Classroom and the Community *(Teachers and Writers) and* More Poetry Comics *(Chicago Review Press). He has coordinated the Wooden Nickel Art Project since 1986. He writes a word-play column for* Word Ways *magazine.*

Alaskan Drinking Song

You know
I know
Juneau
Wino.

A PERFECT POEM

"Alaskan Drinking Song" came about when I went to Alaska with a friend of mine, Dennett Hutchcroft, in the spring of 1977. Walking through Juneau one afternoon, we turned down a side street marked by a painted wooden sign that said Wino Alley. A few hundred feet in, a couple of older men in tattered, dingy clothes were leaning against a chain-link fence and sipping from a brown paper bag. In the yard behind the fence, thousands of empty booze bottles and beer cans glinted in the sun.

"That must be why they call this place Wino Alley," Dennett said pointing at the bottle-and-can mountains.

After rolling the words *wino* and *Juneau* around in my mind, I replied: "You know / I know / Juneau / Wino."

And there it was, a full-blown rhymed poem. It was perfect, too. No rewriting necessary. A rare occasion like this called for a drink.

One traditional definition of perfection in poetry holds that the work should be "the best words in the best order." According to that, "Alaskan Drinking Song" is a perfect poem. Every word in it is necessary: Not one word can be changed to improve it.

It's easy enough to test a poem this short by rewriting it into alternative forms to see if it can be improved.

You know
I know
Anchorage
Wino.

That version fails on three counts: It's not true, its first and third lines don't rhyme, and its regular trochaic rhythm is spoiled by the dactyl in Anchorage (line three). We can try other towns—Fairbanks, Kodiak, Haines, Ketchikan—but none works as well as Juneau.

Another rewrite:

You know
They know
Juneau
Wino.

Similarly, "They know" (line two) is not as good as the original *I know,* which rhymes so well with *wino.* Any other phrase would likewise alter the meaning, the rhythm, or the rhyme—or any combination of the three—to the detriment of the poem.

One more try:

You know
I know
Juneau
Lush.

Clunk. That's way off. So are *drunkard, alkie, boozer, bacchanalian, stiff,* or any other substitute for *wino* (line four). As in previous rewrites, the changes hurt the original rather than help it. In lieu of finding better words, we must conclude that the poem is perfect.

In the infinitely large set of All Possible Linear Poems, the more words a poem has, the more rewrites that can be made. Not all of the alternate versions of a poem need to be examined, but at least enough of the better versions should be tried in order to decide on the best. Because of its tremendous length, we would find it hard to prove that Milton's

"Paradise Lost" is a perfect poem. We couldn't begin sorting through the countless rewrites.[1]

As we consider shorter poems, we see there are fewer possibilities to examine. If the poems have rhyme and rhythm, our job grows even easier. In the set of Rhymed Short Poems, the form, the content, and the length greatly limit the choices of words. "Alaskan Drinking Song" is in the more specialized set of Single-Stanza Trochaic Monometer Quatrains with an *a b a b* Rhyme Scheme, and it's extremely simple to evaluate the few reasonable alternates.

If we look for even smaller sets, we come across the set of Oneword Poems, in which each member is perfect. Take any oneword poem— *dog,* for instance. Does any other word work as well? *Mutt? Collie?* No, they are equally perfect and totally different oneword poems. Is *Dog* with a capital *D* better than our original example? No, it, too, is a different poem. By capitalizing the word *dog,* we change the entire text, not just a single part. In a longer work, such a change would merely alter the poem; but in a oneword poem, it changes every word (the only word). Even a misspelled word is a perfect oneword work, since it's a new word—and thus a new poem.

Let's consider an even smaller set: Oneletter Poems. In the entire English language, there are only fifty-two oneletter poems—twenty-six capital letters and twenty-six small letters—from *a* to *z* and from *A* to *Z.* Is there one oneletter poem that rises to the top and shines above all others? Is *o* better than *c* just because *c* is an *o* with a segment missing?[2] Every letter has its own appeal and charm. The individual reader might prefer one over the other, but that's a purely subjective choice.

---

[1]In fact, the number of versions is directly proportionate to the length of the poem. This is demonstrated by the First Law of Nuclear Poetics, which states that

$$V = w_1 \times w_2 \times w_3 \times \ldots w_n$$

where *V* is the total number of versions and *w* is the number of alternate words which can be placed at each position (indicated by the subscripts *1, 2, 3 . . . n*) in the poem. Example: Shakespeare's Sonnet 30 begins "Shall I compare thee . . ." If we look for reasonable substitutions for those first four words, we find several: *Shall* could be *Will, Should, Could, Can, May, Must,* or *Might; compare* could be *liken; thee* could be *you.* Thus $w_1 = 8$, $w_2 = 1$, $w_3 = 2$, and $w_4 = 2$. Multiplying them together ($8 \times 1 \times 2 \times 2$) gives a total of thirty-two versions of the first four words of Sonnet 30. The complete poem would yield millions upon millions of versions.

[2]In 1973, Joyce Holland solicited lowercase oneletter poems from one hundred four poets and published their submissions in her *Alphabet Anthology.* The letter *o* was submitted by the greatest number of people; the letter *c* wasn't used by anyone. Does it follow that *o* is better than *c* because it's more popular? Or does its popularity imply that it's a cliche?

Dave Morice 155

Finally there is the smallest set of all—the empty set of the Noletter Poem, visible only as the blank page. Nothing can be substituted for nonexistent verse. It has no single author. All of us have written the Noletter Poem. The moment we put a pure, white sheet of paper in front of us, there is the Noletter Poem staring us in the face. When we write over it, putting a multi-word poem in its place, we aren't rewriting it: Behind every visible poem, there's the invisible Noletter Poem hidden like a foundation upon which the new lines are constructed. It exists in every language.

Between "Paradise Lost" and the Noletter Poem, there are many perfect poems. Each achieves perfection through the sense of necessity that its words generate. The poem needs just those words—no more and no less—to make it what it is. "Alaskan Drinking Song," small as it is, is perfect.

Howard Moss *was born in Manhattan in 1922. He was educated at the University of Wisconsin. After teaching English at Vassar College for a year, he joined the staff of the* New Yorker *in 1948 and two years later became the magazine's poetry editor, a post he held until his death in 1987. By his own calculation, he had spent the equivalent of three months of his life in the elevators of the* New Yorker's *building on West Forty-third Street. The Wound and the Weather, the first of his dozen volumes of poetry, appeared when he was twenty-four years old. His* Selected Poems *(1971) won the National Book Award. His* New Selected Poems *(1985) won the Lenore Marshall Prize for Poetry in 1986. Moss was the author of four critical books, including* The Magic Lantern of Marcel Proust *and* Minor Monuments, *and he edited* The Poet's Story, *a collection of prose works by poets. "I would say that the distinction between fiction writers and poets is becoming obsolete, that it might be more useful to think of authors as mirror-writers or window-writers," he wrote in an essay. "In America the two schools stem from two major figures, both poets, who may be viewed as their source: Emily Dickinson, the mirror, and Walt Whitman, the window." Moss died in 1987.*

The Moon

Those who think the word "terrace" unusable
Will never understand the lighting angle
From which I stare at the city tonight—

Its lights and ices, pinnacle heights,
And a single flatiron wedge of weight.
The view out there, more and more like newsprint,

Could it be the stars editing the dark?
Finally we make out what the letters mean:
Forswear the romantic but manage to live it.

A soundless plane's towed over dragging
Pontoons, and on-and-off green and red.
This is the smallest point in the sea.

And how life engages itself in the windows!
Human prospects: suppers, sleeps,
And conversations impossible to hear

About everything under the sun—or the moon
Apparent now with a haze around it,
Telling a story: how it watched the world

And reflects on it without stopping to reflect,
Withholding because it knows too much
That comment that would light up everything.

There were always two competing versions of this poem, though, strangely, the first and last lines never varied. In fact, once I'd hit on the last three stanzas, they remained constant, both in the two-line stanza version of the poem and the present three-line version. The problem was: the poem meant to speak against a romantic view of life while secretly espousing it. And so I knew, when I got to it, that the rather literal point of the poem—*Forswear the romantic but manage to live it*—should either be dropped or somehow brought in so it didn't clobber the reader over the head. More than that, I wanted a true effect, a true emotional response from the reader in regard to the scene I was describing—looking at New York City from a terrace as dusk descends and the moon comes out and a plane goes over. It's when I hit on the notion of dusk as newsprint (though it took several revisions to get there) that I realized I could spell out the "message" of the poem as if it were a headline or a quote—something to be found in a newspaper. That solved one problem, and the rest was a matter of transitions, subtle, I hope, from the first part of the poem (the first four stanzas), announcing its subject, to the last three stanzas, which are meant to be a matter of feeling, and to provide a climax that goes far beyond the confines of the poem itself. I think it is rather typical of my poems to have a phrase as commonplace as "Everything under the sun" used in order to rush on to something more original (I think): the depiction of the moon as a story-teller, somewhat jaded, but kind, mysterious, and, like the sun, impossible to say anything about, just as it refuses to say anything itself, its knowledge being so overwhelming. In the end, "The Moon" is a poem about revelation or the withholding of it, and so it became more and more complex as I worked on it, in spite of being a poem whose action takes place in a relatively brief span of time. I should say, too, that the last line of the poem (once it is sounded) is meant to illuminate retrospectively the text of the poem that leads up to it.

Thylias Moss *was born in Cleveland, Ohio, in 1954. A graduate of Oberlin College and the University of New Hampshire, she has taught at Phillips Academy in Andover, Massachusetts, and at Brandeis University. She joined the faculty of the University of Michigan in 1992.* Pyramid of Bone, *her second book of poems (University of Virginia Press, 1989), was shortlisted for the National Book Critics Circle Award. In 1991 Charles Simic selected her* Rainbow Remnants in Rock Bottom Ghetto Sky *for the National Poetry Series. She has since published* Small Congregations, *a volume of new and selected poetry, and* I Want to Be, *a book for children. Her work has appeared in four volumes of* The Best American Poetry. *She lives in Ann Arbor, Michigan, with her husband and two sons. She was named a Guggenheim Fellow in 1995 and a MacArthur Fellow in 1996. "Many angels are discovered when people trying / to commit suicide ride and tame the air," says the speaker in Moss's poem "The Warmth of Hot Chocolate," adding, "I was just such an accident."*

Renegade Angels

Every night women in love gather outside the window and it
is nothing special; coming out is what stars do, clouds, the

sun when it builds up the nerve and then just has to blurt out. Their thoughts collect there, outside, the window of no value to them unless they marvel at coincidence; the window is just how I know it happens. I am not part of the circle although every game I played as a girl was round. By morning there is fruit on branches not meant to bear witness anymore, that birds avoid and that embarrasses me so I don't taste it; I don't find out if they're edible berries, and even if they were, I'd let them shrink and drop dried; I can see myself snatching berries, especially not from a shrub so brambled, the branches look as if the feet of little birds tangled and broke off to appease beaks that had to get into those berries no matter what. This is the wrong thing to say because someone will start thinking that women in love set traps, bait bushes, trick birds, act out fables in which birds are made to always fly, to exhaust their wings, to be up soaring to death because they can't resort to landing. This is how the great hoverers are made. But women in love can do more than this, making is too traditionally and industrially valued to be a special accomplishment, a reason to gather when light isn't that good and there are no decent shadows, and the lit square and rectangular windows are irregular stars so big in their closeness they can't be wished on and personalized; stars are better the more distant they are so that to wish on them is to empower pinpricks. My eyes do not close without seeing what darkness holds, the letdown hair of women and welcome. And I remember where I was when I was fertilized, where as zygote I was stamped with most destinies but Eagle Scout, where I was when I divided and doubled without taking up additional space for a long time, before testing the limits of the skin that did not fail and being delivered: with a woman, expanding a woman's body from the inside, depending on a woman, filling a woman. This is what I remember while I'm saying that other prayer and singing that song I took, as a girl, as jingle: all day, all night, the angels watching over me. Outside my window. In honor of them for forty years I bleed libation.

On Angels

An interest in angels did not come from the Baptist church of my girl-hood, although they were mentioned there, mostly on Easter and Christmas, when constellations reconfigured themselves into humanoid shapes that differed from humans in the amount of holiness they embodied. The participation of stars was my own interpretation; preachers merely commented that angels descended from heaven, but I felt that I needed graspable angels. Perhaps, too, the participation of stars was born of a confusion that resulted in mergers between fairy godmothers, tooth fairies, and angels wielding magic wands. I liked the size of them, tiny beings that in the tradition of Tinker Bell could reduce themselves to a pinhole of light; they were protons.

Since then, the angel has become for me a transitional being, some-where between deity and mortal, more accessible than deity yet still transcending mortal. In this way is the angel ideal, spared mortal suffering, yet also spared divine responsibility. And in that relaxed position, the angel is able to have options; a god who must ensure a good outcome cannot behave in a way that would ultimately cause evil, but angels may explore a range of attitudes and behaviors; angels for instance may discover, question, spurn, for angels are not omniscient, just blessed and far more privileged than human beings. And angels, as people know, know the frustration at times of being subordinate, as no matter what their demeanor, God is above them.

Angels reveal a higher evolution; they are the ambition I have as I decide who will comprise the company I keep. And I am encouraged that angels too may be ambitious, that they are not necessarily at the limits of their progress, as a god must be. The angel may touch the divine without perishing, for the angel is more nearly spiritually complete than are the people for whom angels are hope. This being, this angel, is the result of desperate human longing, desperate hope that there is a mean-ing to existence that transcends the limits of human knowledge, specula-tion, and invention. It could be that need itself spawned them: human need for a lasting form, human need for a bridge, the angels going up and down and up and down that ladder, the angel as connection, as missing link between what we are and what it is that we hope the creator intended to be our ideal lost form. It is human awareness of human shortcomings that inspires in us the need and ability to conceive of angels, to actually see them, feel their breath weaving warm over and under us soft indestructible nets that give way only when it is time for an angel to suck out of us every evidence of mortal breath leaving then naked and alone for the first time the soul that another or perhaps the same angel adorns and embraces as at that moment, angel and consciousness (it is too difficult and defeating to think that consciousness simply ends, to even for a second suggest that this spirit so powerful within us could cease) realize they are identical. Then a great convergence becomes possible.

The renegade angel is the one with flesh, the one who without dying has the enlightenment that comes the moment after a dying person's last breath. The renegade angel is therefore freer, and more susceptible to experiencing delight, because the renegade angel responds to the angelic part of the self, not the temporary mortal portion that is after all just a casement, just a cocoon in which the renegade grows wings that, as soon as they are fully formed, cut like knives through mortal limitation. This is something I learned in part from the first poem I loved deeply, "The Quarrel" by Lorca. The renegade angel knows what has been suppressed in favor of a benign angel whose purpose involves the shepherding of people. The renegade angel knows that the long history of angels is mostly magic. Angels are powers that God endeavors to keep in check, mostly successfully, but he cannot ultimately control them. Angels do not always operate with God's permission, yet not having it doesn't prevent the operation, so that it seems, correctly or not, that angels are kept in check only so long as they want to be so kept. There are therefore angels with dominion over storms, angels who fall, angels with dominion over memory, an angel who transported to heaven the bodies of deceased Egyptian kings, an angel who compels love, hundreds of angels acting on their assigned or acquired bliss, many of them listed in Gustav Davidson's *Dictionary of Angels*. For me, all angels sing, and they do so better than all humans. I have not heard the singing, for I could not bear it. I have only imagined their mouths or some part of them, for angels need not have mouths as I think of mouths, moving, the songs traveling, healing sometimes what they touch, sometimes destroying.

I place my renegade angels in a prose poem, but it is not really a prose poem. First of all, there is no way to honor an angel but to believe in that angel. They are many and among us, but proving this is impossible. The poem itself is an attempt at honor, but limitations of page, of book, of printing, and my confinement to writing (although sculpture may have been in this case better) have forced me to resort to the only poetic form that encourages the endlessness of the line. Ideally, there would be one long line curving until the poem became a circle. That would pose difficulties for the printer, so the line instead conforms to the page, moving on to the next line only when space runs out. In this way, the line is everything. One line holds all. The margins are simply the edges of the universe. The line cannot exceed the edge of the universe because nothing exists outside the edge. This is the second great achievement of a prose poem, the claiming of the page, the claiming of all available space, the filling of that, the arrogance of that, arrogance that fortifies the renegade angels, who, being so fortified, in turn inspire me. The page, especially the clean blank page, is so often intimidating, but not in the prose poem, not in the steamroller effect of the collective presence of all the words, the neat block of language, even when the subject is not neat at all, the eccentricity encouraged because here the poem breaks free of its most challenging restraint, poetry itself. The prose poem looks like a monument on the page. It does not want, this one did not want, to be economical. It did not want to understate. It is a mountain, an ideal mountain without indentations to facilitate a climb. A rectangle of awe. A renegade structure for the renegades.

Harryette Mullen, *like W. C. Handy,*

was born in Florence, Alabama. She grew up in Fort Worth, Texas, home of Ornette Coleman. She graduated with honors from the University of Texas, Austin, and has graduate degrees from the University of California, Santa Cruz. She is the author of Trimmings *(Tender Buttons, 1991),* S*PeRM**K*T *(Singing Horse, 1993), and* Tree Tall Women *(Energy Earth Communications, 1981). She has worked in the Artists in Schools program sponsored by the Texas Commission on the Arts. More recently she has taught African-American and other U.S. ethnic literatures, postcolonial anglophone literatures of the African diaspora, and creative writing at Cornell University. She now teaches at UCLA.*

From Muse & Drudge

1.

O rose so drowsy in
my flower bed your pink
pajamas zig-zag into
fluent dreams of living ink

carve out your niche
reconfigure the hybrid
back in the kitchen
live alone, buy bread

your backbone slip
sliding silk hipped
to the discography
of archival sarcophagi

pregnant pause conceived
by doorknob insinuation
and no set animal
laminates on DNA

2.

marry at a hotel, annul 'em
nary hep male rose sullen
let alley roam, yell melon
dull normal fellow hammers omelette

divine sunrises
Osiris's irises
his splendid mistress
is his sis Isis.

creole cocoa loca
crayon gumbo boca
crayfish crayola
jumbo mocha-cola

warp maid fresh
fetish coquettish
a voyeur leers
at x-rated reels

3.

married the bear's daughter
and ain't got a quarter
now you're playing the dozens
with your uncle's cousins

sitting here marooned
in limbo quilombo
ace coon ballooned up
without a parachute

use your noodle for
more than a hatrack
act like you got the sense
God gave a gopher

couldn't fold the tablecloth
can't count my biscuits
think you're able to solve
a figure, go ahead and risk it

4.

when memory is unforgiving
mute eloquence
of taciturn ghosts
wreaks havoc on the living

intimidates intimates
polishing naked cactus
down below a bitter buffer
inferno never froze over

to deaden the shock
of enthusiastic knowledge
a soft body when struck
pale light or moderate

smooth as if by rubbing
thick downward curving
bare skin imitative
military coat made of this

5.

Jesus is my airplane
I shall feel no turbulence
though I fly in a squall
through the spleen of Satan

in a dream the book beckoned
opened for me to the page

where I read the words
that were to me a sign

houses of Heidelberg
outhouse cracked house
destroyed funhouse lost
and found house of dead dolls

two-headed dreamer
of second-sighted vision
through the veil
she heard her call

6.

just as I am I come
knee bent and body bowed
this here's sorrow's home
my body's southern song

cram all you can
into jelly jam
preserve a feeling
keep it sweet

so beautiful it was
presumptuous to alter
the shape of my pleasure
in doing or making

proceed with abandon
finding yourself where you are
and who you're playing for
what stray companion

KINKY QUATRAINS

Writing poetry for me is more a matter of texture than form. *Muse &
Drudge* employs a ubiquitously familiar traditional form, the quatrain or
tetrastich, common to ballads and other folk poetry, and well repre-

sented within the history of English verse. However, I was attracted to the form primarily because I saw that, given the surface uniformity and constraint of the four-by-four format as a unit of composition (four quatrains per page), I could make these four-line stanzas actually quite quirky, irregular, and sensuously kinky, in terms of polyrhythm (as opposed to regular meter), polyvocality (as opposed to the persistence of a single lyric voice or narrative viewpoint), a wide range of lexical choice and levels of diction (from the sacred to the profane), variation in line length, the various possibilities of rhyming or not rhyming, using end rhyme or internal rhyme, or odd lines of prose arranged as lines and stanzas to make "found poetry," as well as semantic and syntactic tensions within and between lines.

As in my prose poems *Trimmings* and *S*PeRM**K*T,* I continue to use what Stephen Yenser identified as "multivalent fragments," which produce a layered effect of multiple and sometimes contradictory semantic meanings and cultural allusions. I am also interested in the textural effects enabled by what Roman Jakobson called "subliminal verbal patterning" in literary and folk poetry. Folklorist John Holmes McDowell, referring to children's riddles, calls this aspect of the folk composition "riddling texture" or "aural composition . . . the palpable, sensuous organization . . . metrical and phonological patterning" of the verbal utterance.

My writing process is improvisatory, and certainly I have been influenced by instrumental and vocal improvisations of blues and jazz musicians. Some of the lines I write aspire to certain moments in jazz when scat becomes a kind of inspired speaking in tongues, or glossolalia, moments when utterance is pure music. Improvisatory methods I have used in poetry also follow from my interest in the literary techniques and experiments of Oulipo, as well as Saussure's investigation of anagrammatic, tabular readings of poetic texts, which have been an influence on Steve McCaffery and on Bernadette Mayer, poets whose work I have found useful for its playful preoccupation with the materiality and texture of writing.

Of course I follow in the tradition of poets, including Paul Lawrence Dunbar, James Weldon Johnson, Langston Hughes, Sterling Brown, Margaret Walker, Etheridge Knight, and Gwendolyn Brooks, who often worked with humble, common, and "folksy" materials, such as proverbs, prayers, folk sermons, lullabies, nursery rhymes and children's lore, blues, ballads, jokes, raps, riddles, and toasts. Although simple, such forms are striking in their mnemonic force, aural texture, and pervasive persistence. In a poetic text, simple things can be used for complex effects. I use all of these and other folk-based forms, allusively, along with their mutant offspring: clichés, political slogans, advertising jingles, tabloid headlines, and other linguistic readymades from the mass-culture dumpster. These I recycle in the spirit of Duchamp and of Tyree Guyton's "Heidelberg Houses" in Detroit. Inverted, the urinal becomes a fountain; recontextualized in a gallery or museum, it can be a work of art. For Guyton social transformation of the landscape, and a dynamic confrontation of conflicting views about community are enacted when an abandoned shack used as a crack house becomes a life-sized dollhouse; a vacant lot used for dumping is claimed as a community art park, and only then reviled by politicians as an eyesore. Most influential to me personally is Lorenzo Thomas, whose attention to the communal drum, and commitment to his own offbeat solo music, demonstrates the flexibility of traditions, forms, and genres in the hands of an adept aesthetic innovator.

Muse and Drudge, like the jazz soloist who plays "mysterious" music, locates itself in a space where it is possible to pay dues, respects, and "props" to tradition while still claiming the freedom to wander to the other side of far.

Charles North *was born in New York City in 1941. An active musician in his youth, he played clarinet with his first orchestra at the age of thirteen and spent summers at the music program in Interlochen, Michigan. He received degrees from Tufts College and Columbia University, and briefly attended Harvard Law School. He is the author of seven collections of poetry, most recently* The Year of the Olive Oil *(Hanging Loose Press, 1989) and* New and Selected Poems *(Sun and Moon, 1996). With James Schuyler he edited* Broadway: A Poets and Painters Anthology *(Swollen Magpie, 1979) and* Broadway 2 *(Hanging Loose Press, 1989). He is one of the editors of* The Green Lake Is Awake: Selected Poems by Joseph Ceravolo *(Coffee House Press, 1994). He has received grants from the National Endowment for the Arts, Poets Foundation, and the Fund for Poetry. He is poet-in-residence at Pace University.*

Lineups II

September ss   *(for Mary Ferrari)*
April 2b   "Composed Upon Westminster Bridge" ss
October lf   "The Lucy Poems" 2b
June cf   *Preface to Lyrical Ballads* lf
December 1b   "Tinturn Abbey" lf
March 3b   "Resolution and Independence" rf
January rf   "Michael" 1b
July c   "Mutability" 3b
May p   "The Leech Gatherer" c
     "Ode: Intimations of Immortality" p

Frog 3b
Lightning Bug 2b   Clover cf
Cat lf   Chicory 3b
Dog cf   Daisy ss
Hamster 1b   Sunflower lf
Turtle c   Thistle 1b
Rabbit ss   Dandelion rf
Alligator rf   Queen Anne's Lace 2b
Parakeet p   Milkweed c
     Honeysuckle p

Wittgenstein lf
Heidegger 2b   Simenon lf
Aristotle 1b   Sjöwall (Wahlöö) ss
Kant rf   Conan Doyle cf
Hegel cf   Chandler 1b
Hume ss   Leonard rf
Sartre 3b   Chesterton 2b
Plotinus c   Christie 3b
Plato p   Hammett c
     Poe p

Javelin 2b   Pun ss
110 m. high hurdles ss   Paradox lf
100 m. dash lf   Metaphor cf
1500 m. run cf   Simile rf
Long jump rf   Hyperbole 1b
400 m. dash 3b   Metonymy 3b
Pole vault 1b   Irony c
Shotput c   Understatement 2b
4 × 400 m. relay p   Zeugma p

Mint 3b
Rosemary ss
Thyme lf
Salt 1b
Garlic c
Oregano rf
Dry Mustard cf
Vanilla 2b
Nutmeg p

Williams ss
Hornsby cf
DiMaggio 1b
Ruth c
Mays 3b
Boggs rf
Aaron 2b
Sisler lf
Cobb p

DH Series II

MONTHS—November
PETS—Gecko
PHILOSOPHERS—Derrida
TRACK & FIELD—Marathon
WORDSWORTH—*The Prelude*
WILDFLOWERS—Goldenrod
MYSTERY WRITERS—Spillane
FIGURES OF SPEECH—Synecdoche
HERBS & SPICES—Peppercorn
HITTERS—Mattingly

1b Hamster
2b Chesterton
ss Pun
3b March
lf Wittgenstein
cf Clover
rf Kant/Oregano
c "The Leech Gatherer"
p Cobb
dh November

I wrote the first baseball lineup poem more than twenty years ago for a friend who was struggling with a doctoral dissertation in English. By arranging "major" British poets into a batting order, complete with positions in the field, I was presenting him with a dissertation ready-made. The idea, though outrageous, was valid, I felt—given some knowledge of baseball on the part of the reader, in particular the associations that attach willy-nilly, for the baseball fan, to both position in a batting order and position in the field. Scrappy Alexander Pope was clearly a leadoff man; Milton played first and batted cleanup; Donne pitched (and won thirty games four times).

That same year, in the summer appropriately enough, I came up with nine more lineups and then published them all in a pamphlet. (Actually I must have written sixty before choosing the ten that seemed to mean the most to me—or, more accurately, about which I had the strongest and most lasting intuitions concerning where each "player" hit and played.) Throughout, I felt that the real inspiration was Rimbaud, at least I hoped it was, especially his "Voyelles," which both deranged and rearranged things, was outrageous as well as beautiful, and made no bones about any of it. I wanted my own dearrangements to be somehow systematic—the idea being that the entire world could theoretically be located on metaphorical coordinates of batting order and position; so I invented lineups for cities, colors, parts of the body, vegetables, diseases, rooms, and so forth. A few summers ago I found myself fooling around with the idea again, which resulted in the second set, including a hitters lineup that went the basic premise one better and an all-star team.

Once after a reading, someone complimented me on the three lineups I had read, and then inquired about the little letters and numbers following the names. I guess I've always known that these poems—if they are bona fide poems—can't possibly make sense to everyone. But for those like me who grew up with indelible feelings and memories connected to baseball, there remains a shape and a tone, a *timbre,* to the very notion of shortstop, as there is a timbre not only to the leadoff and cleanup hitters but to the number 5 and number 7 "holes" as well. It interested me to recall, while doing the first set, that as a child I had given colors to both vowels and numerals without feeling that *my* conviction that 5 was orange and always had been, was or had to be everyone's conviction. The individual items that fill the lineups don't, or don't always, represent endorsements—they are as often as not the given, the state of the world—though clearly some intuitive selection process involving personal experience as well as tastes was at work.

Joyce Carol Oates *was born in Lockport,*

New York, in 1938. She currently lives in Princeton, New Jersey, and teaches at Princeton University. She is a coeditor of the Ontario Review. *Her books of poetry include* The Time Traveler *(1989) and* Invisible Woman *(1982). She received the National Book Award for her novel* Them *in 1970. Her other novels include* Expensive People *(1968),* Wonderland *(1971),* Because It Is Bitter, and Because It Is My Heart *(1990),* Black Water *(1992), and* Foxfire: Confessions of a Girl Gang *(1993). She has also written several novels under the pseudonym Rosamund Smith (*Lives of the Twins *and* Nemesis*). Her writings on "the sweet science" have been collected in* On Boxing; *a revised edition of this work was published by the Ecco Press in 1995. "All great poetry is enhanced by the occasion of its discovery, and by the occasion of its savoring," Oates has written. "A poem by night is far more powerful than a poem by day."*

How Delicately . . .

How delicately the fish's
   backbone is being
lifted out of its
   cooked flesh—
the sinewy spine, near-

translticent bones
   gently detached from
the pink flesh—
   how delicately, with
what love, there can be no hurt.

A two-stanza form is necessary for this little poem because its meaning falls naturally into two halves. In the first, focus is upon the literal; in the second, focus is upon the metaphorical. The spare, brief, "floating" lines were chosen in order to suggest the action observed—the lifting of the fish's backbone out of its flesh. The operation is done with such delicacy that one rather forgets the fact that the fish has been killed; not treated with delicacy at all. So with the emotional experience of being, in a way, dissected—one's "backbone" removed. Not all brutal acts are performed brutally, as we all know who have been so treated at one time or another in our lives. There is a pain that comes so swiftly and cleanly it doesn't even hurt. Except in retrospect.

The poem's specific image came by way of immediate observation, one evening at dinner. Someone was performing this operation on a brook trout. The abstract form immediately suggested itself as well: two stanzas, very short plain lines, the irony as subtle and as delayed as possible until the final line—the final word. It is a poem of such smallness that any resounding irony would be heavy-handed and would (in effect) break the translucent bones of the lines. The weight of the poem falls upon the last line but it is meant to fall lightly—delicately.

Form may well have preceded content, which is frequently the case when I am in my poetry phase. I had been writing short poems—very short poems—the shorter the better!—which contain only one image, one metaphor, one governing idea; so I didn't have to experiment with longer forms until I worked my way back to something as short as this. I would have gotten there eventually but it would have taken some time.

Molly Peacock *was born in Buffalo, New York, in 1947. Her collections of poetry include* And Live Apart *(University of Missouri Press, 1980),* Raw Heaven *(Random House, 1984), and* Original Love *(Norton, 1995). She has received fellowships from the Ingram Merrill Foundation, the New York Foundation for the Arts, and the National Endowment for the Arts. From 1989 to 1994 she served as president of the Poetry Society of America. Currently she lives both in New York City and in London, Ontario, Canada, with her husband, the James Joyce scholar Michael Groden. She teaches privately throughout North America.*

She Lays

She lays each beautifully mooned finger
in the furrow on the right and on the left
sides of her clitoris and lets them linger
in their swollen cribs until the wish to see the shaft
exposed lets her move her fingers at the same time
to the right and to the left sides pinning back
the labia in a nest of hair, the pink sack
of folds exposed, the purplish ridge she'll climb
when she lets one hand re-pin the labia
to free the other to wander with a withheld
purpose as if it were lost in the sands when the Via
To The City suddenly appeared, *exposed:*
when the whole exhausted mons is finally held by
both hands is when the Via gates are closed,

but they are open now, as open as her
thighs lying open among the arranged pillows.
Secrets have no place in the orchid boat of her
body and old pink brain beneath the willows.
This is self-love, assured, and this is lost time.
This is knowing, knowing, known
since growing, growing, grown;
revelation without astonishment,
understanding what is meant.
This is world-love. This is lost I'm.

It takes a wealth of chaos in early life to produce a quest for order as emphatic as the one a sonnet imposes. Its severity creates a dense, closed world, one that begins where it ends, and my need for art to order life led to my using it. That, and a feeling that I would like to do what the giants of poetry did, Yeats and Keats and Donne with all their *a b b a*s and *c d d c*s. I was educated at a time—the late sixties—when "formal concerns" were ignored. Because I didn't know a couplet from a dactyl, those who did composed what seemed to me a secret society; feeling excluded from it, I wanted to join.

Now "form" has become a way for me to express something so intimate about myself that, without its transformation into a shimmering, annealed world through measuring and rhyme, would otherwise be prurient or painful. Like everyone, I began writing out of necessity. By college there were things that, held in through childhood and adolescence, I let burst in the happy absence of my parents and hometown. I didn't care so much how it all came out so long as I didn't sound old-fashioned. What I didn't realize then and failed to realize for many years, was that I was trying to use a principle of prose fiction to form my free verse poems.

The shape of a story comes from how it unfolds; the plot of the story governs its form. Allowing a poem to "unfold as it is told" is to write it along narrative lines, and this is how some poems come to sound like broken-up prose. The sweep of a narrative can't ever happily take into consideration the closure of lines. Such a way of writing a poem requires constant decisions about "form," one at the end of each line, with the result that the poem is written to each part rather than to the whole. But with a "formal" method I found I could make an initial decision about the shape of the entire poem, and write both with and against my choice, governing the whole work for better or worse. To me, this is a way of braving an emotion's universe, and because the rules are set, there is an element of play I find beautiful. On the other hand, millions of small decisions in chaos—what writing free verse feels like to me—have about them a sense of overwhelming struggle.

But the problem with a "form" is that the form is perfect, while the feeling it governs is not. "Perfection is terrible," Plath wrote; "it cannot have children." What is distasteful about form is that sort of technical brilliance which becomes so empty when the brilliant words are not deeply felt. It was the work of Elizabeth Bishop that freed me from thinking that imperfections were errors. Bishop just skips a rhyme occasionally. It makes such sense: "form" becomes a way of generally ordering the poem's world, providing a way to express deep feeling, but not within a locked-up grid. It is, after all, this locked-up quality people most object to. A stanza need not be a trap; it is a way. And if "form" is the way of a feeling, it need not be adhered to strictly for itself. Once I felt I could write flawed poems, I felt released to try "formal" poems.

"She Lays" is one of these. It consists of a stanza that is an unmetered sonnet, to which it adds a coda of ten shorter rhymed lines. The reason the coda is there is because I didn't finish the poem when I reached the end of the sonnet. The reason the sonnet is there as a "form" is that there was no way in the world I could write about masturbation without it. I knew I could not write about something so delicate if that delicate thing also had to build its own existence. Facing a blank page, I felt it would be impossible to make up the shape of self-love as I went along. How could this frail subject make its own clumsy masonry? So I chose a "form" as a vehicle to take me to this intimate place. Instead of bewilderment, I chose limitation. The limitations of the lines then became long corridors to freedom—or walls opening on almost unbearably bright vistas.

Choosing a limited number of syllables (in this case, about twelve) both batters me back into density (because I've got to get rid of words which I wouldn't otherwise perceive as "extra" and therefore must recast the line, turning it very far into the subject) and carries me out toward the unmentionable. By this I mean that the limitation also forces me to reach as far outside the subject as I've had to turn in toward it because, for instance, I've got six syllables left and a rhyme to meet, so where will I go now? I would never have gone toward *Via / To The City* if I hadn't reached far away from the heart of the subject to rhyme with *labia.* At the same time, I don't think I would have gone so far inward, into both the act of touching myself *and thinking about it,* if I hadn't had to shut in my language because of the density of such a small number of syllables required. I don't think I would have said "swollen cribs" or "nest of hair" or "purplish ridge" if I had all the line length in the world to describe the flesh. I think I would have been far too frightened. Having everywhere at my disposal, I would not have known where to go.

Robert Pinsky *was born in Long Branch, New Jersey, in 1940. He is the author*

of The Want Bone *(Ecco, 1990) and* History of My Heart, *which won the William Carlos Williams Award from the Poetry Society of America. His first two books, both from Princeton University Press, were* Sadness and Happiness *and* An Explanation of America. *He has published several books of criticism and a translation of Dante's* Inferno, *which was recently published by Farrar, Straus and Giroux. He teaches in the graduate writing program at Boston University. In his poem "Shirt," he writes that it is "Wonderful how the pattern matches perfectly / Across the placket and over the twin bar-tacked / Corners of both pockets, like a strict rhyme / Or a major chord."*

The Want Bone

The tongue of the waves tolled in the earth's bell.
Blue rippled and soaked in the fire of blue.
The dried mouthbones of a shark in the hot swale
Gaped on nothing but sand on either side.

The bone tasted of nothing and smelled of nothing,
A scalded toothless harp, uncrushed, unstrung.
The joined arcs made the shape of birth and craving
And the welded-open shape kept mouthing O.

Ossified cords held the corners together
In groined spirals pleated like a summer dress.
But where was the limber grin, the gash of pleasure?
Infinitesimal mouths bore it away,

The beach scrubbed and etched and pickled it clean.
But O I love you it sings, my little my country
My food my parent my child I want you my own
My flower my fin my life my lightness my O.

FORM AS GROUND ZERO

Form in itself, like "creativity" in itself, is cheap—it is already there: the starting place. All day long forms keep droning that $x = x$, every fulfilled expectation makes a form. And creating all day long the mind chatters like a sewing machine, stitching up its unlikely creatures. A billion per minute.

It is the exception that exhilarates and inspires.

The resistance to form gives form weight and passion, and attentive resistance to the endless mental stream of creation gives the mind shape and action. In this sense, all successful rhyme is slant rhyme: as with metaphor, it is the *un*likeness that delights and illuminates.

The groan of wanting—the plainest English word for desire means not-having—was a physical sound and shape for me, and the form fell out as a procession of almost-having: the rhymes less than full, and rising at the ends of the unfulfilled odd-numbered lines *a* and *c* rather than the even closure of *b* and *d;* the pentameter sprung and oblate rather than fully rounded; the sound and shape of O never repeated to the full rhetorical possibility ("O my fin O my food O my flower my O my O," etc.); all almost filled out or filled in, but not.

This is retrospective, of course; at the time, there was the emotion, the *O,* and maybe a half-formed idea of something nearly florid and juicy, but scorched and spiny instead.

Katha Pollitt *was born in New York City in*

1949. A graduate of Radcliffe College, she is the author of Antarctic Traveller *(Knopf, 1982), which won the National Book Critics Circle Award in poetry. She has also received grants and prizes from the Guggenheim Foundation and the National Endowment for the Arts, a Peter I. B. Lavan Younger Poets Award from the Academy of American Poets, and a Fulbright Fellowship to Yugoslavia. She is an associate editor of the* Nation, *for which she writes a regular column.* Reasonable Creatures, *a nonfiction collection comprising some of her* Nation *columns, was published by Knopf in 1994.*

Playground

In the hygienic sand
of the new municipal sandbox,
toddlers with names from the soaps,
Brandon and Samantha,
fill and empty, fill and empty
their bright plastic buckets
alongside children with names
from obscure books of the Bible.
We are all mothers here,
friendly and polite.
We are teaching our children to share.

A man could slice his way
through us like a pirate!
And why not? Didn't we open
our bodies recklessly
to any star, say, Little one,
whoever you are, come in?
But the men are busy elsewhere.
Broad-hipped in fashionable sweatpants,

we discuss the day—a tabloid
murder, does cold cream work,
those students in China—

and as we talk
not one of us isn't thinking
Mama! Was it like this?
Did I do this to you?
But Mama too is busy,
she is dead, or in Florida,
or taking up new interests,
and the children want apple juice
and Cheerios, diapers and naps.
We have no one to ask but each other.
But we do not ask each other.

When my daughter was small, I spent a great deal of time in the playground in Riverside Park at Ninety-first Street. At first I felt as if I had found the Garden of Eden: big old plane trees, benches and picnic tables, a spigot that sprayed water during the hot Manhattan summer and drove the children wild with glee. It was easy to chat with strangers, since we all had a subject in common—our adorable, ever-fascinating children. After a while, though, I came to see the playground differently, as a kind of cage (complete with iron bars!) for women and children. Where were the fathers? Why did motherhood fence us off from life, instead of placing us in the hot center? Why did it seem to desex us in the eyes of men, when we were all bursting with vitality and milk and blood and sex? And—most important—why couldn't we talk to each other, openly and seriously, about our lives?

"Playground" came out of this experience and reflects it in formal ways. I tried in the opening lines to evoke a tone of depression distanced by irony: everything is pleasant and safe, but also tedious and false. I contrasted semicomical visual details and sociological observations with repetition and end-stopped lines to reproduce the feeling of psychological isolation that the poem is about. Throughout the poem, I used two- and three-beat lines to give it a monotonous ticktock rhythm, which the several outbursts and questions play against.

Behind my poem, of course, lies Philip Larkin's great poem "Afternoons," which is also about mothers in a playground. For Larkin, the mothers' plight, which he depicts with much tenderness and sympathy, is inevitable and quasi-biological: youth and freedom, love and beauty, last but a moment, then dreary old domesticity—so necessary to children but so unrewarding to men and women—takes over. It is nature—the heedless, demanding children, the next generation, the life force—that is pushing the mothers "to the side of their own lives." In "Playground," I wanted to say that this process, which looks like nature, is actually social. The sadness comes not, as in Larkin's poem, because of something inevitable, but because of what needn't be, but is.

Mary Jo Salter was born in Grand Rapids,

Michigan, in 1954, and grew up mostly in Baltimore. A graduate of Harvard University and Cambridge University, she has worked as a staff editor at the Atlantic Monthly. *She was poetry editor of the* New Republic *for three years starting in 1992. Since 1984 she has been a lecturer in English at Mount Holyoke College. Her first collection of poems,* Henry Purcell in Japan *(1985) was followed by* Unfinished Painting *(1989), which won the Lamont Prize for Poetry, and* Sunday Skaters *(1994), all from Knopf. She has also published a children's book,* The Moon Comes Home *(Knopf, 1989). With her husband, Brad Leithauser, she has lived for extended periods abroad in Japan, England, Italy, Iceland, and most recently France. In 1993 she received a fellowship from the Guggenheim Foundation. She and her husband have two children, Emily and Hilary.*

Refrain

> *But let his disposition have that scope*
> *As dotage gives it.*
>
> *—Goneril to Albany*

Never afflict yourself to know the cause,
said Goneril, her mind already set.
No one can tell us who her mother was

or, knowing, could account then by the laws
of nurture for so false and hard a heart.
Never afflict yourself to know the cause

of Lear's undoing: if without a pause
he shunned Cordelia, as soon he saw the fault.
No one can tell us who her mother was,

but here's a pretty reason seven stars
are seven stars: because they are not eight.
Never afflict yourself to know the cause—

like servants, even one's superfluous.
The King makes a good fool: the Fool is right.
No one can tell him who his mother was

when woman's water-drops are all he has
against the storm, and daughters cast him out.
Never afflict yourself to know the cause;
no one can tell you who your mother was.

I've wondered whether anyone would ever ask me how I wrote this poem, first published several years ago, because I wrote only part of it and the rest is brazen plagiarism. The idea for the poem came from a rereading of *King Lear* in which (as happens perpetually with Shakespeare) a new set of correspondences rose to the surface. On this reading it seemed that Shakespeare sought less to assign blame for Lear's and Gloucester's mistakes, or even the evil of daughters and sons, than to suggest that both evil and good are without easily attributable causes, and punishment and reward random. I began to transcribe various lines, spoken by a wide range of characters, supporting this theme. You see some of these lines embedded now in the poem, without my acknowledging all of their sources. In this way I sought not only to borrow Shakespeare's eloquence, but to suggest that "sources," like causes, are not single or simple.

(I was uncomfortable with sources in another way. When I first decided I'd like to hazard an interpretation of the play, I considered composing a scholarly paper. Then I remembered all the background reading and footnoting I'd be in for, and decided a poem would be easier.)

What form of poem, then? I had never written a competent villanelle; irrespective of the subject, each of my stanzas seemed to want to end "Do not go gentle into that good night." Yet Shakespeare's repetition of his theme in so many voices invited the choice of a repetitive form; and a rhymed form might harmonize the cacophony of voices. "Never afflict yourself to know more of it" is what Goneril actually says immediately preceding what was to be the epigraph to my poem; if I changed this to "Never afflict yourself to know the cause" (of her father's madness), which is what she means, I would make my case clear to the reader. I'd also have a rhyme for the other idea that had always fascinated me in *King Lear:* that none of the daughters seems to know who her mother *was.* Well, an off rhyme: now I'd offered myself the freedom to conceive of all the other rhymes in the loosest way, going so far as to employ one only a Briton might think of as a rhyme: *stars* with *was, cause,* etc. Thus the scene in which Lear answers the Fool that there are seven stars because they are not eight at once secured its place in the poem: I was enabled to illustrate, as I might not have in attempting to write an unrhymed poem, that Lear's absurd deduction is one more quite sane reflection on the unattributable causes of things. I was also given, through the rhyming refrain *(cause, was),* the opportunity to imply that the absence of the "mother" of the daughters, even in remembrance, is in some way parallel to the absence of one engendering "cause" of evil in Goneril and Regan and of good in Cordelia. Writing the poem made me see this; the poem's form, rather than forcing me to say something I didn't mean, empowered me to learn the truth of it.

Whatever its faults as a finished work, I have been fond of this poem for the exhilaration I felt in its making: never before or since have I felt form and content mesh so seamlessly. Or quickly. Usually a sluggish procrastinator, I wrote the poem in one day, sensing (for no knowable cause) that tomorrow it would be lost.

Lloyd Schwartz was born in Brooklyn in
1941, *the week after Pearl Harbor was attacked. He has published two books of poems,* These People *(Wesleyan University Press) and* Goodnight, Gracie *(University of Chicago Press), and he coedited* Elizabeth Bishop and Her Art *(University of Michigan Press). He lives in Boston, where he is the Frederick S. Troy Professor of English and codirector of the creative-writing program at the University of Massachusetts, Boston. He is also classical-music editor of the* Boston Phoenix *and a regular commentator on National Public Radio's* Fresh Air. *He has won three ASCAP–Deems Taylor Awards for his articles on music. He won the 1994 Pulitzer Prize for criticism.*

Tom Joanides

Which of these statements is true?

(a) I just got off the boat from Albania; (b) I look like
I just got off the boat from Albania; (c) I'm a master potter,
baking porcelains in a kiln I built myself; (d) I'm a master
pastry chef, sampling the desserts I bake for a famous
downtown hotel; (e) I live on donuts, sometimes one or two
dozen at a time; (f) I'm a diet freak, starving myself
on tofu and brown rice, purging my system with gallons of warm
salted water; (g) I'm an actor—a good one; (h) I've played an
amazing joke: I came home with someone I'd just met, went
into the bathroom, and shaved off my beard; (i) All my clothes
come from Goodwill; (j) I drive a Mercedes; (k) I'm the
artist's oldest friend; (l) I'm unhappy, I hate my life; (m)
Everything changes—give me a minute; (n) None of this is true.

This fourteen-line poem is part (one fourteenth) of a sequence called *Fourteen People,* which is based on an extraordinary series of portraits, also called *Fourteen People,* by Ralph Hamilton. I wanted to write a poem that would be as much about these paintings (and art itself) as about the people in them—fourteen friends I'd have found it impossible to write about so freely without the mediation of a work of art.

There was little question what form this poem had to take. Not only the organization and structure, the numerology, of the paintings—fourteen almost life-size standing figures, an epic "sonnet" of canvases—but also a vigorous American tradition of portrait sonnets (especially those of Edwin Arlington Robinson and Robert Lowell) suggested a basic unit of fourteen lines (or some multiple thereof). The order of the sequence would simply follow the order of the paintings.

The bigger question was how to capture, formally, the variety and drama of the paintings—not only the poignant subtleties of expression and the richness of the juxtapositions but also the kinetic handling of the surfaces themselves, all the more remarkable within formal confines (uniformity of size; absence of "scenery"; the relentless frontality of the poses) as starkly imposed as the strictest forms of versification. I was sure that fourteen literal descriptions would prove monotonous, too essayistic and mechanically dutiful. So I tried to play around with different kinds of responses to works of art, and different points of view, using a wide spectrum of personae and grammatical "persons." The series begins with poems expressing the most external, impersonal (third-person) view of the painted image ("Ralph Hamilton") and speculation about the subject ("Lloyd Schwartz"), and soon moves both inward, to autobiographical (first-person) monologue and direct (second-person) address, and outward to pure dialogue. In "Joyce Peseroff," for instance, we "overhear" an argument about the portrait between two anonymous spectators; in the central poem, "Mr. and Mrs. Hamilton," the artist himself is discussing his relation to his subject—his own parents; in "Robert Pinsky," the speaker is the author, talking to the subject of the painting about the way his image reflects the rewards, and the cost, of a life in art; in the last poem, "Danny and Mary Kelleher," the author, finally speaking directly to the artist, reminisces about two absent, unheard-from friends, both artists, whose complicated lives have become absorbed into their portraits.

The opening poem, about Ralph Hamilton's self-portrait, is the most traditionally formal and sonnetlike, with its nod toward rhyme and hint of a closing couplet. It's the jumping-off point for all the ensuing formal variations, a structural X ray of what might be hidden beneath all the other poems.

"Tom Joanides" is the twelfth "person," one of the least pictorial poems, and formally the most unusual, in the sequence. It's a monologue, a self-portrait, but only the way the "Ithaca" episode in *Ulysses* is a narrative—the truth both revealed and concealed through catechism; here, a questionnaire with only one question and (naturally) fourteen possible answers. It's also a series of turns, a vaudeville routine in which every line is a new punch line, an alphabet of evolving ironies and continually shifting tone (just as each of the fourteen answers begins at a different place on the line). I see this peculiar form, coming so near the end, reflecting the way all Fourteen People keep bumping up against one another—a fourteen-line microcosm of the whole series of poems, paintings, lives.

Charles Simic *was born in Belgrade, Yugoslavia, in 1938, came to the United States at the age of sixteen, went to high school in Oak Park, Illinois, and attended New York University. His first collection of poems was published in 1967. Sixteen others have followed. He received the Pulitzer Prize in 1990 for his book of prose poems,* The World Doesn't End. *His most recent collections are* A Wedding in Hell *(1994),* Hotel In-

somnia *(1992), and* The Book of Gods and Devils *(1990), all from Harcourt Brace. He has had three volumes in the University of Michigan Press's Poets on Poetry Series, most recently* The Unemployed Fortune-Teller *(1994). In an interview Simic described the waitress who had served him coffee and an English muffin at the Cleveland airport the day before. "I wouldn't dare begin writing about her, I couldn't presume to understand, to put myself in her place; but nevertheless, I feel an obligation, a responsibility toward her," Simic said. "I would like to create for her a poem which we could share." He was the guest editor of* The Best American Poetry 1992. *Awarded a MacArthur Fellowship in 1984, he teaches at the University of New Hampshire.*

Theseus and Ariadne

I shall go about with my eyes closed. The streets will no longer be safe. False Messiah, I'm going to step on your tin cup and tambourine. I'll brush against missing children, a few murderers and their sweethearts. Someone with onions on his breath will put a gold watch against my ear. It'll be like silent laughter. I'll be spun around by the crowd like a carousel.

I hope she'll still follow me. I'll cross bridges. I'll reach Jersey meadows if I have to. "He's a lost seeing-eye dog," she'll say. "In the blind universe he wants to be blind like love." O she won't even be there! Up and down Broadway where I play my game.

The Anniversary

I'll walk the streets all day today
With my eyes closed.
I won't bring a white cane and a dog.
I won't carry a doomsday sign.
I won't cheat, I won't peek.

Women will march in protest on the avenue
With their breasts bared proudly.
It will feel like New Year's Eve.
It'll be like Halloween.

Everyone will be wearing a funny hat.
There'll be gorillas in the crowd.

I'll brush against thousands of solitudes,
Bowing and muttering my apologies.
There'll be missing children,
One or two murderers and their sweethearts.
Someone with onion on his breath
Will put a cold wristwatch against my ear.
It'll be like silent laughter.

The lines in the hand foretell the future;
The sore feet know the past.
Somewhere hereabouts I sold tropical fish.
I painted the ceilings in a funeral parlor.
I was an usher in a live sex show.

Ten minutes to closing time,
In a matrimonial agency rarely frequented
A bride will wait for me
Dressed in white lace like my grandmother.

At some construction site, fifty stories up,
I will step on a long beam,
And go to the very tip of it,
My arms spread wide to steady myself
With the wind gusting off the river.

O unknown bride coming to rescue me
With your eyes tightly shut
Over that narrow girder
In your white high-heeled shoes,
The sea gulls snatching your veil,
Your gloved hand groping for mine.

I have a cat who walks around with eyes shut when the sun is too strong. That gave me the idea for the poem. What would it be like, I thought, to walk around New York City with eyes closed? How would one experience the streets one knows so well? The prose poem ("Theseus and Ariadne") was the first attempt to imagine that walk, which seemed to me at the time to be like a walk in a labyrinth with perhaps an Ariadne to guide me.

A year or so after I wrote the prose version, I realized that I hadn't dreamed that dream to the end. So, I started again. Revery led to memories, memories led to sorrow of time passing, and the whole poem got much more complicated. I wanted to recover the feeling of living an incredible and marvelous adventure, the very essence of being young. I suppose what I am saying is that in "The Anniversary" I wanted to return to that point in my life when the world was a wonderful and mysterious place ruled by the hope of an imminent and all-consuming love.

Louis Simpson *was born in Kingston, Jamaica, in 1923. His most recent publications are* Jamaica Poems *(Appletree Alley Press, 1993); a collection of essays and notes on poetry,* Ships Going into the Blue *(University of Michigan Press, 1994); and a book of memoirs,* The King My Father's Wreck *(Story Line Press, 1994). He has also written* A Company of Poets *and* The Character of the Poet, *both published by the University of Michigan Press. His new poems will be published by Story Line Press. Of his life now, he writes, "I retired from teaching two years ago. I can hardly remember teaching—it's like a not very interesting dream. But I remember writing—this was real. The teaching of literature in universities, whether it's by so-called theorists or the people with a political agenda, has very little to do with the understanding of literature. I'm happy to be out of it . . . and just writing."*

STRUCTURE AND IDEA

In the early fifties I worked as an associate editor for a publishing house in Manhattan. The work consisted mainly of reading novels, my feet propped on the bottom desk drawer. There was another associate, the man I have called Mike in "The Precinct Station." Mike wrote articles on jazz; he was writing a novel, and he was an alcoholic. The head editor had a great deal of respect for Mike as a future novelist, and so put up with his coming late to work and not finishing assignments. The head editor would sometimes ask me to do Mike's work for him.

Mike was sleeping with Lorna. She was married, but this seemed to be no obstacle. Then, one night, Lorna was in the emergency ward at Bellevue and Mike was at a police station, under arrest for attempted homicide. In the version that went the rounds, Lorna had picked up a carving knife and Mike had tried to take it away from her, inflicting a wound that required twenty stitches. There was some uncertainty about what she had meant to do with the carving knife. The head editor had gone to the station himself and bailed Mike out. In the sequel Lorna refused to press charges, and Mike continued to work for the publishing house until his absences became flagrant and the head editor regretfully let him go.

Thirty years after the event I wrote a narrative poem about it. My writing usually takes its origin from an actual incident, character, or uttered speech. I included myself, the narrator, as a character in the story. I described my job in publishing, and my first meeting with Lorna. It was in the White Horse Tavern. She was with her husband and Mike introduced us. A few minutes later, in order to illustrate some point in a story she was telling, she unbuttoned her blouse and showed us her breasts. The nipples were small and pink, like tea roses.

I wrote other incidents, as though I were writing a novel. They were strung together like beads on a string. I told myself that I was making leaps, as in cinematography, but what was harder to explain away was the flatness of the language. Then, after many drafts, it occurred to me that the narrator was jealous of Mike, jealous of the sexual favors granted by Lorna to this alcoholic who was habitually late for work. Jealous, too, of the friendship of Mike and the head editor, who would ask the narrator to do Mike's work for him. The narrator had been imposed upon—this poem was his revenge.

From the beginning, the first draft, there had been eight lines that stood out from the rest, describing the precinct station. Here the language was not flat—there were striking images and a compelling rhythm. I had placed these lines in the middle of the poem, but when I saw that it was the narrator's frame of mind that interested me, I moved the lines to the end. They were the objective correlative of his feelings, envy and resentment, lurking like the cockroach under the baseboard at the precinct station.

But would the reader see this? There has been a failure of imagination among readers of poetry. They think that poetry has to be "sincere," by which they mean talking about oneself, one's family, one's friends. They don't want anything to have been "made up," and as for poetry setting out to give pleasure, these latter-day Puritans dislike it wholeheartedly. They want sermons in church, the Church of True Confession, or the Church of Supreme Meditation, whatever. But I am interested in the variety and sensation of real ideas. Poetry makes ideas seem real by removing the detritus of fact and substituting something else that is more to the point.

I did not trust the reader to see the underlying motif. But it would be truer to say that I did not feel that I had carried it off. The incidents, even with this explanation, were strung together; the language remained flat. Something, however, might be salvaged: the part about the precinct station. I amputated this and sent it to *The Georgia Review*. They published it in the fall of 1984.

26th Precinct Station

One night Jake telephoned
to say, "Mike has stabbed Lorna."
He wanted me to call his lawyer . . .
couldn't do it himself, he was tied up.

I called the lawyer, who had just come in
from seeing *Kismet*. We shared a taxi.
All the way down to the station
he kept humming "And This Is My Beloved."

Lorna recovered, and wrote a novel.
Mike married and went to live in Rome.
Jake Harmon died. But I remember
the 26th Precinct Station.

A black woman in a yellow wig,
a purple skirt, and stiletto heels;
a pickpocket; a cripple
arrested for indecent exposure.

The naked light bulb; the crack in the wall
that loops like the Mississippi at Vicksburg;
the shadow of the cockroach
under the baseboard, lurking, gathering his nerve.

When you have published a poem I think you should leave it alone. Rewriting lines and changing titles, revising so as to have a different meaning—the kind of thing Auden did—shows an excessive care to refurbish the past and present oneself in the best possible light. The revised poem is true neither to what one used to write and think nor what one thinks and writes in the present—a flavorless hybrid.

There is always the exception, however, and perhaps in this instance the rule does not apply, for revision of "26th Precinct Station" took place within a few months of the poem's being published, so that publication was merely an interruption of the writing.

I still wasn't satisfied. The lines describing the precinct station still seemed strong, and the lines that came before were as good as I could make them, with a happy, ironic touch—the song title, "And This Is My Beloved." But there was too much explanation and, at the same time, not enough. Something appeared to be missing. I felt that I had cheated the reader and myself—myself being the more seriously injured party.

It has been said before, and has to be said again: structure, or plot, depends on feeling—not the other way round.

I examined my feelings again, going back to the facts of the case. A light flashed on, revealing a fact so obvious that I had not seen it. In the poem I had myself visiting the precinct station. But I had not visited the station—it was the head editor who did so and who got Mike out of trouble. Could this be the key I was looking for? I discarded the lines that described my going to the station and wrote four lines saying that I didn't go and someone else went and bailed Mike out.

The lines about the station now had a reason for being, and for being as they were, grotesque. The naked light; the crack in the wall; the cockroach; the woman in the yellow wig, a threatening female; the pickpocket, one who lived by stealing; the cripple arrested for indecent exposure—were projections of the narrator's unacted desire and his fearful imagining of what would happen if he did act. He had not taken his chances with sex and possibly violence, and therefore, like Coleridge's albatross, the precinct station was hung about his neck and he was compelled to see it again and again.

I wrote a new beginning in four lines that came easily, seeming to write themselves. I changed Lorna to Nancy for the sound of the line, and "stiletto heels" to "heels like stilettos" for the rhythm. Though the purist might object that "stiletto heels" was a standard phrase, I felt that rhythm must take precedence.

The Precinct Station

When Mike stuck a knife in Nancy
I didn't go to the precinct station
to bail him out—someone else did.
But ever since I've had an idea

of what it's like: a woman in a yellow wig,
a purple skirt, and heels like stilettos;
a pickpocket; a cripple
arrested for indecent exposure;

the naked light; the crack in the wall
that loops like the Mississippi at Vicksburg;
the shadow of the cockroach
under the baseboard, lurking, gathering his nerve.

This is a long explanation for twelve lines of verse. But the important struggles need not take place on a wide canvas—they may happen in a corner. The process I went through in arriving at the final structure of this poem would apply to the writing of all my poems. I had to be open to all possibilities, willing to start again from scratch, to say to myself, No. I did not do or feel the things the poem says I did and felt. I'll have to try something else.

There have been writers who did not believe in rewriting. They argue that the first step has been placed in the universe—it is there forever, unchangeable. But the second draft of the poem, and the third—are they not also placed in the universe? So the question of which draft is the best—that is, which moves people most strongly, seems most true—is still to be decided. The best draft may not be the first but the tenth, or the fortieth. The wish simply to speak and have it accepted as poetry is one with the child's wish to utter a cry and be obeyed.

The structure of the poem depends on an idea, and the more the idea proceeds from the character of the poet, the more it compels the poem into a certain form. It may take some examination of one's feelings, and much rewriting, to discover what they mean.

Elizabeth Spires *was born in Lancaster, Ohio, in 1952, and grew up in nearby Circleville. She is the author of four books of poetry, including* Globe *(Wesleyan University Press, 1981),* Swan's Island *(Holt, 1985),* Annonciade *(Viking-Penguin, 1989), and* Worldling *(Norton, 1996). She has also written a book of riddles for children,* With One White Wing *(Simon and Schuster, 1995). She was the Amy Lowell Travelling Poetry Scholar in 1986–87 and has had fellowships from the Guggenheim Foundation and the National Endowment for the Arts. A Vassar alumna, she interviewed Vassar alumna Elizabeth Bishop for the* Paris Review. *For the University of Michigan Press's Poets on Poetry series, she is editing a collection of Josephine Jacobsen's critical prose. She lives in Baltimore and teaches at Goucher College and in the Writing Seminars at Johns Hopkins University.*

On the Island

for Josephine Jacobsen

One ferry arrives as one is pulling out.
July was a high point, hot, bright and buttery.
August is huge and blue, a glittering gemstone
curving dangerously at either end into what precedes
and follows it. The ferry begins as a small white point
on the horizon and gradually enlarges into an event
we don't know whether to dread or impatiently wait
    for.
Those who have just disembarked look stunned and
    hopeful.
The trip has been long for them. Down the gangplank
they come, with dogs and bicycles and children,
the sun glaring down, the narrow streets of the town
crowded and loud. Weekends are always busiest.
Up the beach, we who have been here for weeks
are grateful to be going nowhere, to be innocent
bystanders to scenes of greeting and farewell.
We have lived through too many beginnings and ends,
and will again, but not today, thank goodness, not
    today.
Today we lean back lazily, our chairs set low in the
    sand,
happy to sit in the safe shadow of a big beach
    umbrella
and stare out at wide water, our minds emptying
like the plastic watering cans the children use
to wet down the sand. We coexist with them,
    dreaming
our dreams as they dream theirs, building our castles
in air, in sand, not minding when waves or wind
flood the moats and take down careful curling walls,
calmly rebuilding with the patience of clouds,
the dream we were dreaming beginning all over again.

But there is one among us who does not dream . . .
Waist-deep in rolling water, a woman, a grandmother,

stands in a skirted suit, a bright blue bathing cap
neatly fastened under her chin. Rock-solid, she strides
deeper into the cold blue water, calling back
to her two granddaughters, "Try to keep up with me,
    girls!"
Out beyond the breakers, she swims rapidly back and
    forth
between two unmarked points, then rests for a while,
her blue head buoyantly bobbing down and up.
Beaches are big enough for big thoughts that meander
like dogs, sniffing the truth out about themselves.
Will I, too, as I have secretly hoped, give myself up
one day to waves and water, no longer a watcher?
Will I lead the small ones out, fearlessly lead them out,
as if to say, "Courage, dear ones! Beauty will go.
    Pride, too.
We must take the plunge now or throw in the white
    towel!"

Like a huge bassoon, the inbound ferry sounds,
shaking the island. To leave here, all must ride it.
Some before others. Some at summer's end and some
    tomorrow.
Some never to return, and some to come back,
summer after summer, weaving a bright thread of
    constancy
into inconstant lives. Babies will change
into children, children will awkwardly grow up,
girls will find their slender beauty stolen,
and mothers will wake up grandmothers, they will
    wake up.
Pursued by change, they will run to the end of their
    lives,
no other choice left to them, and plunge into
an element darker than sunlight, darker than night.
The ever-widening wake of the inbound ferry
cannot shake the resolve of the woman in the waves.
She follows it out, waving her arms wildly
as she goes, not in distress, oh no,

but simply to give the ones going away a good
 goodbye.
Soon they will reach the mainland, the summer quickly
becoming a good dream to them, no turning point.
All will go on as it has. Or will it?
They point at the sight of a woman alone in a
 churning ocean
held up by . . . What holds her up? She waves and
 waves.
And they, not yet caught up in the life ahead of them,
wave back at her. They wave back.

TWO VOICES

"On the Island" began with an overheard remark. Several summers ago, on a weekend in July, I had just arrived by ferry with my husband and daughter on Block Island. After dropping off our suitcases in the house we were renting, we hurried out onto the beach. Almost immediately, as if the scene had been waiting to happen, a woman in her late sixties or early seventies who was standing at the ocean's edge dashed into the waves and called back to two adolescent girls (her granddaughters, I supposed), "Try to keep up with me, girls!" Often I see or hear things that seem to be the germ of a poem, and this small scene was just such a case. I scribbled it down in my notebook. I was struck by the older woman's verve and energy, perhaps because I had been feeling so little myself for some months.

But the *idea* for a poem, no matter how "ecstatic" the occasion, isn't the poem itself, even when a setting or character is charged with resonance and possibility. Other factors come into play. I had not written a poem I had been satisfied with for over a year, and I felt at a loss about how to proceed on this one. The penciled notes in my notebook stayed there until late summer when I came upon two poems, "The Woods" and "Hourglass," by a friend of mine, Josephine Jacobsen, in *The Best American Poetry 1991* and *The Best American Poetry 1993*, respectively. Now Josephine is a poet who, like the woman on Block Island, has lost none of *her* vital energy. The main character in "Hourglass," an older woman living in a retirement community, "perfectly understands the calendar / amid the sun's passage. But she grips the leash / and leans on the air that is hers and is here." The voice in both of Jacobsen's poems was as sure of itself, as *present,* as the other voice I had heard on Block

Island. There was absolutely no vacillation, no tentativeness—traits that I am constitutionally plagued with and struggle against—in either woman's declarations. Jacobsen's poems had an implied imperative, a secret message meant only for me, as if to say, "Well, what are you waiting for? Write the poem!" Her voice, rhythms, directness, and self-assurance catapulted me into my own poem the way the apocryphal mother throws her child into the swimming pool and the child, miraculously, swims.

Poets are indebted to each other for the poems they write although they often would rather not acknowledge the fact. The plain title I chose, almost generic, is one Jacobsen uses for one of her short-story collections. I hope she doesn't mind it coming around again and crossing genres, a kind of literary recycling. I acknowledge my debts, obvious and not so obvious, here and now.

A final note, about the poem's free-verse lines and stanzas. What little I had written in the year preceding "On the Island" was short and constrained, poured into tight stanzaic structures that felt like an emotional straitjacket. In contrast, the lines in "On the Island" unrolled in waves or breakers, the shape and length of the poem, like the beach setting, "big enough for big thoughts that meander / like dogs, sniffing the truth out about themselves." Nothing but long, expansive lines would have suited the action, but form and content, as is often the case, came into being *simultaneously,* not one before the other. The act of writing "On the Island" was a breaking through and breaking out of unhappy constraint into something larger and freer, two lively voices outside of myself leading me back into my own.

Jon Stallworthy *was born in London in 1935. An Oxford graduate, he*

worked as an editor at Oxford University Press for many years before becoming the Anderson Professor of English Literature at Cornell University. In 1986 he returned to Britain to take up a teaching appointment at Wolfson College, Oxford. He is Wilfred Owen's biographer and has edited Owen's complete poems. In collaboration with Peter France, he translated Boris Pasternak's Selected Poems *(Norton, 1983). His books include* The Anzac Sonata: New and Selected Poems *(1986) and* The Guest from the Future *(1989). His* Louis MacNeice: A Biography *(Norton, 1995) proves in several ways that MacNeice "has been fortunate in his champions and critics."*

At Half Past Three in the Afternoon

On one side of the world
I was watching the waterfall
shake itself out, a scroll unfurled
against a gray slate wall,
when on the other side—
it would be half past nine, and you
in bed—when on the other side
the night was falling further than I knew.

And watching the water
fall from that hole in the sky
to be combed into foam, I caught
a glimpse in the pool's dark eye
of us, eating our bread
and cheese, watching the falling light
crash into darkness. "Look," you said,
"a rainbow like a dragonfly in flight."

On one side of the world
at half past five in the afternoon
a telephone rang, and darkness welled
from a hole in the sky,
darkness and silence. Soon,
in search of a voice—how to recall
"a rainbow like a dragonfly
in flight"—I walked back to the waterfall.

The trees had lost their tongues—
as I did, coming face to face
with the glacial skeleton hung
beside our picnic place.
The spine was broken, cracked
the ribcage of the waterfall.
The pond under its cataract
knew nothing of us, knew nothing at all.

And what did I know, except
that you, the better part of me,
did not exist? But I have kept
your anniversary

today—or, there, tonight—
returning to the creek, and trying
to understand. I saw the light
falling, falling, and the rainbow flying.

We have been taught to consider experience as flux, a stream of random sense impressions most faithfully recorded by the stream-of-consciousness method. Contrariwise (and some will think more contrary than wise), I am continually aware of patterns of recurrence and, since it is these perceptions—rather than perceptions of flux—that seem to generate my poems, patterns of recurrence are a natural feature of my writing. Perhaps I should explain what I mean by natural.

When I learned that my mother had died, in England, at a moment when I, in America, had been watching a waterfall beside which we had picnicked two years before, I found the coincidence strange and comforting. It suggested a connection at a moment when one was painfully aware of disconnection.

In due course, the first phrases of what was to be the first stanza of a poem came into my head: "at half past three, on one side of the world . . . at half past nine, on the other side." The sentences that grew from these phrases determined their own line breaks, their own pattern of rhymed and rhythmic recurrence. I did not plan a stanza of two halves, two quatrains representing this side and that side, light and darkness, voice and silence, falling and flying. Rather, I allowed the poem to find its own pattern of recurrence, and instinctively it found one that would reflect these emerging polarities. It was born with its voiceprint as a child with its fingerprint, and once that pattern of lines was established (trimeter, two tetrameters, two trimeters, two tetrameters, pentameter; rhyming *a, b, a, b, c, d, c, d*), it would have seemed unnatural to alter it in subsequent stanzas. On the other hand, such a pattern of recurrence seemed to produce, naturally, the necessary repetitions, the echoes (line seventeen of line one, for example, or line twenty of line ten) of the stanzas that follow. Such echoes can have ironic vibrations, as in the return of line thirty-two to both the place and the rhyme of line twenty-four. Conversely, an established pattern sets up expectations in attentive readers that need not be fulfilled if the poem's intention is to surprise them: hence, after an unbroken series of masculine rhymes, the final feminine one that tries to lift the poem into the air.

But will it fly? Only time will tell.

Mark Strand

was born of American parents on Prince Edward Island, Canada, in 1934. Educated at Antioch College, he had wanted to paint and had gone to the Yale Art School to study with Josef Albers before turning to poetry. His books include Sleeping with One Eye Open *(1964),* Reasons for Moving *(1968),* The Story of Our Lives *(1973),* The Continuous Life *(1990), and* Dark Harbor *(1993). He has also published short stories, translations from the Spanish and the Portuguese, and a monograph on Edward Hopper. "When I was a child what I saw of the world I saw from the backseat of my parents' car," Strand writes, explaining his kinship with Hopper. "It was a world beyond my immediate neighborhood glimpsed in passing. It was still. It had its own life and did not know or care that I happened by at a particular time. Like the world of Hopper's paintings, it did not return my gaze." In 1990 he became the fourth Poet Laureate of the United States. He was the guest editor of* The Best American Poetry 1991. *For a number of years he taught at the University of Utah. He is currently the Elliott Coleman Professor of Poetry at Johns Hopkins and lives with his wife and son in Baltimore.*

Two De Chiricos
for Harry Ford

1. The Philosopher's Conquest

This melancholy moment will remain,
So, too, the oracle beyond the gate,
And always the tower, the boat, the distant train.

Somewhere to the south a Duke is slain,
A war is won. Here, it is too late.
This melancholy moment will remain.

Here, an autumn evening without rain,
Two artichokes abandoned on a crate,
And always the tower, the boat, the distant train.

Is this another scene of childhood pain?
Why do the clockhands say 1:28?
This melancholy moment will remain.

The green and yellow light of love's domain
Falls upon the joylessness of fate,
And always the tower, the boat, the distant train.

The things our vision wills us to contain,
The life of objects, their unbearable weight.
This melancholy moment will remain,
And always the tower, the boat, the distant train.

2. *The Disquieting Muses*

Boredom sets in first, and then despair.
One tries to brush it off. It only grows.
Something about the silence of the square.

Something is wrong; something about the air,
Its color; about the light, the way it glows.
Boredom sets in first, and then despair.

The muses in their fluted evening wear,
Their faces blank, might lead one to suppose
Something about the silence of the square,

Something about the buildings standing there.
But no, they have no purpose but to pose.
Boredom sets in first, and then despair.

What happens after that, one doesn't care.
What brought one here—the desire to compose
Something about the silence of the square,

Or something else, of which one's not aware,
Life itself, perhaps—who really knows?
Boredom sets in first, and then despair . . .
Something about the silence of the square.

About two years ago, I was asked by the Art Institute of Chicago to write
a poem or a short piece of prose to accompany a painting from their
collection. They were going to publish a book of reproductions alongside the "texts" by other writers they had asked. At about the same time,
the University of Iowa asked me to contribute a poem to a similar
project. Since each collection included a De Chirico, I chose his work. At

first, I thought I should write prose, especially since I took a dim view of most poems written in response to paintings. But then I changed my mind when I realized how difficult it would be to communicate in prose De Chirico's perplexing stillnesses, his repetitions, his mysterious retrievals. I chose to try my hand at writing villanelles. It is a form, after all, that shares a great deal with De Chirico's paintings. That is, it uses repetition to compensate for notions of loss. With each repeated line, it supplies the reader with a replenishing fullness, allowing him to take pleasure in what ordinarily would be a cause for unhappiness. In De Chirico's paintings, certain objects—trains, towers, flags—are carried over from work to work. In what otherwise would be an ominous world of twilight and absence a rearrangement of familiar things occurs. They find their places again and again, each acquiring a new finality—like the lines of a villanelle.

Richard Stull was born in Mt. Gilead, Ohio, in

1951. After studying classics and English literature at the University of Cincinnati, he received an M.F.A. from the University of Iowa. He has received a grant from the Ingram Merrill Foundation and had a residency at Yaddo. His poems have appeared in Boulevard, New American Writing, Chelsea, Poetry, *and the* Paris Review. *A chapbook,* Adoration of the Golden Calf, *was published by Groundwater Press. Since 1979 he has lived in New York City, where he works in publishing.*

Romance

The enigma was plagued with vertigo.
While summer lasted, its familiar flame
Was not forgotten. Circling the tableau,
Disdaining oxygen, the stranger came
To quiz the private group: a specimen,
Too fine a proof that late believers
Must also suffer, like Wyatt, from fevers.

These new impressions burned confidently
And afflicted with time (doomed to return),
Distressed our memories permanently.

Glaring incidents angled in an urn
Charge days; and life, or its idea, must turn
At last like a startled face in the park,
Swaying but painfully clear in the dark.

Distractions were logically engineered
Which we followed. Personal seriations,
Spied from windows, quietly disappeared.
Cool, deep rooms seemed some retaliation
For the tensions of our congregation
Which if it could would live without regret—
A consistent infusion at sunset.

Ruined but successful empires are rare.
Like senses in timelessness, they know grief
Disguises real pain. Pope's lock of hair
Is trivial next to the handsome thief's
Need for it. And our embittered motifs
Loosened our grip on tone as we confused
Certain ranges of color, especially blues.

Imagine how this conditioned the day.
Each one's forgotten love was a mirror
Of present deliriums. A new way
To meet anxious selves who glided nearer
Until finally the nights became clearer
Directives to the past than simple tense
Would indicate: the first, pure routes of sense.

A residue of permanent shapes bled
From the projector while certain scenes were
Laid within the sleepers' grasp. Overhead,
A couple undressed. Each in a cold blur
Crawled toward the other's land: worshippers
Implying a blinding rain, but unsaid—
A sigh in a dramatic poem, a thread.

In the end, the lovers left unannounced.
The veiled country house was put up for sale,
And the once wishful forest was denied.
Thus, in this romance, an unknown detail

Slowly pulled the lovers from their jail,
Where sensibility outlasts death, to
A further vividness of darker hue.

A friend has suggested to me that although the word *romance* is popularly associated with the stylized and often ritualistic beginning of an amorous relationship, it might just as easily refer to the ending of one. I think that my poem "Romance" could be accurately described in these terms; that is, as a "stylized dissolution."

The stanza form of "Romance" might be characterized as a lazy *rime royal*. The rhyme and the syllabic line contribute much to the idealization of the characters and their actions toward one another. I remember noting while working on the poem that the rhyme was forcing me to "position" the lovers in a certain way, both in relation to one another and in relation to objects in the house. As a result, I found people strolling through a park at night, sitting about sumptuous rooms, or drifting in a dream about their own sleeping heads. I would even venture to say that my understanding of the examples of *rime royal* that I was reading at the time, especially Thomas Wyatt's, encouraged my rather decorative escape from any realism that might have crept into my descriptions. Such realism is something that a writer of different temperament might have desired.

The interlocking rhyme scheme produced a further effect. The intricate relationships among the characters seem to dissolve Houdini-like in the very bonds established for them. Without having foreseen the consequences, I had, in effect, willed this dissolution: the form itself granted me a brief respite from the feelings that haunted me and led me to compose the poem. This mysterious cessation may in fact be the very subject of the poem.

James Tate was born in Kansas City, Missouri, in 1943. He was awarded the Yale Younger Poets Prize in 1966 for The Lost Pilot. His Selected Poems (Wesleyan/University Press of New England, 1991) won the Pulitzer Prize for poetry in 1992. Worshipful Company of Fletchers (Ecco) received the National Book Award in 1994. Other recent books include Constant Defender (Wesleyan, 1983), Reckoner (Wesleyan, 1986) and Distance from Loved Ones (Wesleyan/University Press of New England, 1990).

He has taught at the University of Massachusetts since 1971 and lives in Amherst. Asked about the humor in his work, Tate has said, "Poetry-reading audiences invariably giggle at the most tragic passages. My own thinking about this is that the depressing truths about the world are obvious. I don't use humor as a weapon. I don't think of myself as a satirist, as one reviewer recently suggested. I don't even think of myself as 'using' humor. It is just there; *it is a part of the world as I see it."*

Peggy in the Twilight

Peggy spent half of each day trying to wake up, and the other half preparing for sleep. Around five, she would mix herself something preposterous and '40s-ish like a Grasshopper or a Brass Monkey, adding a note of gaiety to her defeat. This shadowlife became her. She always had a glow on; that is, she carried an aura of innocence as well as death with her.

I first met her at a party almost thirty years ago. Even then it was too late for tragic women, tragic anything. Still, when she was curled up and fell asleep in the corner, I was overwhelmed with feelings of love. Petite black and gold angels sat on her slumped shoulders and sang lullabies to her.

I walked into another room and asked our host for a blanket for Peggy.

"Peggy?" he said. "There's no one here by that name."

And so my lovelife began.

The prose poem has its own means of seduction. For one thing, the deceptively simple packaging: the paragraph. People generally do not run for cover when they are confronted with a paragraph or two. The paragraph says to them: I won't take much of your time, and, if you don't mind my saying so, I am not known to be arcane, obtuse, precious, or high-fallutin'. Come on in.

What the prose poem does not admit is that it is capable of employing all but one of the devices of a regular poem, the obvious exception being the line break. Image, metaphor, rhythm, syntax, all are available to the prose poem in their full variety.

Harder to describe is why a certain poem wants to be a prose poem and not a poem in lines. Since I believe that the appearance of a more relaxed line is, for the most part, an illusion in prose poems, it must be the illusion itself that occasionally attracts me to them.

And when, by the end of a prose poem, a revelation or epiphany of some sort has been achieved, it is particularly satisfying. You look at it and you say, Why, I thought I was just reading a paragraph or two, but, by golly, methinks I glimpsed a little sliver of eternity.

Lewis Turco *was born in Buffalo, New York, in 1934, but was raised in Meriden, Connecticut. He founded the Cleveland Poetry Center at what is now the Cleveland State University in the early 1960s, and the program in writing arts at the State University of New York, Oswego, in 1968, which he has directed ever since. He has published some thirty-five books, chapbooks, and monographs of various kinds, including* The New Book of Forms *(University Press of New England, 1986);* Visions and Revisions of American Poetry *(University of Arkansas Press, 1986), a book of criticism that won the Melville Cane Award of the Poetry Society of America;* The Shifting Web: New and Selected Poems *(University of Arkansas Press, 1989);* The Public Poet *(Ashland University Poetry Press, 1991);* Dialogue *(Reader's Digest Books, 1991); and* Emily Dickinson, Woman of Letters *(State University of New York Press, 1993). Also in 1993, he was inducted into the Meriden Hall of Fame, other members of which include diva Rosa Ponselle and his Meriden High School classmate of 1952, Tomie DePaola. He is currently writing a literary handbook for Oxford University Press,* The Oxford Handbook of Literary Forms.

Winter Bouquet
On Lines from Emily Dickinson's Letters

It storms in Amherst five days—
it snows, and then it rains, and then
soft fogs like veils hang on all the houses,
and then the days turn topaz

like a lady's pin. The hills
take off their purple frocks and dress
in long white nightgowns. The men were
mowing the second hay not

long since—the cocks were smaller
than the first, and spicier. I
would distill a cup, bear it to my friends,
drinking to summer no more

astir, make a balloon of
a dandelion, but the fields
are gone where children walked the tangled road,
some of them to the end, some

but a little way, even
as far as the fork. Remembrance
is more sweet than robins in May orchards.
Today is very cold, yet

I have much bouquet upon
the window pane—of moss and fern.
I call then saints' flowers, because they do
not romp as other flowers

do, but stand so still and white.
I enjoy much with a precious
fly, not one of your blue monsters, but a
timid creature that hops from

pane to pane of her white house
so very cheerfully, and hums
and thrums—a sort of speck piano. I
have one new bird and several

trees of old ones. A snow slide
from the roof dispelled the sweetbrier.
There are as yet no streets, though the sun is
riper. This is a landscape

of frost and zeros. I wish
"the faith of the fathers" didn't
wear brogans and carry blue umbrellas.
The doubt, like the mosquito,

buzzes round my faith. My heart
has flown before, my breaking voice

follows—that bareheaded life under grass
worries me like a wasp—life

of flowers lain in flowers—
what a home of dew to come to!
We reckon by the fruit. When the grape gets
by, and the pippin and the

chestnut—when the days are a
little short by the clock, and a
little long by the lack—when the sky has
new red gowns and a purple

bonnet, I am glad that kind
of time goes by. Twilight is but
the short bridge, and the moon stands at the end.
With Nature in my ruche, I

shall not miss the spring, the seasons falling
and the leaves—the moulting goldfinch singing.

A Sampler of Hours

During the winter of 1980 I was reading a book that contained an essay about Emily Dickinson, and in that essay there were quoted some lines from Emily Dickinson's letters: "The Moon rides like a girl through a topaz town." "Tonight the Crimson Children are playing in the west." "The lawn is full of south and the odours tangle, and I hear today for the first the river in the trees." "Not what the stars have done, but what they are to do is what detains the sky."

I was so struck by these sounds and images, which were more modern, I felt, than even the lines of Dickinson's poetry, that I immediately set to work writing poems that included, and tried to live up to, these lines.

This was, no doubt many people will feel, a foolhardy thing to do, but I had attempted the same sort of thing with Robert Burton's seventeenth-century book, *The Anatomy of Melancholy*, and I produced a manuscript of poems based on Burton's lines titled *The Compleat Melancholick*, subtitled "A Sequence of Found, Composite, and Composed Poems" (St. Paul: Bieler Press, 1984). I felt, and feel, that the poems did little damage to Burton and that some of them are among my better work.

When I had finished the first four Dickinson-based poems, I went to the library and checked out her collected letters, hoping to find other lines I might quarry. Much later I was fortunate enough to find a copy I could purchase for my own library. Now, four years later, I have written sixty poems in a series I have titled *A Sampler of Hours*. One of these poems is "Winter Bouquet." People who read these pieces sometimes want to know which lines are Dickinson's and which are mine. At first I had tried italicizing her words, but that practice seemed to break up the poems badly. Sometimes internal evidence will provide clues, but not always. At times, I have done little more than select lines and cast them into syllabic prosody, letting the first few lines fall as naturally as possible into their own lengths in the first stanza and then casting succeeding lines into the same pattern as the first. More often, I have taken lines from various letters and "arranged" them in some sort of order. Reasonably often I have "augmented" her lines with my own—some poems are more mine than Dickinson's. But the shortest poem in the series may serve as an example of the method of composition I used most often:

The Gift
A one-armed man conveyed the flowers.
I gave him half a smile.

The first line is Dickinson's, the second is mine.

On one occasion—when I was giving a reading from these poems in Portland, Oregon—I was accused by a woman of "tampering with an American classic," but this is not so. I have touched nothing of the canon of that classic—the poems themselves—only her letters, which few people read. If any of these poems work, then all I've done is bring to the attention of a modern audience a number of Emily Dickinson's beautiful and startling observations that would otherwise have stayed buried in the bulk of her prose.

This, it seems to me, would have been a shame. I have never met a person who had such a brilliantly wide-ranging mind, or such an ability to toss off, seemingly at random and on any occasion, images as arresting and colorful as any in American poetry, or to match in depth of perception and succinctness of expression the flowers of anyone's intellectual garden.

John Updike

was born in Shillington, Pennsylvania, in 1932. He attended the local public schools, Harvard College, and the Ruskin School of Drawing and Fine Art. He worked for two years as a "Talk of the Town" reporter for the New Yorker, to which he has contributed poems, short stories, essays, and book reviews. Since 1957 he has lived in Massachusetts as a freelance writer. He is the author of some forty books. His sixteen novels include Rabbit, Run *(1960),* Couples *(1968),* Rabbit Redux *(1971),* The Coup *(1978),* Rabbit Is Rich *(1981),* Roger's Version *(1986),* Rabbit at Rest *(1990), and* Brazil *(1994). Among his books of short stories are* Bech: A Book *(1970),* Bech Is Back *(1982), and* The Afterlife and Other Stories *(Knopf, 1995). He won the National Book Critics Circle Award in criticism for* Hugging the Shore *(1983) and in fiction for* Rabbit at Rest *(1990). He recently published his* Collected Poems, 1953–1993 *(Knopf). "The idea of verse, of poetry, has always, during forty years spent working primarily in prose, stood at my elbow, as a standing invitation to the highest kind of verbal exercise—the most satisfying, the most archaic, the most elusive of critical control," Updike has written.*

The Naked Ape
(Following, Perhaps All Too Closely, Desmond Morris's Anthropological Revelations)

The dinosaur died, and small
   Insectivores (how gruesome!) crawled
From bush to tree, from bug to bud,
   From spider-diet to forest fruit and nut,
Developing bioptic vision and
   The grasping hand.

These perfect monkeys then were faced
   With shrinking groves; the challenged race,
De-Edenized by glacial whim,
   Sent forth from its arboreal cradle him
Who engineered himself to run
   With deer and lion—

The "naked ape." Why naked? Well,
   Upon those meaty plains, that *veldt*

Of prey, as pellmell they competed
    With cheetahs, hairy primates overheated;
Selection pressure, just though cruel,
    Favored the cool.

Unlikeliest of hunters, nude
    And weak and tardy to mature,
This ill-cast carnivore attacked,
    With weapons he invented, *in a pack.*
The tribe was born. To set men free,
    The family

Evolved; monogamy occurred.
    The female—sexually alert
Throughout the month, equipped to have
    Pronounced orgasms—perpetrated love.
The married state decreed its *lex
    Privata:* sex.

And Nature, pandering, bestowed
    On virgin ears erotic lobes
And hung on women hemispheres
    That imitate their once-attractive rears:
A social animal disarms
    With frontal charms.

All too erogenous, the ape
    To give his lusts a decent shape
Conceived the cocktail party where
    Unmates refuse to touch each other's hair
And make small "grooming" talk instead
    Of going to bed.

He drowns his body scents in baths
    And if, in some conflux of paths,
He bumps another, says, "Excuse
    Me, *please."* He suffers rashes and subdues
Aggressiveness by making fists
    And laundry lists,

Suspension bridges, aeroplanes,
    And charts that show biweekly gains

And losses. Noble animal!
  To try to lead on this terrestrial ball,
With grasping hand and saucy wife,
  The upright life.

The poem I have chosen—"The Naked Ape"—is light verse, of which I
once wrote a great deal. Light verse adhered to rhyme and metrical
strictness long after serious poets had gone the way of *vers libre,* and for
a good reason: there is something comic, something of the imposition of
the mechanical upon the organic which Henri Bergson defined as the
essence of the comic, about poetic form in the old sense, and many a
solemn Victorian chant now rings in our ears rather humorously. Lewis
Carroll needed to twit Isaac Watts's hymns very little to turn them into
jokes.

In my poem, I was amused by the something overdeveloped, we
might say—mechanical, indeed—about Desmond Morris's reconstruction of our sexual evolution in his "Naked Ape," and I thought that
simply turning his theories into stanzas and rhymes might lead a reader
to share my amusement. The first stanza came, and then the challenge
was to duplicate its rather intricate form repeatedly. The rhyme scheme
is blunt enough—*a a b b c c*—but the tetrameters are varied by a
pentameter in the fourth line and a dimeter in the sixth. Oddly enough, I
notice now that my first and model stanza in fact violates this intended
form with a pentameter fifth line as well; no doubt the polysyllabic
words tricked me into thinking I had a four-beat line here and not a five-.
But two pentameters per stanza would be too many; the tetrameter line
preserves bounce whereas pentameter tends to lose it amid the caesuras
of conversational rhythm. The effect of this poem depends upon the
complexities of scientific explanation as they fall into a plainly audible,
rather balladic form.

It took effort, of course, to work the sense into the pattern; off-
rhymes are resorted to (e.g., the fourth stanza) and occasional strain can
be felt, as in the penultimate stanza. But the perils of adhering to a strict
form (stiffness, awkwardness, padding) are balanced by the seren-
dipitous delights that the form forces us to create. The fifth stanza, for
instance, struck me at the time, and still strikes me, as especially happy.
In the third stanza, the "pellmell," taken with "veldt" and "prey" and
"competed," gives us a touch of that *extra* music without which light
verse is merely wooden and fails to earn the extra trouble its formalism
asks of reader and writer both. Where the music must be so strictly
tended to, inadvertencies that a freer form would gladly absorb annoy;

the "make" of stanza eight and the "making" of stanza nine are an unwelcome pair, and if I could think of any way around them ("forming fists / And laundry lists" is possible but farfetched) I would take it. To write in a strict form exposes one to constant consciousness of imperfection; to write without an overt form softens such consciousness, perhaps too mercifully. The case was neatly put by the informal Frank O'Hara: "As for measure and other technical apparatus, that's just common sense: if you're going to buy a pair of pants you want them to be tight enough so everyone will want to go to bed with you." This attractive tightness, until a century ago, has been almost unanimously sought by poets in the fit of fixed metrical form; but no doubt it can be obtained by other means of tailoring as well, and with stitching that doesn't so much show.

Mona Van Duyn was born in Waterloo, Iowa, in 1921, and moved

to Eldora, Iowa, at the age of one. Having earned an M.A. at the University of Iowa, she went on to teach there while earning her Ph.D. She then taught writing and literature at the University of Louisville. Since 1950 she has lived in St. Louis. She served as the Poet Laureate and Consultant in Poetry to the Library of Congress in 1992–1993, and describes her duties as follows: "I commuted to Washington every month for five days, appointed the readers for the year's poetry and literature series and introduced them, gave an inaugural reading and a final lecture (since printed by the Library of Congress), gave seventy-two interviews on television, radio, National Public Radio, and for newspapers and magazines in the U.S., Russia, Europe, China, etc., answered all the many letters written to the Laureate, gave readings in the area, and wrote three public poems. I also saw two books through the press, If It Be Not I: Collected Poems, 1959–1982 *and* Firefall, *a new book. These two books, along with* Near Changes, *all published by Knopf, contain my life's work."*

The Ballad of Blossom

The lake is known as West Branch Pond.
It is round as a soapstone griddle.
Ten log cabins nose its sand,
with a dining lodge in the middle.

Across the water Whitecap Mountain
darkens the summer sky,
and loons yodel and moose wade in,
and trout take the feathered fly.

At camp two friendly characters
live out their peaceful days
in the flowery clearing edged by firs
and a-buzz with bumble bees:

Alcott the dog, a charming fool
who sniffs out frog and snake
and in clumsy capering will fall
from docks into the lake,

and Blossom the cow, whose yield is vaunted
and who wears the womanly shape
of a yellow carton badly dented
in some shipping mishap,

with bulging sack appended below
where a full five gallons stream
to fill puffshells and make berries glow
in lakes of golden cream.

Her face is calm and purged of thought
when mornings she mows down fern
and buttercup and forget-me-not
and panties on the line.

Afternoons she lies in the shade
and chews over circumstance.
On Alcott nestled against her side
she bends a benevolent glance.

Vacationers climb Whitecap's side,
pick berries, bird-watch or swim.
Books are read and Brookies fried,
and the days pass like a dream.

But one evening campers collect on the shelf
of beach for a comic sight.

Blossom's been carried out of herself
by beams of pale moonlight.

Around the cabins she chases Alcott,
leaping a fallen log,
then through the shallows at awesome gait
she drives the astonished dog.

Her big bag bumps against her legs,
bounces and swings and sways.
Her tail flings into whirligigs
that would keep off flies for days.

Then Alcott collects himself and turns
and chases Blossom back,
then walks away as one who has learned
to take a more dignified tack.

Next all by herself she kicks up a melee.
Her udder shakes like a churn.
To watching campers it seems she really
intends to jump over the moon.

Then she chases the cook, who throws a broom
that flies between her horns,
and butts at the kitchen door for a home,
having forgotten barns.

Next morning the cow begins to moo.
The volume is astounding.
MOOOAWWW crosses the lake, and MAWWWW
from Whitecap comes rebounding.

Two cow moose in the lake lift heads,
their hides in sun like watered
silk, then scoot back into the woods,
their female nerves shattered.

MOOOAWWW! and in frightened blue and yellows
swallows and finches fly,
shaping in flocks like open umbrellas
wildly waved in the sky.

In boats the fishermen lash their poles
and catch themselves with their flies,
their timing spoiled by Blossom's bawls,
and trout refuse to rise.

MAWWOOOO! No one can think or read.
Such agony shakes the heart.
All morning Alcott hides in the woodshed.
At lunch, tempers are short.

A distant moo. Then silence. Some said
that boards were fitted in back
to hold her in, and Blossom was led
up a platform into the truck,

where she would bump and dip and soar
over many a rocky mile
to Greenville, which has a grocery store
as well as the nearest bull.

But the camp is worried. How many days
will the bellowing go on?
"I hope they leave her there," one says,
"until the heat is gone."

Birds criss-cross the sky with nowhere to go.
Suspense distorts the scene.
Alcott patrols on puzzled tiptoe.
It is late in the afternoon

when back she comes in the bumping truck
and steps down daintily,
a silent cow who refuses to look
anyone in the eye.

Nerves settle. A swarm of bumblebees
bends Blue-eyed grass for slaking.
A clink of pans from the kitchen says
the amorous undertaking

is happily concluded. Porches
hold pairs with books or drinks.

Resident squirrels resume their searches.
Alcott sits and thinks.

Beads of birds re-string themselves
along the telephone wire.
A young bull moose in velvet delves
in water near the shore.

Blossom lies like a crumpled sack
in blooms of chamomile.
Her gaze is inward. Her jaw is slack.
She might be said to smile.

At supper, laughter begins and ends,
for the mood is soft and shy.
One couple is seen to be holding hands
over wild raspberry pie.

Orange and gold flame Whitecap's peak
as the sun begins to set,
and anglers bend to the darkening lake
and bring up a flopping net.

When lamps go out and the moon lays light
on the lake like a great beachtowel,
Eros wings down to a fir to sit
and hoot* like a Long-eared owl.

Usually I do not wish to participate in symposia of this kind, or in interviews, which require me to inspect my own creative processes. I'm afraid they remind me of the women's lib fad for examining one's own reproductive organs (one of the funniest clippings a friend ever sent me was an article suggesting a speculum as the ideal gift for every woman on one's Christmas list). I prefer to leave that sort of probe to the critic-doctor, either male or female. But the chance to say something on behalf of the pleasures of working with the for-so-long-beleaguered formal poem tempts me.

My love of poetry came from nursery rhymes and continued to be nourished on the rhymed verse in school anthologies of that day; college

---

*The Long-eared owl's hoot resembles the whistle of tribute to the sight of something beautiful and sexy: wheé *whée-you*.

reading offered me an alternative love in the earlier surge of free-verse fashion, which included Whitman, Masters, Sandburg, A. Lowell, H.D. and others, and I have continued to write in both forms, according to the whim of the poem at hand. But I confess to a preference for the poem that comes to me expressing, by whatever mysterious means—the donnée of a line, a vague sense of musical pattern, a nudge of the will to collaborate appropriately with an "idea," or something unanalyzable—a wish to be formal. Why? A friend's son who has recently begun to write stories said in surprise and wonder, "It's the most satisfying thing you can do all by yourself," thereby speaking for us all, it seemed to me. For me, writing a formal poem increases that satisfaction by deepening and intensifying the out-of-body concentration, with its little flares of joy when the right word comes, which we all seek and find in writing poems of whatever kind.

"Why rhyme?" John Hollander asks in his poem "Footnote To A Desperate Letter" (*New York Review of Books,* 25 October 1984). "To make it harder . . . When files of words are labelled 'Shut'?" Yes, otherwise-perfect words are excluded, the labor of love becomes still more arduous, and the mind escapes its habitual limits. I only wish to add that the opposite may happen too, and "locked," or at least stuck, files of words may open. I must speak autobiographically here: When one spends many years of one's life in small towns, even though one is a reader-writer, one's use-vocabulary normally is small and plain. In a city, one may communicate daily with like-minded people, and also employ speech for jostling, competing with, insulting, swaying others. In small towns, where one must spend close daily life with unchosen fellows, the major use of speech is to accommodate. A small-town reader-writer has an island of use-vocabulary, set in a vast sea of recognition vocabulary, which using rhyme forces him to embark upon. Words that he loves, but that do not readily come to mind for use, are found by rowing out after rhyme. Free verse, which draws from the island of speech, does not force this quest. (I have sometimes tried, unsuccessfully, to persuade city critics of the virtues of certain examples of small-town Middlewestern free verse. Unwilling to look past the plain style for other qualities, they take it as simple-minded.) Concentration is also deepened by the constraints of meter, of course, with its constant questions of when to be regular, when to open up the foot, and so on. As a result, I can freely leave an unfinished free-verse poem to prepare a meal, sleep, have a drink with friends, but a formal poem follows me everywhere, makes me hard to live with, and gives me pleasure approaching the ecstatic.

I cannot now remember with certainty how the choice of form came to me for this poem, but I think it was by receiving the first two lines. I do remember the delight with which, some months after leaving Maine, and after some years of preoccupation with aged and ailing parents and a few consequent poems dealing with endings, I arrived at the idea of a poem in celebration of sexuality, where it all begins. I do not often use received forms, but I do sometimes enjoy the attempt to reanimate them, and I have always loved the ballad. For wholly private enjoyment I used to write light verse ballads during my high school years. When the poem and I chose its form, I was of course faced with the memory of two brilliant modern ballads, Elizabeth Bishop's "The Burglar of Babylon" and James Merrill's "Days of 1935"—a daunting confrontation. I decided to rhyme, for my own pleasure, not only the second and fourth lines of the stanza, as Bishop does, but also the first and third, as Merrill had done. As I wrote, I came close to regretting that choice, for it seemed to me that a rhyme was required almost before I could move the poem more than an inch across the page, before I could take a step in any narrative or descriptive direction.

I wanted a light tone for my serious subject and so decided, as I wrote, on clipped, closed stanzas (the third through sixth stanzas are my longest run-on in the poem). But I wanted also to paint in the scene and found that the short, closed stanza confined me to the merest short brushstrokes of depiction. I remember very clearly one instance of what can happen when one searches through rhyming words for the right one (for this search includes a continuous discarding of the many words that rhyme too heavily in the wrong place, rhyme too habitually, or simply do not serve one's purposes). As I looked for a rhyme for "yellows" my mind tossed me "umbrellas," and with an inward smile, I discarded it as absurdly useless. One instant later I *saw* the startled flocks of swallows and finches in the Maine sky, and they looked exactly like wildly waved open umbrellas. This now seems to me the most accurately observed descriptive detail in the poem, and I would not have seen it at all if I had not been working in rhyme.

Paul Violi was born in New York in 1944 and grew up in Greenlawn, Long Island. After studying English literature and art history at Boston University, he traveled through Africa, Europe, and Asia, and then returned to New York, where he was managing editor of the Architectural Forum and worked on special projects for Universal Limited Art Editions. He helped organize a reading series at the Museum of Modern Art for many years, and, *with Charles North, edited and published a series of books by contemporary poets. He has received two fellowships in poetry from the National Endowment for the Arts as well as grants from the Fund for Poetry, the New York State Council for the Arts, and the Ingram Merrill Foundation. His books include* The Curious Builder *and* Likewise *from Hanging Loose Press,* Splurge *and* Harmatan *from Sun Press, and* In Baltic Circles *from Kulchur Press. In England in 1993 he curated an exhibition of Kenneth Koch's collaborations with artists.*

Index

Analysis of important works:
  Wine glass with fingerprints
  Nude on a blue sofa
  The drunken fox trappers
  Man wiping tongue with large towel
  Hay bales stacked in a field
  Self-portrait
  Self-portrait with cat
  Self-portrait with frozen mop
  Self-portrait with belching duck 135
Correspondence with Cecco Angolieri 136
Dispute over attribution of lines: "I have as large supply of
  evils / as January has not flowerings." 137
Builds first greenhouse 139
Falling out with Angolieri 139
Flees famine 144
Paints *Starved cat eating snow* 145
Arrested for selling sacks of wind to gullible peasants 146
Imprisonment and bewildment 147
Disavows all his work 158
Invents the collar stay 159
Convalescence with third wife 162
Complains of "a dense and baleful wind blowing the words
  I write off the page." 165
Meets with Madame T. 170
Departures, mortal premonitions, "I think I'm about to
  snow." 176
Disavows all his work 181
Arrest and pardon 182
Last days 183
Last words 184, 185, 186, 187, 188, 189, 190

To say that the form and subject of "Index" came to me simultaneously and continued to modify each other as I wrote the poem, may sound a bit convenient, but that is what usually happens when I use a prose form. I had been reading an autobiography—I forgot whose, a completely unnecessary book by an egregiously self-indulgent man—and I noticed that the author's egotism even seeped into the end papers, especially the index which by condensing his life seemed to magnify his faults. A different character came to mind, one who was not quite the master of his fate, and an index, with its fragmentary lines, suggested a way to catch both the quick, haphazard changes such a character would endure and his increasingly scrambled perception of them. As I assembled the poem it began to resemble a chronology. This helped define the character more clearly for me and gave the static index, which was developing imagistically, a linear movement as well. The page numbers, initially tacked on as decoration, worked like dates, punctuating the events they paralleled. From then on it was like a run of blind luck in putting a jigsaw puzzle together. The pieces fell into place with little shifting or revision. By going back and indenting all the lines after the first I hoped to imply that the poem was an extract from an index to a larger book, a collection of lives that never made it into Vasari. One change that seems trivial, quirky, in retrospect was misspelling Angiolieri's name (it often appears with variant spelling) but I was going on the impression that indexes are not as carefully proofread as texts. In a way, when I use a prose form I feel I'm adapting a persona, one that speaks a mock-prose. With "Index" I knew I'd set-off and continued to play-off an "argument" between the neutral if not deadpan tone and the wild particulars of the life it described. With regard to formal considerations, how much is a deliberate choice and how much just happens I can't say, but when I do use such forms I assume I'm employing a simple metaphor, a familiar if not trite context yet a very accessible one, by which I don't mean to celebrate the ordinary but to subvert it.

Rosmarie Waldrop *was born in Kitzin-*
gen, Germany, in
1935. Her books of poetry include Lawn of Excluded Middle *(Tender Buttons),* The Reproduction of Profiles *(New Directions), and most recently,* A Key into the Language of America *(New Directions). She has also published two novels,* The Hanky of Pippin's Daughter *and* A Form/of Taking/It all *(Station Hill). She lived in Paris in 1970 and 1971 and regards that experience as a turning point in her career. She has translated the work of Edmond Jabes, Jacques Roubaud, Paul Celan, and Friederike Mayrocker. She was recently a guest of the DAAD Artists Program in Berlin. She lives in Providence, Rhode Island, where she and Keith Waldrop are codirectors of Burning Deck Press.*

Shorter American Memory of the American Character according to Santayana

All Americans are also ambiguous. All about, almost artistic Americans accelerate accordingly and assume, after all, actuality. But before beams, boys break. Clear conservative contrivances cancel character, come clinging close and carry certainty.

An American does, distinguishes, dreams. Degrees, experience, economy, emergencies, enthusiasm and education are expected. For future forecasts, forces far from form fall and find fulfilment. Good God. Gets growing, goes handling himself and his help (hardly happy).

Immediate invention. Intense imagination? Ideals instead. He jumps, it is known. Life, at least Leah, her left leg. Much measured material might modestly marry masterly movement.

Nature? Never. Numbers. Once otherwise. Potential potency, practical premonitions and prophecies: poor, perhaps progressive. Quick! Reforms realize a rich Rebecca. Same speed so successfully started stops sympathetic sense of slowly seething society. Studious self-confidence.

Time. Terms. Things. The train there, true. Ultimately understanding vast works where which would.

It was an important moment for me when I realized consciously that the encounter of a poem-nucleus with an arbitrary pattern (like a rhyme scheme) would tend to pull the nucleus out of its semantic field in unforeseen directions. The tension always generates great energy, not just for bridging the "gap" between original intention and the pattern, but for pushing the whole poem farther. When it works, the poem grows richer for being "stretched."

I'm spelling out what Ashbery and others have called the liberating effect of constraints. But what matters is that *any* constraint, *any* pattern can be generative in this way. It does not need to be one of the traditional forms with their heavy closure effect of regularity and recurrence.

"Shorter American Memory of the American Character according to Santayana" is an extreme case of constraints. I set out to write an abecedarium, limiting myself to the words used in Santayana's essay "The American Character." The only freedom I allowed myself was the arrangement and articulation of the words beginning with the same letter.

This kind of extreme formalism rarely works to my satisfaction. More often I use a pattern (e.g., the grammatical structure of a given text), but *also* let the words push and pull in their own directions. Since I make the rules, I also feel free to break them.

Rosanna Warren was born in Connecticut

in 1953. Her books of poetry include Each Leaf Shines Separate *(Norton, 1984) and* Stained Glass *(Norton, 1995). A contributing editor of* Partisan Review, *she is assistant professor at Boston University in the University Professors Program, the English department, and the modern foreign languages department. Her most recent publication is a translation of Euripides'* Suppliant Women *(with Stephen Scully), which Oxford University Press published in 1995. She edited and contributed to* The Art of Translation: Voices from the Field *(Northeastern University Press, 1989). She is working on a biography of Max Jacob with the support of a three-year writer's award from the Lila Wallace–Reader's Digest Fund.*

Poetry Reading

manibus date lilia plenis

—*Aeneid VI*

It is a promise they bear in their hands.
Feathers waver in the ghostly crests.
Rome is an iron glint in the eyes,
a twitch at swordhilt. Down the long avenue
through silted shadow and pale leaking light
stalks the future. Power,
whispers the father, power bounded
only by the edge of earth, the rim of heaven.
The arts of peace, the rule of law:
the Capitol, aqueducts, legions, circuses.

Disorder chained in the temple. Abundant calm.
In such love you have given yourself.

But who is that young one, pallid
in armor with darkened brow
and night coming on at his heels,
scent of crushed lilies, a bruise—

Here the reading breaks off.
The Emperor's sister breaks into hysterical tears,
patrons and literati disband.
Servants clear away winecups, platters of cake.

And Aeneas climbs back into daylight
through the Gate of false dreams.

"Poetry Reading" is obviously a form of minor commentary on book VI
of *The Aeneid,* where Virgil imagines his hero receiving a promise of an
imperial future from the shade of his father, Anchises. The poem was
composed in response to a request from the *Washington Post* for a poem
"about" the inauguration of President Clinton. Having at first confessed
my ineptitude at any such task, I found myself haunted by the figure of
another young man presented with a vision of great power and great
responsibility. I was haunted as well by the ironies attendant upon the
relations of poets to political authority, particularly in an imperial structure such as Augustan Rome, where the emperor was the patron and in
some sense instigator of the poem. My little poem, with its deliberately
deadpan and emphatic meter (iambic, with many spondees, trochaic
reversals, and some hobbyhorse anapests) explores the crack in the vision of grandeur, the mortal failure and grief at the death of Marcellus,
Augustus's young nephew who was thought to be the hope of Rome. By
extension, then, it introduces elegy into an occasion of celebration, tragic
premonition into the assumption of success. It tries to do so in a tight-
lipped style, in end-stopped clauses and fairly unadorned presentation,
with a metrical contraction to trimeter in the final couplet suggesting
other potential contractions of overblown hopes.

Marjorie Welish was born in New York City
in 1944. She is an art critic
as well as a poet and has taught regularly at Brown University and

Pratt Institute. Her most recent books of poems are The Windows Flew Open *(Burning Deck, 1991) and* Casting Sequences *(University of Georgia Press, 1993). She has received grants from the Fund for Poetry and the New York Foundation for the Arts. Her art criticism has appeared in such magazines as* Arts Magazine, Bomb, Partisan Review, *and* Salmagundi. *She lives in New York City.*

Street Cries

I think I shall end by not feeling lonesome,
only scoured by the lengthy light of everyone.
Nice, fine milk, fine milk, the best of all milk.

Balancing the persuasive long pole
of friendship on a stone,
I think I shall end by not feeling lonesome.

I have lived and eaten simply.
I have leaned against the shape of handsome choices.
This almanac conceals a pasture you would like.

The universe is cast in consequences.
Draw my name in milk on canvas.
I doubt I shall end by not feeling lonesome,

but this is outrageous:
come buy my ground ivy, come buy my water cresses.
The ink is wrong, but a battered almanac is not a heartless
    almanac.

But is it time to combine and speak out?
The day gazes helplessly at time.
I think I shall end by not feeling lonesome,
the pamphlets yellow, the milk also: milk, the fine milk.

The garland of sentiment that characterizes a villanelle prevails over almost any attempt at informality. Even indulging in relaxed line lengths, three rhymes instead of the prescribed two, does not erode the lyrical form of the villanelle very much. Nor, I found, do the intrusive subjects and rhythms of traditional street cries delivered by peddlars.

It has often been said that a strict form like the villanelle sets up expectations and gives pleasure as these expectations are fulfilled or resisted. I enjoyed resisting expectations of lyricism by inviting the "noise" of seventeenth-century London to add harshness and relentlessness to the courtly repetitions the villanelle provided as a frame. My aim: to achieve affective complexity through this fusion of cry and song. (Incidentally, a French street cry Guillaume Apollinaire admired puts in a cameo appearance here.) In any event, a form kept in mind while composing a poem urges strong criteria of excellence that will help structure the process and final product, for a poem does not have to illustrate a given form to emulate and be empowered by it.

Bernard Welt was born in Houston, Texas, in 1952, and raised in Arlington, Virginia. He received an M.A. in creative writing at the Johns Hopkins University and a doctorate in literary studies from the American University. He has been awarded a creative writing fellowship from the National Endowment for the Arts. His book of poems, Serenade, was published by Z. Press. He is the chairman of the Department of Academic Studies at the Corcoran School of Art in Washington, D.C., and a contributing editor of Art Issues, for which he has written a series of articles on fantasy in film, television, and other popular arts, including essays on Michael Jackson, Star Trek, The Wizard of Oz, The Simpsons, and Dr. Seuss. He is currently working on an interlinked set of short plays: My Instrument, The Couch, and The Siegels.

Prose

What is the subject? It looks like a paragraph,
Like an analyst's pencil. It's not a pipe,
But that much is obvious, or flowers in a vase,
Or a nude disguised as so much fabric. Rhetoric,
You single out faces from deepening crowds,
To turn them on lathes till they come to resemble us.

I was marooned—I mean metaphorically—
And the solitude in that tall vegetation
I found stifling, though I understood perfectly
Once I was there I was appointed caretaker.
The sconces lighting the halls I also shrank from
And looked for relief from the sound of the breakers.

My friends the animals helped me, for which
I spare them the naming. They offered me
Images of maps and small tombs, and valium
To assuage fear of eternity. Still in my infancy,
I escaped happiness and that textured plantation,
Grateful acknowledgment being hereby made.

The occasion for this poem was a desire to respond to Mallarmé's "Prose pour des Esseintes," which suggested the poem-as-desert-island metaphor of the second stanza. The opening question came separately, and was only later fitted together with some almost absurdly prosaic statements—"It looks like a paragraph" and "I mean metaphorically"—to establish the central idea of some laboring to state the obvious in the midst of much confusion—which is not such a bad way to look at poetry, come to think of it.

The basic structure of the poem was already determined. Since I have been writing mostly long pieces in prose lately, I began using this improvisatory form of three six-line stanzas to accommodate less ambitious projects, and things that really seemed to need to be in verse, for the sake of the sound. The strict framework of beginning, middle, and end provides the sense of an argument without making argument itself necessary, and perhaps lends conviction through mere orderliness. I like being able to make a new start with each new stanza—it gives me the feeling of covering a great distance in a few lines. One clear advantage of the form is that it provides an alternative to the sonnet, and guards me from the temptation to take on and violate an established convention when that isn't genuinely a part of the poem's intent.

With the skeletal form, the occasion, and a few phrases settled, the development of the poem was the extension of these basics, drawing them nearer each other through various kinds of association—of sound, for instance. Thus *rhetoric* suggested *fabric,* and *eternity, infancy,* and the dactyllic rhythm of the introduction kept recurring sporadically. I like quirky rhythms and strange echoes better than stately measures and exact rhymes, and I think this is more than just a matter of taste: I want to impose order on my thoughts, but I look for an order that is loose and subtle enough to allow them to grow into new forms.

In the absence of the traditional conventions of prosody, however, there seems to be a special pressure on tropes to do the work of the poem, to generate new ideas and pleasing language. For most people, it is the figures of speech that mark writing as "poetic." Like rhyme and meter, they alert the reader to the fact that language is being stretched beyond its pragmatic, everyday use. The controlling trope in this poem is self-reference, or Romantic irony; at least, it is what unified the poem for me, applying the paradox of the title, which challenges the status of the poem, to the poem's opening question, and raising it again at the end. This makes the problem of form especially vexing, if the form of a poem is conceived as a vehicle for ideas, since here the ideas all seem to lead back to the poem itself. It was my attempt to decipher Mallarmé that started all of this, you'll recall, and I found I could respond to his paradox only with one of my own—not an explication but an appreciation, an attempt to employ his method. I can feel some sympathy, then, toward the speaker in "Prose," who considers himself lucky to be leaving the world of the poem behind, just as, in the closing line, he discovers a purpose for it: to dedicate the poem to those "friends" that have helped him escape it. Even if it creates a circle of reasoning that seems inescapable, I hope this assures that the poem *does* have a purpose and that the question posed at its beginning has been answered.

Susan Wheeler *was born in Pittsburgh in 1955. Her first book,* Bag 'o' Diamonds *(University of Georgia Press, 1993) was selected by James Tate to receive the Poetry Society of America's Norma Farber First Book Award, and was short-listed for the Los Angeles Times Book Awards. Her poems have appeared in the 1988, 1991, 1993, and 1996 editions of* The Best American Poetry *as well as in the 1994 Pushcart Prize anthology. She lives in New York City, where she teaches at the New School for Social Research. Until February 1995 she was director of public affairs for Arts and Science at New York University. She was the Thornton Writer in Residence at Lynchburg College in Virginia in spring 1995.*

Ezra's Lament

I owed the baker three dollies with heads.
I owed the singer a way to recoup.
I owed the bookmaker my mother's own sauce.
I owed the outfielder plenty, plenty.

I owed the swimmer a new way of speech.
Lucky I was that the view of the villa

Prevented my pitching the book overboard.
I owed the industrialist pinafore threads.

I owed the waters drops from my lenses,
I owed the bereaved, I owed a tiger,
A dentist, a hobbyist, a smallish crook,
The maîtresse d'hôtel—the shiniest stones.

What breath employs me whose salary should be
Paid in tenders I don't understand?
The bankruptcy makes ichnites of heirlooms
Strung across oxidized fiberboard pegs.

I owed Winslow a flowering grove, a bower.
I owed a simpleton plenty, plenty.
I owed the gentlest of Barbie collectors
A wracked afflicter and a soupçon of sand.

Machinate carefully, o if you should go there,
Clicking the debts like a rotary phone
Where the lifeline is sparked in the vectors.
That frantic believing will break you in two.

I owed who raised me the still of my back,
The television's glint in the model set store,
And I owed my brother a bike.
I owed the fence these colorform 'toons.

The parch in the Playland is criminogenic.
I owed the insects swarming the creditors
Their own salt hearts, brittling the trees.
The army, and air force, plenty I owed.

O if you should go there in your twenty years
Remember the wank that you cannot repay,
O if you should, there in your twenty years.

The closer the poem is to my bone, the stricter I tend to make its setup, although the setup generally evolves while I'm working, and rarely is it a kind of initial "self-assignment." (When it is, I don't seem to have the skill to make it more than illustrative: illustrating the formal idea and not much more.) Here, the premise that quickly evolved as I worked out the first few lines was a long series of varied assertions, many beginning "I owed," that modulated its density of stressed syllables so as to mix an almost children's-rhyme rhythm with one that alternated between tumbling (through many unstressed syllables) and abrupt truncation.

Modulation in the types of sentences also seemed important, and this, too, evolved as I went along. I have always been a fan of the cinematic extending of a scene long past reasonable tolerance (as in Cassavetes, Warhol, Godard), and within the fairly clippy pace of this poem I tried in two places—the second stanza and the fourth—to make a couple of static moments over two lines that would brake the speed at the beginning. Directives to the reader intrude in another two places, and in others, strings of clauses, a rhetorical question, and the repetition of "plenty"—identically structured in two lines and altered in its third appearance—helped to modulate the series.

This was critical because of the gravity of tone I felt the poem needed in order to get the full of "Ezra's Lament." Named for the poet obsessed with debt and its interest, the poem and "owing" itself needed simple words and images to anchor its abstract operation (thus "baker," "my mother's own sauce," "the shiniest stones"). "Tougher" words, however, and especially those with hard consonants ("ichnites," "afflicter," "machinate"), seemed to give the simpler assertions some bite. With that, I hoped they helped to get across the combination of a child's diction with that of a rather obsessive adult who is accustomed to a more Latinate English (a lawyer? a scientist? another "industrialist"?). It's a trick of which Pound was the master.

Finally, I wanted to hint at the full tragedy of this "owing," and so I issued directives to the reader through the time-honored notion of a cautionary tale, instead of simply asserting the speaker's own state: "That frantic believing *will break you* in two" instead of "*broke me* in two." I hoped that this indirection might, through reticence alone, deepen the sense of loss.

The stanzas just shook out at four lines each as I began it, and the final tercet echoes the absence of "go" in the final line.

Richard Wilbur was born in New York City in 1921, and raised on a farm in New Jersey. After graduating from Amherst College into World War II, he served for two years in Europe with the 36th Infantry Division.

*After his service, he went to graduate school at Harvard University,
spent three years in Harvard's Society of Fellows, and taught for "some
decades" at Harvard, Wellesley College, Wesleyan University, and Smith
College. He and his wife have four children. His wife has been the chief
advisor in his translation work (he has translated seven plays by Molière
and two by Racine) and the chief critic of his poems, the bulk of which
were gathered into* New and Collected Poems *in 1988. He has also
done some editing, some criticism, some Broadway lyrics, some children's books, and spent a year as Poet Laureate. Commenting on his
own work, Wilbur notes that his poems tend "to favor a spirituality that
is not abstracted, not dissociated and world-renouncing. A good part of
my work could, I suppose, be understood as a public quarrel with the
aesthetics of Edgar Allan Poe."*

Thyme Flowering among Rocks

This, if Japanese,
Would represent grey boulders
Walloped by rough seas

So that, here or there,
The balked water tossed its froth
Straight into the air.

Here, where things are what
They are, it is thyme blooming,
Rocks, and nothing but—

Having, nonetheless,
Many small leaves implicit,
A green countlessness.

Crouching down, peering
Into perplexed recesses,
You find a clearing

Occupied by sun
Where, along prone, rachitic
Branches, one by one,

Pale stems arise, squared
In the manner of *Mentha,*
The oblong leaves paired.

One branch, in ending,
Lifts a little and begets
A straight-ascending

Spike, whorled with fine blue
Or purple trumpets, banked in
The leaf-axils. You

Are lost now in dense
Fact, fact which one might have thought
Hidden from the sense,

Blinking at detail
Peppery as this fragrance,
Lost to proper scale

As, in the motion
Of striped fins, a bathysphere
Forgets the ocean.

It makes the craned head
Spin. Unfathomed thyme! The world's
A dream, Basho said,

Not because that dream's
A falsehood, but because it's
Truer than it seems.

Because I have sent off the worksheets of "Thyme Flowering among Rocks" to a library, I am reduced to making confident guesses as to how its form came about. One thing I know is that I have never deliberately set about to "write heroic couplets" or "write a sonnet." Poetry is both art and craft, but I abominate formal exercises and am stuck with the Emersonian feeling that a poem is something which finds out what it has to say, and in the process discovers the form which will best stress its tone and meaning. It may seem improbable to some poets of the last thirty years that such a process could result in, let us say, a rondeau; but that is because such poets are free-verse practitioners who lack my generation's instinctive sense—got both by reading and by writing—of the capabilities of certain traditional forms.

    Though I commonly work in meters, my way of going about a poem is very like the free-verse writer's: that is, I begin by letting the words find what line lengths seem right to them. Often this will result in a stanza of some sort, which (though the ensuing stanzas keep the metrical pattern) will still be flexible enough to permit the argument to move and speak as it likes. All of my poems, therefore, are formally *ad hoc;* quite a few are, so far as I know, without formal precedent, and none sets out to fulfill the "rules" of some standard form. However, I have wakened in the middle of the night to realize that a poem already under way called for the logic of the rondeau; and another poem (I have read my Villon, and translated some of him) told me rather early in the game that it wanted to be a ballade.

The present poem happened because my herb patch reminded me of the miniature landscapes of Japanese gardens, and because grovelling amongst herbs reminded me how much we lose of the world's wonder by perceiving things in an upright posture from usual distances. I expect that the brief way the first lines fell had much to do with expressing minuteness and a moment-by-moment concentrated observation; and that they then, together with the word "Japanese," gave me the notion of using the haiku form as a stanza. I was familiar with the form through such poets as Edmund Blunden, and through Harold G. Henderson's book on the subject. It seems to me that the haiku is the only syllabic form in which the Anglo-American ear can hear quantity with some assurance. Still, because the Japanese register syllables more readily than we, many English haiku rhyme the first and third lines for the sake of greater definition. I chose to rhyme in that manner (or found myself doing it) both for the reason given, and because I was going to write a poem of many haiku, in which variation of rhythm and likely linkages between stanzas would make the haiku pattern less consistently audible. There are poems like Auden's marvelous "In Praise of Limestone" in which we simply do not hear the syllabic structure—the lines in that poem being, if I remember rightly, as long as eleven and fourteen syl-lables. This inaudibility is not a defect, since the poet was after resistance and self-discipline rather than a clear quantitative effect. What I hope to have got in my little experiment is a quantitative structure of which the reader will be aware, playing against a speech rhythm which carries the motion and emotion.

Charles Wright was born in Pickwick Dam, Hardin County, Tennessee, in 1935. He grew up in Tennessee and North Carolina. He attended

Davidson College, the University of Iowa, and the University of Rome. From 1957 to 1961 he was in the Army Intelligence Service, stationed for most of the time in Verona, Italy. In 1963–65 he was a Fulbright student in Rome, translating the poems of the Italian poets Eugenio Montale and Cesare Pavese. In 1968–69 he was a Fulbright Lecturer at the University of Padua. From 1966 until 1983 he taught at the University of California, Irvine. Since 1983, he has been professor of English (since 1988, Souder Family Professor of English) at the University of Virginia. He has published ten books of poems, including Country Music, *which was a cowinner of the National Book Award in 1983, and* The World of the Ten Thousand Things. *With the University of Michigan Press's Poets on Poetry Series, he has published two books of prose,* Halflife (1988) *and* Quarter Notes (1995). Chickamauga, *a new book of poems, appeared in 1995. He lives in Charlottesville, Virginia. "Language is the element of definition, the defining and descriptive incantation. It puts the coin between our teeth," Wright told an interviewer. "It whistles the boat up. It shows us the city of light across the water."*

Bar Giamaica, 1959–60

Grace is the focal point,
                          the tip ends of her loosed hair
Like match fire in the back light,
Her hands in a "Here's the church . . ."
                                   She's looking at Ugo Mulas,
Who's looking at us.

Ingrid is writing this all down, and glances up, and stares hard.

This still isn't clear.

I'm looking at Grace, and Goldstein and Borsuk and Dick Venezia
Are looking at me.
                   Yola keeps reading her book.

And that leaves the rest of them: Susan and Elena and Carl Glass.
And Thorp and Schimmel and Jim Gates,
                             and Hobart and Schneeman

One afternoon in Milan in the late spring.

Then Ugo finishes, drinks a coffee, and everyone goes away.
Summer arrives, and winter;
                          the snow falls and no one comes back

Ever again,
     all of them gone through the star filter of memory,
 With its small gravel and metal tables and passers-by . . .

"Bar Giamaica, 1959–60" is from a section of *The Southern Cross* where each poem—and there are twenty in the section—answers to some technical problem I gave myself. Since technical, these problems are formal by definition, some more exaggerated than others. One poem contains no verbs, for instance, while the following one has a verb in every line. There is a poem which tries to imitate, however shallowly, a musical form, and another which tries to assemble itself as a painting might be composed. There are portraits of the poet with people he could not possibly have been seen with, a poem written entirely in hotel rooms (very difficult for me), a poem that was written at one sitting, and without changing one word later (a first for me), a poem that has two endings, one on top of the other, a poem with no reference point, two poems whose major imagery comes from the work of another poet. And so on. All great fun to do and, as is the case in all formal choices, I hope no hindrance to the finished product. The problem should be invisible. Two of the poems were concerned with photography, one of which being an attempt to create a photograph which I should have taken but never did. That's "Bar Giamaica, 1959–60."

 Going through a book of photographs by the Italian photographer Ugo Mulas one evening, I was struck by the familiarity of scene in one of the pictures. Looking down at the title, "Bar Giamaica, 1953–54," I realized it was the small courtyard of a bar I used to frequent occasionally in 1959–60 in Milan. I was living in Verona at the time, and the Giamaica, as it was called, was an artists' bar we almost always went to when in Milan. Looking at the picture, I recognized no one, of course, but began thinking of some of the people I had known back then, both in Verona and Milan, many of whom I'd spent time with in the Giamaica, and became somewhat sad that I had no like picture of my time there and my friends. So I decided to take Ugo's picture and replace the people in it with the people I'd known. Ugo still takes the picture, but it's six years later and the chairs and spaces are occupied now with my friends. The poem is an almost exact replica, descriptively, of the photograph, only the names have been added—all real names—to give me the photograph I'd never been able to take. Or a version of it, at least. Even the two unknown passersby, the metal caffe tables and the river gravel in the courtyard are included. Only the Birra Italia fluorescent sign was omitted. Some pictures may be worth a thousand words. This one was worth one hundred forty-five. . . .

As for the lineation—it was part (and still is for me) of a larger problem: how to use *all* of the page in structuring a poem, the way a painter uses all the canvas (the way Pollock used all four sides, for example), or a photographer uses all his frame. By using the dropped line, the "low rider," you can use both sides of the page at once, left- and right-hand margins, the conjunction of line and surface, and you can carry the long line on as an imagistic one, rather than a discursive or laboriously rhetorical one. Speed in the line is everything.

John Yau *was born in Lynn, Massachusetts, in 1950, shortly after his parents immigrated from China. His publications include poetry,* Radiant Silhouette: New and Selected Work: 1974–1988 *(Black Sparrow Press, 1989) and* Edificio Sayonara *(Black Sparrow Press, 1992); fiction,* Hawaiian Cowboys *(Black Sparrow Press, 1994); and criticism,* A. R. Penck *(Abrams, 1993) and* In the Realm of Appearances: The Art of Andy Warhol *(Ecco Press, 1993). A visiting professor at the University of California, Berkeley, in the spring semesters of 1994 and 1995, he is currently organizing a retrospective of the paintings and drawings of Ed Moses for the Museum of Contemporary Art in Los Angeles, and writing a book on the film star Anna May Wong.*

Broken Off by the Music

With the first gray light of dawn the remnants
of gas stations and supermarkets assume their
former shapes. A freckled, red headed boy
stares into the refrigerator, its chrome shelves
lined with jars, cans, and bottles—each
appropriately labeled with a word or a picture.
For some of the other inhabitants of the yellow
apartment house, the mere vapor of food
in the morning is sufficient nourishment.

Along the highway dozens of motorists have pulled
onto the shoulder of the road, no longer guided
by the flicker of countless stars dancing over
the surface of the asphalt. Three radios

disagree over what lies ahead. It is morning,
and sand no longer trickles onto the austere
boulevards of the capital.

Outside, on the sidewalk, two girls kneel down
and pray in front of a restaurant closed for
vacation. A breeze reminds everyone that ice
is another jewel—the result of snow gleaming
at night. "I used to play on this street,
but now it is different," says the older girl.
The younger one, who might be her sister, nods
solemnly. Across the street is a store
no one will enter.

Distance can hardly lend enchantment to the remnants
of a supermarket where faces are torn, as always,
between necessity and desire. With the first gray
light of evening a freckled girl assumes her former
shape—each limb appropriately labeled with words
of instruction. The younger boy skips away from
the others, while singing a song full of words
he stumbles over.

Outside the capital, two motorists disagree over
the remnants of a refrigerator. Three boys stare
at what lies behind the stars. A breeze reminds
everyone of their former shapes, while evening
lends an austere enchantment to the yellow window
of a gas station.

Snow can hardly lend enchantment to a sidewalk
where two girls shiver uncontrollably
while looking for the doorway of a store
that is closed. Nearby, a woman labels
gray shapes with songs of disagreement.

Three supermarkets disagree over the food vapors
in a refrigerator. Along the highway sand
becomes a song of chrome enchantment. A young boy
kicks the remnants of his brother's radio.
"I used to pray on this street, but now it is

sufficient to return each afternoon," he whispers,
as if someone were listening.

A woman stops in front of a gas station and stares
at the surface of the stars drifting through the
clouds. The breeze reminds the motorist that the
first gray light of dawn is the remnant of a jewel.

Thousands of radios begin flickering throughout
the apartment complex.

The shoulders of the younger sister are covered
with snow. The sidewalk in front of the restaurant
is littered with sleeping motorists, each of them
staring at the breeze trickling from the clouds.
But at night, the sky is a window full of earrings,
each lost in its blue velvet box.

Two boys nod solemnly in front of their former shapes.
Someone has embroidered the remnants of sufficient
    enchantment.

The world is matter and juxtaposition, a democracy in which anything,
everything leans on something else. The words of "Broken Off by the
Music" were to enter, leave, and return. Context and objects were to be
interchangeable in a fluid realm. An ingrown sestina, a whirlpool I tried
to follow until I reached its center. The influences were Richard Art-
schwager, Wallace Stevens, and Luis Buñuel.

Stephen Yenser was born in Wichita, Kansas, in 1941. He received his

*Ph.D. in English from the University of Wisconsin and is currently a
professor of English at the University of California, Los Angeles. He has
also taught for a year each at the University of Baghdad, the University
of Pau in France, and the University of Athens, the last two on Fulbright Teaching Fellowships. He received the Bernard F. Connors Poetry Prize from the* Paris Review *and the Walt Whitman Award for his
book of poems,* The Fire in All Things *(1993). His books of criticism
are* Circle to Circle: The Poetry of Robert Lowell *and* The Consuming

Myth: The Work of James Merrill. *He writes frequently for the* Yale Review.

Ember Week, Reseda

Back here the fall, spreading down the hills,
Scatters its fire through the Modesto ash
And gingko, the occasional pistache,
The sour gum and the purple plum alike.
Here and there a liquidambar burns
Wickedly as it turns

Its deep flame up. The fire in all things loves
The end of them. Underfoot the leaves
Crackle like crumpled letters. Even the rain,
Dripping its last at midnight from the eaves,
Pops and snaps out on the front porch steps.
Watching the logs give in

And glow, the fire like memory revise
Those other windblown trees' slow-motion blaze,
Your brush lick at a glaze of crimson lake
Somewhere in the dreamlike, liquid world
The heat's a window on, I catch myself
Again, falling awake.

The final poem in a sequence worked at intermittently over a period of several years, "Ember Week, Reseda" seems to welcome the opportunity for closure. Each of the preceding fourteen poems in the sequence had been in three six-line stanzas, so there was no question of deviating from that pattern here. From the outset, too, the normative line had been iambic pentameter (as usual in my case, so that not to write from this metrical base is more like a decision than to write from it). But while the fundamental form had declared itself long before this poem, I'd exercised throughout the sequence the options to vary the line length, and to rhyme or not, so the poems meet their minimal obligations differently. The comparative prominence of rhyme and the fixed shape of the stanzas in this instance owe something to the knowledge that it was to be the sequence's last poem. As the drafts accumulated, the stanzas looked more and more like one another prosodically, and the variations in line length themselves became regularized in the trimeters—which had originated when the first stanza's last line turned up the quick rhyme with the fifth. But these short lines too might have filled out if they hadn't seemed to fall in with the fall—and if the sequence hadn't begun with a trimeter. If I'd once wanted another end rhyme in the concluding stanza—to balance those in the first stanza and to close the sequence even more firmly—I settled for the one full rhyme on the final word and the internal rhymes. Are these last extravagant? A similar passage appears in about the same position in the sequence's opening poem, also set in the fall, and this hint of symmetry seemed a plausible justification. Moreover, while I knew that the rich surfaces of the sequence's painter were beyond me, I must have hoped that these lines would borrow something from her glazes and scumbles.

A BRIEF GLOSSARY
of Forms and Other Terms

Acrostic: A poem in which the initial letters of the lines, read downward, spell out a message or a name. It could be the author's name, for example, or that of his valentine; or it could amount to a cipher, a more or less concealed message that subverts the text itself. The form is designed to incorporate something of the bilateral, down-and-across motion of a cross-word puzzle. Variations abound. In a *mesostic* (or mesostich), the middle letters of successive lines form the message; in a *telestich,* the terminal letters do so. Edgar Allan Poe's "A Valentine" is a *cross acrostic* in which the name Frances Sargent Osgood appears diagonally down the page, spelled out by the first letter of the first line, the second letter of the second line, the third letter of the third line, and so forth.

An abecedarium (or abecedarius) operates on a similar principle. Here the initial letters run from *A* to *Z* in alphabetical order. The form immediately suggests children's verse but needn't be restricted to same. Tom Disch has written a *zewhyexary*—his coinage—which begins with *Z* and works its way backward. Walter Abish elevated the logic of the abecedarium into a structural ideal in his ingenious novel *Alphabetical Africa.* The book's first chapter is limited to words beginning with *A;* the second chapter allows words beginning with *A* and *B;* the third chapter, words beginning with *A, B,* and *C.* The pattern continues until chapter *Z* is reached and all the letters are covered—at which point the process is reversed, and with each succeeding chapter, the letters start dropping out one by one until we're back again at *A.*

Anagram: An anagram is the epitome of a verbal metamorphosis: the letters in a word are rearranged to form another word or phrase. *Keats* yields *steak;* the name *Spiro Agnew* might make mischievous minds meander to *grow a penis.* Lewis Carroll took apart *William Ewart Gladstone* and reassembled him as *Wild agitator! Means well.* Making anagrams out of *T. S. Eliot* remains a literary litmus test and a parlor game that anyone might play. W. H. Auden, whom Eliot published, opted for *litotes.* Vladimir Nabokov, who held no brief for Eliot, leaned to *toilets.* Turning away from plays on names, we can't be startled to find that *evil* is *live* backwards or that *horse* leads to *shore* where, perhaps, *heroes* may be found. Dmitri Borgmann has compiled extravagant lists of clever anagrams (e.g., *halitosis* equals *Lois has it!*) and *antigrams.* In the latter, the equation involves a reversal of meaning: it's the *militarist* who loudly says *I limit arms.*

The anagram is not a poetic form, but it can easily generate one. A poem inspired by the sort of wordplay found in a Nabokov novel might entail including in every line at least one anagram for a word appearing in the previous line. Here is a villanelle consisting exclusively of anagrams for the name *Wystan Hugh Auden:*

Why shun a nude tag?
Why stun a huge hand?
Hug a shady wet nun.

Why stand a huge Hun?
Why gash a dune nut?
Why shun a nude tag?

Guy hands u new hat,
Haw, the Sunday gun.
Hug a shady wet nun.

Why aghast, unnude?
Why a gash, untuned?
Why shun a nude tag?

Ashen guy dun what?
Why? Nag a shut nude.
Hug a shady wet nun.

Why daunt a snug he?
Why dun a gaunt she?
Why shun a nude tag?
Hug a shady wet nun.

Anaphora: The systematic repetition of a word or a phrase can serve as the organizing principle of a poem, as in Christopher Smart's celebrated litany of praise, "For I Will Consider My Cat Jeoffrey." Joe Brainard's *I Remember* consists entirely of sentences beginning "I remember." The book begins: "I remember the first time I got a letter that said 'After Five Days Return To' on the envelope, and I thought that after I had kept the letter for five days I was supposed to return it to the sender."

Apostrophe: In an apostrophe, an absent person or a personified abstraction is addressed as though present and alive. Epics frequently begin with an apostrophe to the muse. Many of Richard Howard's poems take the form of intimate apostrophes to past artists. In "Decades," for example, Hart Crane is punningly addressed as "Dear Hart."

Canzone: The canzone is like the sestina, only more so; both are based on a strictly controlled pattern of end-word repetition rather than rhyme. The canzone comprises five twelve-line stanzas and a closing five-line envoy, with each of five end-words recurring thirteen times. In the opening stanza, the end-words occur in the following sequence: 1-2-1-1-3-1-1-4-4-1-5-5. In stanza two, the pattern is 5-1-5-5-2-5-5-3-3-5-4-4. Stanza three: 4-5-4-4-1-4-4-2-2-4-3-3. Stanza four: 3-4-3-3-5-3-3-1-1-3-2-2. Stanza five: 2-3-2-2-4-2-2-5-5-2-1-1. Envoy: 1-2-3-4-5. Clearly, each stanza is dominated by one of the chosen words. The most brilliant modern example of the form is James Merrill's "Samos" in *The Changing Light at Sandover*. Merrill's end-words are *sense, water, fire, land,* and *light:* the four elements plus our faculty for apprehending them. Merrill naturally works changes on the repeated words: we come across *magnifier* and *sapphire, chrysolite* and *leit-/motifs, ascents* and *innocence, island* and *inland, water* as a verb and as a noun.

Carmen Figuratum: Latin for "a shaped poem." The variable line lengths of George Herbert's "The Altar," for example, suggest the appearance of an altar. Included in Guillaume Apollinaire's typographically adventurous *Calligrammes* is a poem in the shape of a tie and pocket watch; a poem with five long vertical lines running down the page is called "Il pleut" ("It's Raining"). A contemporary master is John Hollander, in whose *Types of Shape* we encounter a light bulb, a bell, an arrow, and a swan with its mirrored shadow in a pond.

Catalogue: In an essay on Walt Whitman, Randall Jarrell quotes a representative passage from "Song of Myself" and exclaims: "It is only a list—but what a list! And how delicately, in what different ways—likeness and opposition and continuation and climax and anticlimax—the transitions are managed, whenever Whitman wants to manage them." Kenneth Koch superbly demonstrates the poetic attractions—and humorous possibilities—of the list or inventory in a number of poems in his volume *Thank You.* "Taking a Walk With You" is a catalogue of the poet's misunderstandings:

I misunderstand "Beautiful Adventures"; I also think I probably
    misunderstand *La Nausée* by Jean-Paul Sartre . . .
I probably misunderstand misunderstanding itself—I
    misunderstand the Via Margutta in Rome, or Via della Vite, no
    matter what street, all of them.
I misunderstand wood in its relationship to the tree; I
    misunderstand people who take one attitude or another about it . . .
Spring I would like to say I understand, but I most probably
    don't—autumn, winter, and summer are all in the same boat
(Ruined ancient cities by the sea).

Clerihew: A form of light verse invented by, and named after, Edmund Clerihew Bentley, the same E. C. Bentley who wrote *Trent's Last Case.* The two couplets in a clerihew irreverently characterize the usually famous person whose name supplies one of the rhymes. W. H. Auden's *Academic Graffiti* gives us the clerihew at its best:

When Karl Marx
Found the phrase 'financial sharks,'
He sang a Te Deum
In the British Museum

Collage: A literary composition consisting entirely or mainly of quotations from various sources—poems, novels, the newspaper, textbooks, government reports, a dictionary of quotations, etc. Ever since T. S. Eliot incorporated a mosaic of quotations in "The Waste Land," the collage has been a popular device. It "brings strangers together, uses its 'ands' to suggest an affinity without specifying what it is, and produces, thereby, a low-level but general nervousness," writes William Gass in his book *Habitations of the Word.* "It is one of the essential elements of a truly contemporary style." The *cento,* a type of collage, is an anthology poem; every line is culled from another poem, whether by one author or by many. Here is a fragment from John Ashbery's cento "To a Waterfowl":

Calm was the day, and through the trembling air
Coffee and oranges in a sunny chair
And she also to use newfangleness . . .
Why cannot the Ear be closed to its own destruction?
Last noon beheld them full of lusty life.
Unaffected by "the march of events,"
Never until the mankind making
From harmony, from heavenly harmony
O death, O cover you over with roses and early lilies!

The lines are taken, in order, from poems by Spenser, Stevens, Wyatt, Blake, Byron, Pound, Dylan Thomas, Dryden, and Whitman. "To a Waterfowl" is the title of a poem by William Cullen Bryant. See also *Touchstones.*

Creative writing: When the subject of creative writing is brought up, some people automatically respond with a snicker, a sneer, or a groan. Critics argue that the writing of poetry can't be taught. Extreme critics think that our general cultural blight can be summed up in the word *workshop* (as in "we workshopped my sestina today"), just as Hitler thought that the popular dance called the shimmy was the perfect metonymy for all the idiocy of America. The impulse to mock the creative-writing racket is understandable. "I, too, dislike it," as Marianne Moore would say.

But though inspiration cannot be taught, there are ways of coaxing the imagination into action. And though workshops can disintegrate into group therapy sessions, there are ways of keeping the focus on language and its possibilities, forms and styles, strategies and methods of composition, metaphors and similes, acrostics and anagrams.

I find there is no substitute for regular poetry-writing assignments, the more inventive the better. Here are some assignments I have used: (1) Write the last paragraph of a novel that does not exist. (2) Write a poem in a style or manner not your own. (3) Write a poem in which one noun in every line means something different from what it usually means. (4) Explain baseball to an Englishman.

Certain parlor games stimulate the imagination. A Tarot reading can generate a poem. So can the "landscape game." In this game the players are asked to picture a house and then to imagine taking a walk and coming across a key, a bowl, a body of water, a wild animal, and a wall, in that order. The assignment is to write a narrative connecting the elements.

Robin Behn and Chase Twichell have compiled an excellent book of writing assignments. *The Practice of Poetry: Writing Exercises from Poets Who Teach* was published by HarperCollins in 1992.

Cut-up: Samuel Johnson improved a James Thomson poem by omitting every second line—a method that certain contemporary poets might be advised to apply to their own compositions.

Double dactyls: A light-verse form invented by Anthony Hecht and expertly handled by the various poets represented in *Jiggery Pokery: A Compendium of Double Dactyls,* which Hecht edited collaboratively with John Hollander. According to the editors, the form calls for "two quatrains, of which the last line of the first rhymes with the last line of the second. All the lines except the rhyming ones, which are truncated, are composed of two dactylic feet. The first line of the poem must be a double dactylic nonsense line, like 'Higgledy-piggledy.' . . . The second line must be a double dactylic name. And then, somewhere in the poem, though preferably in the second stanza, and ideally in the antepenultimate line, there must be at least one double dactylic line which is *one word long.* . . . But, and the beauty of the form consists chiefly in this, once such a double dactylic word has successfully been employed in this verse form, it may never be used again." An example, from the Hecht oeuvre:

Professionalism

Higgledy-piggledy,
Quintus Tertullian

Drew on his Rhetoric
With his last breath,

(Sesquipedalian
Valedictorian)
Boring his near ones and
Dear ones to death.

Form: While no entry can begin to do justice to all the permutations of this term, here are three quotations that struck the editor's fancy when he was preparing the manuscript of this book.

From Boris Pasternak's *Doctor Zhivago*, as quoted by Frank O'Hara: "As he scribbled his odds and ends, he made a note reaffirming his belief that art always serves beauty, and beauty is delight in form, and form is the key to organic life, since no living thing can exist without it, so that every work of art, including tragedy, expresses the joy of existence."

"Form is not tradition," wrote E. M. Forster. "It alters from generation to generation. Artists always seek a new technique, and will continue to do so as long as their work excites them. But form of some kind is imperative. It is the surface crust of the internal harmony, it is the outward evidence of order."

Form

We were wrong to think
form a frame, a still
shot of the late
beloved, or the pot thrown
around water. We wanted
to hold what we had.

But the clay contains
the breaking, and the man
is dead—the scrapbook
has him—and the form of life
is a motion. So from all this
sadness, the bed being touched,

the mirror being filled,
we learn what carrying on
is for. We move, we are moved.
It runs in the family.
For the life of us
we cannot stand to stay.

—Heather McHugh

Glose: The glose's forty-four lines are divided into one four-line stanza followed by four stanzas containing ten lines each. The opening quatrain supplies the poem's rhymes and refrains. The first line in the poem recurs as the final line of stanza 2; the second line concludes stanza 3; the third line, stanza 4; the fourth line, stanza 5. It's customary to rhyme the sixth, ninth, and tenth lines of each stanza. A more intricate and demanding rhyme scheme can, of course, be imposed.

Haiku: Japanese in origin, the classical haiku consists of three lines totaling seventeen syllables. The first and third lines contain five syllables apiece; the middle line gets the remaining seven. Ron Padgett illustrates in his poem "Haiku":

First: five syllables
Second: seven syllables
Third: five syllables

The haiku is a thoroughly ritualized form: the very word connotes a quick, impressionistic, but precise sketch of a scene in nature conjuring up a whole season. American poets need no license to take liberties with the customary associations and traditional subject matter of the haiku. A Japanese haiku written by a tourist in Tokyo follows:

O-kanjo-O,
O-negai-shimasu,
O-nei-san.

This translates roughly as

Check,
please,
waitress!

which situates us accurately in a Midwest diner in 1956.

With the haiku as with many other forms, American poets are divided between those favoring a strict, and those favoring a broad, construction of the rules. As a formal restraint, a strict enforcement of the five-seven-five syllabic pattern would seem indispensable. Those who would relax the rule argue that the American idiom requires a line unit based on speech—and that seventeen syllables might prove extravagant, since an American speaker can get the job done even faster.

Here is Bashō's most celebrated haiku rendered strictly according to Hoyle:

At the ancient pond
A solitary frog leaps—
The sound of water.

And here is the same haiku rendered with brevity as the governing principle:

Pond—
Frog—
Splash!

In a *tanka,* two seven-syllable lines are added to the haiku structure. The haiku is also the basis for the longer form called *linked verse.* "Generally three or more poets took part, composing alternate verses of 7, 5, 7 syllables and 7, 7 syllables," Donald Keene explains. In linked verse, each two-line stanza functions as the conclusion of one poem and as the opening of another in a seamless series. Thus, "any three links taken from a sequence should produce two complete poems." Here, in Keene's translation, is a brief excerpt from the hundred-stanza-long *Three Poets at Minase,* written collaboratively by Sogi, Shohaku, and Socho, three Japanese poets of the fifteenth century:

> Heedless of the wishes
> Of piping insects,
> The grasses wither.

> When I visited my friend
> How bare the path to his gate!

> Remote villages—
> Have the storms still to reach you
> Deep in the mountains?

The use of the haiku as a stanza form—in effect, a building block—has not yet caught on in the United States, but there are hints that it might. Elizabeth Spires works variations on the form in "The Haiku Master," in which haikulike fragments, linked together, form (as she notes) "a kind of elliptical narrative (haiku with a plot!)." David Trinidad's "Reruns" consists of seventeen stanzas, one for each syllable in a haiku. Each stanza is a haiku, adhering strictly to the five-seven-five syllabic pattern; each is devoted to a different television sitcom from the 1960s. Both the Spires and the Trinidad poems appear in *The Best American Poetry 1991.*

Limerick: No one yet has figured out a way to put the limerick to anything but lighthearted use. Its five lines amount to a rhyme sandwich—an eminently suitable form for naughty wit. The best limericks are bawdy but too good-natured to seem truly obscene. Here's a famously anonymous example:

> The breasts of a barmaid of Crale
> Were tattooed with the price of brown ale,
> While on her behind
> For the sake of the blind
> Was the same information in braille.

Or:

> There was a young man of St. John's
> Who wanted to bugger the swans

So he went to the porter
Who said "Have my daughter!
The swans are reserved for the dons."

The British poet Gavin Ewart took the latter and rewrote it as "Two Semantic Limericks," replacing the words with their dictionary definitions. The
punch line, as defined by the shorter Oxford English Dictionary of 1933, is
as follows:

> "Hold or possess as something at your disposal my female child! The
> large web-footed swimming-birds of the genus *Cygnus* or subfamily
> *Cygninae* of the family *Anatidae,* characterized by a long and gracefully
> curved neck and a majestic motion when swimming, are set apart,
> specially retained for the Head, Fellows and Tutors of the College."

Lipogram: A piece of writing that deliberately excludes one or
more letters of the alphabet. Georges Perec, the late French novelist and
member of the Oulipo, wrote an entire novel—titled *La Disparition*—without the vowel *e,* the letter that otherwise recurs with the greatest frequency
in French as in English.

Musical Forms: In this broad category falls any concerted effort
to approximate a musical form in verse. In Eliot's *Four Quartets,* themes are
developed and orchestrated as they might be in a sequence of interlocking
string quartets. Other notable examples are Paul Celan's great "Death
Fugue" and Weldon Kees's "Round," both of which are built around the
contrapuntal repetition of key phrases. With its symphonic structure and its
insistent musical metaphors and puns, Wallace Stevens's "Peter Quince at
the Clavier" reads like a series of chord progressions—or like a score,
complete with instrumentation. The elders watching Susanna bathe are said
to have felt

The basses of their beings throb
In witching chords, and their thin blood
Pulse pizzicati of Hosanna

The rhythm of John Ashbery's poem "The Songs We Know Best"
derives from the song "Reunited (and it feels so good)"; the calypso section
of his "Variations, Calypso and Fugue on a Theme of Ella Wheeler Wilcox"
is made up of intentionally silly, singsong rhymes:

But of all the sights that were seen by me
In the East or West, on land or sea,
The best was the place that is spelled H-O-M-E.

Oulipo: An acronym for *Ouvroir de Littérature Potentielle,* which
translates as "charity bazaar of potential literature." Founded by Raymond

Queneau and François LeLionnais in 1960, the Oulipo is a primarily French association of mathematicians and writers committed to the discovery or invention of strict and unusual literary forms. In the name of literary potentiality, Oulipians have developed new variants of old forms, adapted structures borrowed from symbolic logic, and derived methods of composition from word games and lexicographic permutations. Oulipian inventions include the $N + 7$ strategy, where N stands for all the nouns in a given passage of prose or verse; each noun is replaced by the seventh ensuing noun in the dictionary (or, in an $N - 7$ procedure, by the seventh noun preceding it). Harry Mathews, an American member of the Oulipo, used a pocket American Heritage Dictionary to transmute "Mighty oaks from little acorns grow" into "Mighty oaths from little acrimonies grow." Kant's "There can be no doubt that all our knowledge begins with experience" can become "There can be no donut that all our knuckle-joints begin with expiation." To produce *definitional literature,* the Oulipian poet replaces the words in a text with their dictionary definitions, in *semi-definitional literature,* the writer substitutes oblique definitions (such as crossword puzzle clues). *Atlas de littérature potentielle* (Gallimard, 1981) is a comprehensive anthology of Oulipo stratagems. In English, Mathews gives an excellent account of the Oulipo in the May 1976 issue of *Word Ways: The Journal of Recreational Linguistics* and in an essay on Georges Perec in *Grand Street,* Autumn 1983.

Pantoum: A Malayan form consisting of a series of four-line stanzas. The second and fourth lines of each stanza repeat as the first and third lines of the next stanza. The first and third lines of the opening stanza repeat as the second and fourth lines of the final stanza, thus completing the circle: the same line both opens and closes the poem. J. D. McClatchy's "The Method" is a singular example inasmuch as it consistently substitutes witty approximations for exact repetitions. "The hearth's easy, embered expense" turns into "The heart's lazy: remembrance spent." "When you're away I sleep a lot," the poem begins. It ends: "When you're away, asleep, or lost."

Prose Poem: Prose poems go free verse one better: they do away with lines themselves as the basic unit of composition. John Milton prefaced *Paradise Lost* with the remark that rhyme was "no necessary Adjunct or true Ornament" of poetry; practitioners of the prose poem operate on the assumption that verse itself is similarly expendable. The prose poem as a genre was baptized by Charles Baudelaire in his volume *Petits Poèmes en prose* (also sometimes called *Spleen de Paris*). Baudelaire's prose poems come in the form of parables, diary entries, dialogues, manifestoes, anecdotes, ruminations, and personal essays. Arthur Rimbaud's prose poems in *Illuminations* resemble hallucinatory fragments, dream episodes, the visions of a youthfully debauched seer. The prose poem is the characteristic form of expression of a quartet of distinguished French poets: Max Jacob, René Char, Francis Ponge, and Henri Michaux. While it has never quite become a genre in England or the United States, the prose poem has given rise to some memorable experiments. The examples that instantly come to mind are staggeringly diverse. Consider Gertrude Stein's *Tender Buttons,* William Carlos Williams's *Kora in Hell,* W. H. Auden's *The Orators* and his "Caliban to the Audience," John Ashbery's *Three Poems,* and Geoffrey Hill's *Mercian Hymns.* The speaker of Frank O'Hara's poem "Why I Am Not A Painter," a verse poem, reflects the modern poet's love affair with prose. Apropos of an earlier production titled "Oranges," he proudly declares: "It is even in / prose, I am a real poet."

Sestina: Devised by the Provençal troubador poet Arnaut Daniel in the late thirteenth century, the sestina owes its Italian name to the notable use of it made by Dante and Petrarch. It has thirty-nine lines—hence a Tom Disch sestina about reaching the age of forty calls itself "The Thirty-Nine Articles"—which divide into six six-line stanzas plus a terminal triplet (or envoy). The same six words, or *teleutons,* end all the lines in the poem. James Merrill's "Tomorrows" virtually defines as it exemplifies the form. The successive lines in stanza one of Merrill's poem conclude with the words "one," "two," "three," "four," "five," and "six." In Merrill's second stanza, the teleutons reappear as "Sikhs," "one," "five," "two," "for," and "three," in that order. Each subsequent stanza applies the same 6-1-5-2-4-3 ratio to its immediate predecessor, so that by the time we reach the end of the sixth stanza (where, in "Tomorrows," the words *into, before, classics, five-, three,* and *someone* designate the correct order) we've come full circle. Merrill's envoy contains, as it must, *one, three,* and *five* in the middle of the lines and *two, for,* and *six* as end-words.

Modern poets have treated the sestina as a test of their virtuosity and technical dexterity or, alternatively, as an invitation to surrender their initiative to the words themselves, allowing chance to become a determining element in the composition. Since the last word of any stanza must recur as the last word of the opening line of the next stanza, there's a built-in transitional effect that makes the sestina an unlikely but effective vehicle for narrative poetry. A common tactic is to choose five of the teleutons from one paradigm and the sixth from a radically different one. In W. H. Auden's "Paysage Moralisé" (i.e. "moralized landscape"), *sorrow* moralizes the five landscape words *valleys, mountains, water, islands,* and *cities.* In Elizabeth Bishop's "A Miracle for Breakfast," *miracle* is the odd word out, imposing an order on the five neutral nouns *coffee, crumb, balcony, sun,* and *river.* Puns and homophonic substitutions are acceptable, and so the writer of a sestina may gravitate precisely to teleutons with multiple meanings. The word *pound* for example, may indicate a unit of weight or of currency, a kennel, or the action of a hammer on an anvil; capitalized, it refers to the author of *The Cantos;* and it can also appear as the suffix of words like *impound, compound,* and *propound.*

Inevitably, the sestina has called forth bravura displays and self-referential antics. In Harry Mathews's "Age and Indifferent Clouds," the rhyming teleutons are the deliberately antipoetic *hippopotamus, geranium, aluminum, focus, stratum,* and *bronchitis.* It's two sestinas in one: the beginning of all the lines pun on the names of six out-of-the-way plants. The "sea anemone" becomes "An enemy, who was seen . . ." and "sixty enemas"; the Jew's harp reappears in the guise of "the deuce of hearts" and "fused harps"; in one of its incarnations, Aaron's rod is transformed into "Erin's colorful rood." Alan Ansen's sestina "A Fit of Something Against Something" offers a condensed history of the form as a progressive loss of glory. The poem opens in full rhetorical flower:

> In the burgeoning age of Arnaut when for God and man to
>   be
> Shone a glory not a symptom, poetry was not austere.
> Complicated laws it followed, generosity through order,
> Dowered acrobats with hoops trapezing laurels undergone.
> Fountainlike gyrations earned the free trouvère the name of
>   master,
> And the climax of his daring was the dazzling sestina.

To suggest our fall from the grace of "the burgeoning age of Arnaut," each stanza in Ansen's poem has shorter lines than the previous stanza. Here's what happens to the sestina as we approach the inglorious present:

> Its zing's all gone,
> It's no master.
> Get lost, sestina,
> Go way, austere.
> You'll always be
> Out of order.

With the envoy the shrinking effect is complete:

> *Sestina order,*
> Austere master,
> BE GONE!!!

Concealed in part two of T. S. Eliot's "The Dry Salvages" is a meta-sestina that does away with the envoy and with the 6-1-5-2-4-3 rule of thumb. The six end-words recur in identical order, but in each case with rhyming substitutions. For example, the opening stanza's "wailing," "flowers," "motionless," "wreckage," "unprayable," and "annunciation" become, a stanza later, "trailing," "hours," "emotionless," "breakage," "reliable," and "renunciation." The original six words (with "unprayable" turning into "barely prayable") reassert themselves in the sixth stanza.

Sonnet: The most venerable of all English verse forms. Several major subcategories of the sonnet, and innumerable minor ones, have established themselves. The *Petrarchan* or Italian sonnet is composed of an octet and a sestet; the *volta* or "turn" between stanzas accompanies a turn in the argument, as from thesis to antithesis, whether or not an actual stanza break calls attention to it. The *Shakespearean* or English sonnet, by contrast, relies on three quatrains to advance a theme, followed by a culminating couplet. The *Spenserian* sonnet is something of a cross between the Italian and English varieties, while the *Miltonic* sonnet obtains its distinctive effect by the simple expedient of postponing the turn. Rupert Brooke's "Sonnet Reversed" stands the English sonnet on its head. Brooke begins with a romantic couplet:

> Hand trembling towards hand; the amazing lights.
> Of heart and eye. They stood on supreme heights.

From this climax, we move to the prosaic post-honeymoon future, capped off by this quatrain:

> They left three children (besides George, who drank):
>   The eldest Jane, who married Mr. Bell,
> William, the head-clerk in the Country Bank,
>   And Henry, a stockbroker, doing well.

If in the sestina modern poets saw an undeveloped form that was ripe for exploitation, in the sonnet they confronted the full weight of literary tradition. The sonnet therefore seemed a particularly inviting target for modern iconoclasts: the need to evade a daunting predecessor goes hand in hand with the temptation to draw a mustache on the Mona Lisa. Already in the nineteenth century, poets arbitrarily discarded or altered the standard conventions, with the effect that only the abstract idea of a sonnet was retained. The fifty "sonnets" in George Meredith's *Modern Love* are each sixteen lines long; Gerard Manley Hopkins tried out a twelve-line sonnet. It was nevertheless with a certain provocative insistence that the French poet Arthur Rimbaud, still in his teens, titled a paragraph of prose—part two of his prose poem "Jeunesse" ("Youth")—"Sonnet."

"Shadow sonnets" seems a good name for the unrhymed, unmetered, fourteen-line poems that have lately become a common feature on the literary landscape. And, of course, the fourteen-line rule of thumb continues to go by the boards on occasion. "Dido," the first of the "Two Sonnets" in John Ashbery's *The Tennis Court Oath,* is one line shy of the requisite total; the fragmented sonnet was invented in the process. "So I am cheated of perfection" is the poem's terse comment on itself. John Hollander virtually reinvented the rules of the sonnet sequence in his aptly titled *Powers of Thirteen:* 169 poems—that's thirteen squared—each containing thirteen lines, each line limited to thirteen syllables.

Inveterate sonneteers continue to put the old form to dazzlingly elaborate uses. The twenty sonnets in Daryl Hine's "Arrondissements" correspond to sections of Paris. Anthony Hecht's "Double Sonnet" in *A Summoning of Stones* offers a sixteen-line "octet" followed by a twelve-line "sestet." One sonnet interrupts, and is contained by, another in James Merrill's "The Will." The six stanzas of Kenneth Koch's "The Railway Stationery" tell a narrative first and are sonnets only upon inspection. The sonnet is also used as the narrative stanza of Paul Muldoon's long poem "The More A Man Has The More A Man Wants." Vikram Seth's *The Golden Gate* (1986), a novel in verse about yuppiedom in San Francisco, consists of close to six hundred sonnets in a sprightly iambic tetrameter; everything from the book's dedication, acknowledgments, and contents page to the author's bio note is in the sonnet form, the model being Pushkin's sonnet stanza in *Eugene Onegin*.

A *Crown of Sonnets* comprises seven linked sonnets, the last line of each serving as the first line of the next. In "The Labours of Hercules," the British poet John Fuller added some desirable thorns to the Crown. Fuller's poem is composed of fifteen sonnets, the last of which is simply the reiteration, in sequential order, of the first lines of the previous fourteen.

The opening eight lines of Edwin Denby's "On the Home Front— 1942" show that a contemporary American idiom is admirably adaptable to the demands of the sonnet form:

> Because Jim insulted Harry eight years previous
> By taking vengeance for a regular business loss
> Forwardlooking Joe hints that Leslie's devious
> Because who stands to lose by it, why you yourself boss.
> Figures can't lie so it's your duty to keep control
> You've got to have people you can trust, look at em smile
> That's why we're going to win this war, I read a man's soul
> Like a book, intuition, that's how I made my pile.

Things to Do: James Schuyler invented the "Things to Do" genre with his poem of that title. Here's how it concludes:

> Complain to laundry
> *any laundry*. Ask for borrowed books back.
> Return
> junk mail to sender
> marked, Return to Sender.
> Condole. Congratulate.
> " . . . this sudden shock . . ."
> " . . . this swift surprise . . ."
> Send. Keep. Give. Destroy.
> Brush rub polish burn

mend scratch foil evert
emulate surpass. Remember
"to write three-act play"
and lead "a full and active life."

The best "Things to Do" poems begin with the mundane particulars of
the daily round and manage to ascend the heights of poetic refreshment
while remaining true to the homely occasion. Ted Berrigan was a master.
Among his triumphs are "Things to Do in Anne's Room," "Things to Do in
New York (City)," and the moving "Things to Do in Providence."

Touchstones: A specialized form of the cento, consisting of a
selection of the poet's favorite lines juxtaposed strategically. The form derives from Matthew Arnold's essay "The Study of Poetry": "Indeed there
can be no more useful help for discovering what poetry belongs to the class
of the truly excellent, and can therefore do us most good, than to have
always in one's mind lines and expressions of the great masters, and to apply
them as a touchstone to other poetry." The following example was composed on a five-hour bus journey from the Port Authority in Manhattan to
Ithaca, New York:

Touchstones

That, in Aleppo once, where
With nectar pure his oozy locks he laves,
Bloom, O ye amaranths! bloom for whom ye may,
Till elevators drop us from our day . . .

And would it have been worth it, after all,
To let the warm love in
Or stain her honor or her new brocade
To a green thought in a green shade?

As though to protect what it advertises,
Surely some revelation is at hand;
My music shows ye have your closes,
And to die is different from what anyone supposed, and luckier.

Blind mouths! as from an unextinguished hearth,
Me only cruel immortality
Consumes: whatever dies was not mixed equally
But does a human form display

Alone and palely loitering, like a rose rabbi.
O could I lose all father now! for why
I wretch lay wrestling with (my God!) my God,
Honey of generation had betrayed.

These modifications of matter into innocent athletes
Whose action is no stronger than a flower
Through Eden took their solitary way.
I, too, dislike it. With rue my heart is laden.

If you are coming down through the narrows of the river Kiang,
Where knock is open wide,
Fear death by water. To begin the morning right,
The small rain down can rain

Where ignorant armies clash by night
Though I sang in my chains like the sea.
Nor law, nor duty bade me fight,
Nor, in thy marble vault, shall sound

Joy's grape, with how sad steps, Oh Moon,
With naked foot stalking in my chamber.
The dark italics it could not propound,
And so—for God's sake—hock and soda-water!

Triolet: Of the eight lines of the triolet, five are taken up by the
two refrain lines. Line one of the poem returns as lines four and seven; line
two doubles as line eight. John Hollander illustrates:

Triolets' second lines refrain
From coming back until the end;
Though the first one can cause some pain
Triolets' second lines refrain
From coming back yet once again.
(The form's too fragile to offend.)
Triolets' second lines refrain
From coming back until the end.

Typography: Typography can help establish the poem's formal
action. What might seem idiosyncratic in ordinary discourse can become
strategic in verse. That is why the editors who regularized Emily Dickinson's
poems were doing her no favor; all those dashes—those emphatic pauses or
interruptions or hesitations—are crucial to the rhythm and pace of her
poems. Similarly, it's central to our experience as readers that, for example,
Frank O'Hara "played the typewriter"; that W. S. Merwin does away with
conventional punctuation; that Jorie Graham substitutes blanks for words in
some of her poems; that Robert Creeley favors lowercase letters and short
lines; that Frank Bidart makes liberal use of italics, ellipses, and capital
letters to raise his dramatic monologues to fever pitch; and that both A. R.
Ammons and James Schuyler use colons where periods or semicolons might

have been expected, thereby effecting a sense of continuity rather than closure.

In *The Changing Light at Sandover*, James Merrill entrusts the typewriter keyboard with the all-important task of distinguishing his otherworldly speakers from his human voices. Merrill's use of uppercase letters for the former, and lowercase for the latter, advances the idea of a divine hierarchy, an idea at the heart of the visionary experience that was his poem's "ecstatic occasion."

Villanelle: Like the pantoum, an example of chained-verse. The villanelle's nineteen lines are spread out over five tercets and a closing quatrain. The rhyming first and third lines of the poem become its refrains: the latter concludes stanzas three, five, and six; the former concludes stanzas two and four and is the penultimate line of stanza six. The second lines of all the stanzas rhyme with one another; thus, there are only two rhymes in a villanelle. No form more elegant exists. A compendium of villanelles could scarcely afford to omit Theodore Roethke's "The Waking," Elizabeth Bishop's "One Art," Dylan Thomas's "Do Not Go Gentle into That Good Night," and, among lesser known examples, James Schuyler's fine "Poem" ("I do not always understand what you say"). In the most famous of W. H. Auden's villanelles, the two refrains are "Time will say nothing but I told you so" and "If I could tell you I would let you know." This is the way the poem ends:

> The winds must come from somewhere when they blow,
> There must be reasons why the leaves decay;
> Time will say nothing but I told you so.
>
> Perhaps the roses really want to grow,
> The vision seriously intends to stay;
> If I could tell you I would let you know.
>
> Suppose the lions all get up and go,
> And all the books and soldiers run away;
> Will Time say nothing but I told you so?
> If I could tell you I would let you know.

Auden playfully titled the poem "But I Can't."

A *terzanelle* looks like a villanelle, retaining the five tercets and the closing quatrain, but with a strong nod toward *terza rima*. In the terzanelle, the second line of each stanza repeats as the third line of the following stanza; lines one and three of every stanza rhyme. The first and third lines of the poem reappear as, respectively, the second (or, in some cases, the third) and the fourth lines of the quatrain.

Word Golf: A word association game that can be used as a warmup for a poem. Playing word golf, one goes from, say, *lead* to *gold* by changing one letter at a time. One may take the most direct route (*lead* to *load* to *goad* to *gold*) or amiably follow detours (*leaf, loaf,* and *loan* intervene between *lead* and *load; goad* leads to *goat, coat, colt,* and *cold* before emerging as *gold*). The exercise might result in a makeshift form requiring the poet to include in every line a transformed word from the previous line.

FURTHER READING

Beckson, Karl, and Arthur Ganz. *A Reader's Guide to Literary Terms.* New York: Farrar, Straus and Giroux, 1960.

Behn, Robin, and Chase Twichell, eds. *The Practice of Poetry: Writing Exercises from Poets Who Teach.* New York: HarperCollins, 1992.

Benedikt, Michael. *The Prose Poem: An International Anthology.* New York: Dell, 1976.

Bombaugh, C. C. *Oddities and Curiosities of Words and Literature.* Edited and annotated by Martin Gardner. New York: Dover, 1961.

Brotchie, Alastair, and Mel Gooding, *A Book of Surrealist Games.* Boston and London: Shambhala Redstone Editions, 1995.

Conte, Joseph M. *Unending Design: The Forms of Postmodern Poetry.* Ithaca: Cornell University Press, 1991.

Dacey, Philip, and David Jauss, eds. *Strong Measures: An Anthology of Contemporary American Poetry in Traditional Forms.* New York: Harper and Row, 1985.

Disch, Thomas M. *The Castle of Indolence: On Poetry, Poets, and Poetasters.* New York: Picador USA, 1995.

Friebert, Stuart, and David Young, eds. *Models of the Universe: An Anthology of the Prose Poem.* Oberlin: Oberlin College Press, 1995.

Fussell, Paul. *Poetic Meter and Poetic Form.* Rev. ed. New York: Random House, 1979.

Gilbert, Roger. *Walks in the World: Representation and Experience in Modern American Poetry.* Princeton: Princeton University Press, 1991.

Gioia, Dana. *Can Poetry Matter? Essays on Poetry and American Culture.* St. Paul, Minn.: Graywolf Press, 1992.

Glück, Louise. *Proofs and Theories: Essays on Poetry.* Hopewell, N.J.: The Ecco Press, 1994.

Hollander, John. *Rhyme's Reason: A Guide to English Verse.* New Haven: Yale University Press, 1981.

Howard, Richard, ed. *The Best American Poetry 1995.* New York: Scribner, 1995.

Kinzie, Mary. *The Cure of Poetry in an Age of Prose: Moral Essays on the Poet's Calling.* Chicago: University of Chicago Press, 1993.

Lehman, David. *The Line Forms Here.* Ann Arbor, Mich.: University of Michigan Press, 1992.

McCorkle, James, ed. *Conversant Essays: Contemporary Poets on Poetry.* Detroit: Wayne State University Press, 1990.

McHugh, Heather. *Broken English: Poetry and Partiality.* Middletown, CT: Wesleyan/University Press of New England, 1993.

Morice, Dave. *The Adventures of Dr. Alphabet: 104 Unusual Ways to Write Poetry in the Classroom and the Community.* New York: Teachers and Writers Collaborative, 1995.

Padgett, Ron. *Handbook of Poetic Forms.* New York: Teachers and Writers Collaborative, 1987.

Padgett, Ron, and Nancy Larson Shapiro, eds. *The Point: Where Teaching and Writing Intersect.* New York: Teachers and Writers Collaborative, 1983.

Pinsky, Robert. *Poetry and the World.* New York: The Ecco Press, 1988.

Rich, Adrienne. *What Is Found There: Notebooks on Poetry and Politics.* New York: Norton, 1993.

Shapiro, Karl. *Essay on Rime.* New York: Reynal and Hitchcock, 1945.

Stillman, Frances. *The Poet's Manual and Rhyming Dictionary.* New York: Thomas Y. Crowell, 1965.

Strand, Mark, ed. *The Best American Poetry 1991.* New York: Scribner, 1991.

Turco, Lewis. *The New Book of Forms: A Handbook of Poetics.* Hanover, N.H.: University Press of New England, 1986.

Williams, Miller. *Patterns of Poetry: An Encyclopedia of Forms.* Baton Rouge: Louisiana State University Press, 1986.

ACKNOWLEDGMENTS

An early version of this anthology appeared in the Fall–Winter 1983 issue of *Epoch*. Grateful acknowledgment is made to *Epoch* and its former editor, Cecil Giscombe, for his encouragement, support, and permission to reprint material that first appeared in *Epoch*. Of the prose statements collected in this book, twenty-four appeared, in the same or different form, in *Epoch;* the others are published here for the first time.

A. R. Ammons: "Serpent Country" and "Inside Out" appeared in the Fall–Winter 1983 issue of *Epoch*. Reprinted by permission of the poet.

John Ashbery: "Variation on a Noel" from *A Wave* by John Ashbery. Copyright © 1984 by John Ashbery. Reprinted by permission of Viking Penguin, Inc., Carcanet Press Ltd., and the author. The poem and accompanying statement appeared in the Fall–Winter 1983 issue of *Epoch*.

Frank Bidart: "To the Dead" appeared in *The New York Review of Books,* 8 November 1984. Reprinted with permission from *The New York Review of Books*. Copyright © 1984 Nyrev, Inc.

Eavan Boland: "The Harbor." Reprinted by permission; Copyright © 1995 Eavan Boland. Originally in *The New Yorker*.

Donald Britton: "Winter Garden" appeared in the Fall–Winter 1983 issue of *Epoch*. Reprinted by permission of the poet.

Lucie Brock-Broido: "Hitchcock Blue" appeared in the Fall–Winter 1983 issue of *Epoch*. Reprinted by permission of the poet.

John Cage: "Writing through a text by Chris Mann" and the accompanying statement are published by permission of Mr. Cage.

Maxine Chernoff: "Phantom Pain" from *Utopia TV Store* by Maxine Chernoff (The Yellow Press, 1979). Reprinted with the permission of the Yellow Press and the author.

Amy Clampitt: "Portola Valley" appeared in *The New Republic,* 19 November 1984. Reprinted with the permission of *The New Republic* and the author.

Marc Cohen: "Silhouette" appeared in the Fall–Winter 1983 issue of *Epoch*. Reprinted by permission of the poet.

Wyn Cooper: "Fun" is reprinted by permission of the poet.

Alfred Corn: "Infinity Effect at the Hôtel Soubise" from *All Roads at Once* by Alfred Corn (Viking, 1976). Copyright © 1976, © 1986 by Alfred Corn. Reprinted by permission of the poet.

Douglas Crase: "Once the Sole Province" appeared in *Poetry in Motion,* Winter 1979, and in the Fall–Winter 1983 issue of *Epoch.* Reprinted by permission of the poet.

Robert Creeley: "The Whip" from *For Love: Poems 1950–1960* by Robert Creeley. Copyright © 1962 Robert Creeley. Reprinted with the permission of Charles Scribner's Sons. Reprinted from *Poems 1950–1965,* by Robert Creeley, by permission of Marion Boyars Publishers Ltd.

Tom Disch: "Buying a Used Car" originally appeared in *Boulevard* (vol. 9, no. 3, 1994). Reprinted by permission.

Jim Dolot: "Dictionary Jazz" appeared in *The Stud Duck,* 1994. Copyright © Jim Dolot 1994. Reprinted by permission.

Rita Dove: "Rive d'Urale" reprinted by permission of the author from *Callaloo,* Vol. 17, No. 2. Copyright © 1993 Rita Dove.

Maria Flook: "Discreet" first appeared in *Poetry,* September 1983. Copyright © 1983 by the Modern Poetry Association. Reprinted by permission of the poet and of the editor of *Poetry.*

Alice Fulton: "Everyone Knows the World Is Ending" appeared in the Fall–Winter 1983 issue of *Epoch* and in *Palladium* by Alice Fulton (University of Illinois Press, 1986). Reprinted with the permission of the author and of the University of Illinois Press.

Jonathan Galassi: "Our Wives" by Jonathan Galassi appeared in *The Nation,* 20 November 1982. Reprinted with the permission of the author and of *The Nation.*

Amy Gerstler: "Commentary" is reprinted by permission of *New American Writing.*

Dana Gioia: "Lives of the Great Composers" has appeared in *The Hudson Review,* Autumn 1981, *Epoch,* Fall–Winter 1983, and *Daily Horoscope* by Dana Gioia (Graywolf Press, 1986). Reprinted by permission of the poet.

Debora Greger: "Memories of the Atomic Age: Richland, Washington" originally appeared in *The Gettysburg Review* (vol. 6, no. 4) and is reprinted here by permission of the editors.

Marilyn Hacker: "Letter from the Alpes-Maritimes," copyright © 1983 by Marilyn Hacker. Reprinted from *Assumptions,* by Marilyn Hacker, by permission of the author and of Alfred A. Knopf, Inc.

Rachel Hadas: "Codex Minor" appeared in the Fall–Winter 1983 issue of *Epoch* and in *A Son from Sleep* by Rachel Hadas (Wesleyan University Press, 1987). Copyright © 1987 by Rachel Hadas. Reprinted by permission of the poet.

Mac Hammond: "Golden Age" appeared in the Fall–Winter 1983 issue of *Epoch*. Reprinted by permission of the poet.

William Hathaway: "My Words" and the accompanying statement are published by permission of the poet.

Anthony Hecht: "Meditation" was first published in *Vogue*, November 1981. Copyright © 1986 by Anthony Hecht. Reprinted by permission of the poet.

Gerrit Henry: "Cole Porter's Son" appeared in *American Poetry Review*, March–April 1981. Reprinted with the permission of the poet and of *American Poetry Review*.

Daryl Hine: "Si Monumentum Requiris" and the accompanying statement are published here by permission of the poet.

Edward Hirsch: "Fast Break" from *Wild Gratitude* by Edward Hirsch. Copyright © 1985 by Edward Hirsch. Reprinted by permission of the author and of Alfred A. Knopf, Inc.

John Hollander: The twenty-six untitled quatrains beginning "Why have I locked myself inside / This narrow cell" from *In Time and Place* by John Hollander (The Johns Hopkins University Press, 1986). Copyright © 1986 by John Hollander. Reprinted by permission of the poet and publisher.

Paul Hoover: "Poems We Can Understand" from *Somebody Talks A Lot* by Paul Hoover (The Yellow Press, 1982). Reprinted with the permission of the author and of the Yellow Press.

Richard Howard: "At the Monument to Pierre Louÿs" from *Lining Up*. Copyright © 1984 Richard Howard. Reprinted with the permission of Atheneum Publishers, Inc.

Colette Inez: "Apothegms and Counsels" from *Alive and Taking Names* by Colette Inez (Ohio University Press, 1978). Reprinted by permission of the poet and of Ohio University Press.

Phyllis Janowitz: "Change" appeared in *Spazio Umano*, Settembre 1984. Reprinted by permission of the poet.

Lawrence Joseph: "That's All" and the accompanying statement are published here by permission of the poet.

Donald Justice: "Pantoum of the Great Depression." Reprinted by permission; Copyright © 1994 Donald Justice. Originally in *The New Yorker* under the title "Pantoum of the Depression Years."

Richard Kenney: Excerpt from "The Encantadas" first appeared in *Poetry*, April 1983. Copyright © 1983 by the Modern Poetry Association. Reprinted by permission of the poet and of the editor of *Poetry*.

John Koethe: "The Substitute for Time" appeared in *Epoch,* Fall–Winter 1983, and in *The Late Wisconsin Spring* by John Koethe. Copyright © 1984 by Princeton University Press. Reprinted with permission of the poet and of Princeton University Press.

Yusef Komunyakaa: "Trueblood's Blues" first appeared in *AGNI Magazine,* Issue #40, in 1995. Reprinted by permission.

Ann Lauterbach: "Psyche's Dream" appeared in *Epoch,* Fall–Winter 1983, and in *Before Recollection* by Ann Lauterbach (Princeton University Press). Reprinted by permission of the poet.

David Lehman: "Amnesia" from *An Alternative to Speech* by David Lehman (Princeton University Press, 1986). The poem first appeared in *Poetry,* July 1984.

Brad Leithauser: "Post-Coitum Tristesse" appeared in *Epoch,* Fall–Winter 1983, and in *Cats of the Temple* by Brad Leithauser (Knopf, 1986). Copyright © 1983, 1984, 1985 by Brad Leithauser. Reprinted by permission of the poet, of Alfred A. Knopf, Inc., and of International Creative Management, Inc.

William Logan: "The Lost Birds of Venice" is reprinted by permission of *The New Republic.*

Michael Malinowitz: "Glose" appeared in *Epoch,* Fall–Winter 1983. Reprinted by permission of the poet.

Harry Mathews: "Condition of Desire" appeared in *Epoch,* Fall–Winter 1983. Reprinted by permission of the poet.

William Matthews: "Merida, 1969" appeared in *Hubbub* magazine (Reed College, Portland, Oregon). Reprinted by permission of the poet and of the editors of *Hubbub.*

J. D. McClatchy: "The Method" appeared in *Grand Street,* Summer 1984, and in *Stars Principal* by J. D. McClatchy (Macmillan, 1986). Reprinted by permission of the poet and of *Grand Street.*

Heather McHugh: "Form" appears in *A World of Difference* (Houghton Mifflin) and *Hinge & Sign: Poems 1968–1993* (Wesleyan / UPNE 1994), both by Heather McHugh. Copyright © 1980 Heather McHugh. Originally in *The New Yorker.*

Heather McHugh: "Nihil Privativum in the House of Ken" appeared in *The Colorado Review,* Spring 1995. Reprinted by permission.

James Merrill: "Snapshot of Adam" appeared in *Raritan,* Fall 1982, and *Epoch,* Fall–Winter 1983. Reprinted by permission of the poet.

W. S. Merwin: "Ancestral Voices" reprinted with permission from *The New York Review of Books.* Copyright © 1994 Nyrev, Inc.

Susan Mitchell: "Venice" was originally published in *The Paris Review,* issue 134, spring 1995. Reprinted by permission.

Robert Morgan: "Grandma's Bureau" and "Good Measure" appeared in the Fall–Winter 1983 issue of *Epoch.* Reprinted by permission of the poet.

Dave Morice: "Alaskan Drinking Song" and "A Perfect Poem" appeared in the Fall–Winter 1983 issue of *Epoch.* Reprinted by permission of the poet.

Howard Moss: "The Moon" first appeared in *The New Yorker,* 3 March 1986. Reprinted by permission; copyright © 1986 Howard Moss.

Thylias Moss: "Renegade Angels" appeared in *The Colorado Review,* Fall 1993. Reprinted by permission.

Harryette Mullen: Six sections from "Muse and Drudge" appear here for the first time by permission of the poet. Copyright © 1995 Harryette Mullen.

Charles North: "Lineups II" from *The Year of the Olive Oil* (Hanging Loose Press) and from *New and Selected Poems* (Sun & Moon Press). Copyright © 1989, 1995, Charles North. Reprinted by permission.

Joyce Carol Oates: "How Delicately . . ." and the accompanying statement appear by permission of the author.

Molly Peacock: "She Lays," copyright © 1982 by Molly Peacock. Reprinted from *Raw Heaven,* by Molly Peacock, by permission of the poet and of Random House, Inc. The poem and prose statement appeared in the Fall–Winter 1983 issue of *Epoch.*

Robert Pinsky: "The Want Bone" appeared in *The Threepenny Review.* Reprinted by permission of the poet and of the editor of *The Threepenny Review.*

Katha Pollitt: "Playground." Reprinted by permission; Copyright © 1990 Katha Pollitt. Originally in *The New Yorker.*

Mary Jo Salter: "Refrain" from *Henry Purcell in Japan* by Mary Jo Salter (Knopf, 1985). Copyright © 1984 Mary Jo Salter. Reprinted with the permission of the poet and of Alfred A. Knopf, Inc. The poem initially appeared in *The Kenyon Review.*

Lloyd Schwartz: "Tom Joanides" initially appeared in *Shenandoah,* vol. 34, no. 1, 1982–83. Copyright © 1984 by Washington and Lee University. Reprinted from *Shenandoah: The Washington and Lee University Review* with the permission of the editor.

Charles Simic: "The Anniversary" appears here by permission of the poet. Reprinted by permission; Copyright © 1994 Charles Simic. An earlier version originally appeared in *The New Yorker.*

Louis Simpson: An early version of "The Precinct Station," quoted in Mr. Simpson's discussion, appeared in the Fall 1984 issue of *The Georgia Review*. Reprinted with the permission of the editor of *The Georgia Review*.

Elizabeth Spires: "On the Island" originally appeared in *Boulevard* (Vol. 10, Nos. 1 and 2). Reprinted by permission.

Jon Stallworthy: "At Half Past Three in the Afternoon" appeared in the Fall–Winter 1983 issue of *Epoch,* in *Poetry Review* (72, 2), and in *The Anzac Sonata: New and Selected Poems* by Jon Stallworthy (Chatto & Windus, 1986). Reprinted with the permission of the author.

Mark Strand: "Two Villanelles" appear here by permission of the poet. Copyright © 1995 Mark Strand.

Richard Stull: "Romance" and the accompanying statement are published here by permission of the poet.

James Tate: "Peggy in Twilight" appears here by permission of the poet. Copyright © 1995 James Tate.

Lewis Turco: "Winter Bouquet" is published here by permission of the poet.

John Updike: "The Naked Ape" copyright © 1968 by John Updike. Reprinted from *Midpoint and Other Poems* by John Updike (Knopf, 1969) by permission of the author, of Alfred A. Knopf, Inc., and of Andre Deutsch Ltd.

Mona Van Duyn: "The Ballad of Blossom" from *Letters from a Father and Other Poems*. Copyright © 1982 Mona Van Duyn. Reprinted with the permission of Atheneum Publishers, Inc.

Paul Violi: "Index" appeared in *Splurge* by Paul Violi (SUN, 1982) and in the Fall–Winter 1983 issue of *Epoch*. Reprinted with the permission of the author and of SUN.

Rosmarie Waldrop: "Shorter American Memory of the American Character According to Santayana" appeared in *Grand Street,* Autumn 1983. Reprinted by permission of the publisher of *Grand Street*.

Rosanna Warren: "Poetry Reading" appeared in *The Washington Post,* January 1, 1993. Copyright © 1993 Rosanna Warren. Reprinted by permission of the author.

Marjorie Welish: "Street Cries" and the accompanying statement are published here by permission of the poet.

Bernard Welt: "Prose" and the accompanying statement are published here by permission of the poet.

Susan Wheeler: "Ezra's Lament" appears here by permission of the poet. Copyright © 1995 Susan Wheeler.

Richard Wilbur: "Thyme Flowering Among Rocks" from *Walking to Sleep* by Richard Wilbur (Harcourt Brace Jovanovich, 1969). Copyright © 1969 by Richard Wilbur. Reprinted by permission of Harcourt Brace Jovanovich and of Faber and Faber Ltd.

Charles Wright: "Bar Giamaica, 1959–60" from *The Southern Cross* by Charles Wright (Random House, 1981). Copyright © 1981 by Charles Wright. Reprinted by permission of Random House, Inc.

John Yau: "Broken Off By the Music" from *Corpse and Mirror* by John Yau (Holt, Rinehart and Winston, 1983). Copyright © 1983 by John Yau. Reprinted by permission of the poet and of Henry Holt & Co.

Stephen Yenser: "Ember Week, Reseda" appeared in *The Yale Review,* Winter 1981, and in *Clos Camardon* by Stephen Yenser (Sea Cliff Press, 1985). Reprinted by permission of the poet, the Yale Review, and Sea Cliff Press.

Acknowledgment is also made to the following for permission to reprint copyrighted material:

Alfred A. Knopf, Inc., for material from *The Collected Poems of Wallace Stevens,* copyright © 1954 by Wallace Stevens.

Random House, for material from *W. H. Auden: Collected Poems,* edited by Edward Mendelson, copyright © 1976 by Edward Mendelson, William Meredith and Monroe K. Spear, executors of the Estate of W. H. Auden; and for material from *The Complete Poems* by Edwin Denby, edited by Ron Padgett, copyright © 1975 by Edwin Denby.

Faber and Faber, Limited, for material from W. H. Auden's *Collected Poems,* edited by Edward Mendelson, and for material from *The Collected Poems of Wallace Stevens.*

W. W. Norton & Company for material from *The Selected Poems 1951–1977* by A. R. Ammons. Reprinted by permission of the author and the publisher, W. W. Norton & Company, Inc. Copyright © 1977, 1975, 1974, 1972, 1971, 1970, 1966, 1965, 1964, 1955 by A. R. Ammons.

Atheneum Publishers, Inc., for "Professionalism" by Anthony Hecht from *Jiggery-Pokery: A Compendium of Double Dactyls* by Anthony Hecht and John Hollander. Copyright © 1966 Anthony Hecht and John Hollander. Reprinted with the permission of Atheneum Publishers, Inc.

The editors of *Shenandoah* for "Wystan Hugh Auden: A Villanelle" by David Lehman. Reprinted from *Shenandoah: The Washington and Lee University Review,* vol. 34, no. 1, 1982–83, with the permission of the editor. Copyright © 1984 by Washington and Lee University.

Yale University Press for the triolet in John Hollander's *Rhyme's Reason: A Guide to English Verse.* Copyright © 1981 by John Hollander.

Wesleyan University Press for material from *Disorderly Houses* by